PRAISE FOR
IT'S BETTER TO LAUGH...

"Kathy Levine's book is like the legendary show host herself—full of down-to-earth credibility, a great sense of humor and always entertaining."

—Susan Lucci

"Kathy is a lovable woman and her book reveals it even more. She speaks candidly about herself and her life in a way that should be most inspiring to millions of women around the country."

—Diane von Furstenberg

"Kathy is one of the most lovably irreverent people I've ever met. Her story is written like a personal letter to a trusted friend, where it's OK to reveal personal intimacies, truths, tears, and laughter. Anyone who wants to know why we all love Kathy so much should read *IT'S BETTER TO LAUGH...*"

—Bob Bowersox

A Selection of the Literary Guild

KATHY LEVINE

It's Better To Laugh...

Life,
Good Luck,
Bad Hair Days,
and QVC

KATHY LEVINE
WITH JANE SCOVELL

WITH AN INTRODUCTION BY
Joan Rivers

POCKET BOOKS
New York   London   Toronto   Sydney   Tokyo   Singapore

POCKET BOOKS, a division of Simon & Schuster Inc.
1230 Avenue of the Americas, New York, NY 10020

Copyright © 1995, 1996 by Kathy Levine

ISBN 978-1-4516-6191-0

First Pocket Books paperback printing September 1996

10 9 8 7 6 5 4 3 2 1

POCKET and colophon are registered trademarks of
Simon & Schuster Inc.

Family photo from 1960 (page five of insert) courtesy of
Sam Smith—Allentown, PA

Cover photo by Kimberly Butler

Printed in the U.S.A.

For my mother, Pat Seinfeld,
who never said "never"—
you are the wind beneath my wings.

Acknowledgments

- Sandi Donaldson, who pushed, barked, growled and shoved. I am eternally grateful, and love you dearly.

- Ellie Einhorn, who watched QVC, recognized my story-telling talent, and nudged her daughter Amy.

- Amy Einhorn, my editor, who had the good sense to listen to her mother.

- My dad, Arnold Kauffman, who assisted in raising three fabulous kids, and who, under better circumstances, would be proud as hell.

- Ron and Bruce Kauffman, my brothers, who have always been there and have always made me laugh. I couldn't have picked better.

- Andrea Sample—for loving my Chelsea as her own and for helping me chase my dream.

- My oldest and dearest girlfriends: Monica, Barkie, Rener and Philly. We are "lifers" and I am rich with your friendship.

- Frank Montemurro, who understands the difference between PBS and PMS and knows not to bother me in the middle of either. Thank you for your love and guidance.

- Stephen Breimer and Peter Dekom—for your legal savvy and your gentle manner.

- Susan Ginsburg—for your literary advice and moral support.

Acknowledgments

❖ Gina Centrello, Liz Hartman, Cindy Ratzlaff, and all the people at Pocket Books—for championing the dark horse. I hope we all win the race.

❖ Jane Scovell (co-author)—the light of this project, the voice of my thoughts. I'd laugh to the poorhouse or the bank with you. Either way, I had a ball (see afterword).

❖ Joe Segal (QVC founder)—for your vision, your soft-spoken class. Thank you for opening the door of opportunity when I knocked.

❖ Doug Briggs (president of QVC)—for letting me spread my wings and fly.

❖ Joan Rivers—for your graciousness and generosity. Thanks for letting me hold on to your coattails for this magic ride.

❖ To the QVC support staff—Jack and Robb ('cause you made me do this!). Telephone reps, customer service, information services, correspondence, buyers, programmers, quality control, and especially my buddies, the product coordinators, producers, technical gang, et al. Thank you for transforming a job into a mega-hit great-place-to-work retail giant.

❖ Ellen Rubin and Kim Hannum, QVC's P.R. mavens. You are wonderful.

❖ The QVC program hosts—the ones who've been on the front line making this company #1 from the get-go. You have covered for me on rough days, and you have laid me out in laughter during those interminable host meetings. We have grown together, and I am proud to be part of the finest sales force in the country.

❖ You, the viewers. Thank you for inviting me into your living rooms, for letting me be zany, goofy, klutzy, and just plain Kathy. You have supported my antics, my hair colors, and my ongoing search for the perfect date. Sit back and enjoy—eat a little, shop a little, read a little, and laugh a lot.

Love,
Kathy

As always, I gratefully acknowledge my three children, Amy, Lucy and Bill Appleton, who never fail to listen and inspire. Ditto for Sydney Sheldon Weldon.

My gratitude to Amy Einhorn, an enthusiastic and adept editor, and to Susan Ginsburg, as great a friend as she is an agent. Also, my personal thanks to Frank Montemurro, Monica Singleton, and David Stephens.

And finally, to the one-and-only Kathy Levine. Working with her was a constant delight, and because of her I am addicted to QVC.

—Jane Scovell

Contents

❖ ❖ ❖

Introduction by Joan Rivers   xiii

1   **TV or Not TV**   1

2   **Hair Wins by a Nose**   17

3   **Little (Ha!) Kathy Kauffman**   34

4   **"Was It *Bueno* for You?"**   51

5   **The Boss and Groom**   70

6   **Friendly Fire**   111

7   **Thee and Me and QVC**   123

8   **Here's the (Real) Jeffery**   142

9   **The Happy Hawker**   167

10 **Diller Meets Diva**   193

Contents

11   **To Bee or Not to Bee**   224

12   **Who's Afraid of the Big B.H.D.?**   243

13   **The Stars Are Out Tonight**   245

14   **Life Is Short, Death Is Long . . . Eat Dessert First!**   270

Glossary   **Vaddaya Mean?**   277

Afterword   279

Introduction
by Joan Rivers

❖ ❖ ❖

I came to QVC in 1990 to sell jewelry and got more than I bargained for when Kathy Levine was named my cohost. In those early appearances it was business first—pearls, bracelets, bangles, and bee pins. From the beginning, Kathy showed extraordinary sales talent; and little by little her warm, witty qualities crept out. We laughed, we cried, we lamented saggy boobs, broadening rear ends, and disastrous dates, and in the process grew to know and enjoy each other. Now Kathy has written her story and all her viewers can get to know her.

Autobiographies usually come in two flavors—candy-coated lies or bitter-pill truths. I'm sure it would have been easy for Kathy to turn her life into the equivalent of a glamorous, perfumed Danielle Steele novel (probably the first with a hardworking Jewish heroine), but she didn't. She's told her story truthfully and honestly and with style, wit, humor, and flair.

Kathy Levine is a pioneer in televised home shopping, the revolutionary system of retailing that burst on the scene only a short time ago. Linked by televi-

sion and phone technology, her network—I call it Ka-
thyland—joins Kathy and her on-camera guests (me
included) with the viewers. I'm a working woman and
for me the hallmark of Kathy's network is its super-
equality. Can you think of any other place where sex,
race, appearance, or age are never issues?

An autobiography declares that one significant part
of your history has come to a conclusion; this leaves
the reader wondering what's going to come next. I've
given some thought to Kathy's future, and taking into
consideration her huge and powerful legion of fans,
here's my idea: I think she's the ideal presidential candidate. And I'm not saying this simply because I would
be named Secretary of Gorgeous Jewelry. No, I think
it's a logical conclusion, and I'm urging her to get in
the race. In the meantime, I cordially invite you to
read this book and meet a funny girl who at times
didn't find her life all that funny. For anyone who is
at a crossroads, this story may inspire you to choose
something good, something better, and to learn to
laugh at life's ups and downs.

And don't forget to wear pearls.

"Have fun. Be good to yourself.
Don't hurt anyone.
And—make a difference."

It's Better To Laugh...

1
TV or Not TV

❖ ❖ ❖

Who ever thought a not-so-beautiful, not-so-brilliant, smartass Jewish girl from Allentown, Pennsylvania, would become a television personality? Not me ... and certainly not my father.

"What are you going to do with your life?" he asked me when I was a twenty-year-old college student.

"I don't know. Have a good time, I guess," I replied.

"A good time? Life isn't a good time, young lady. Every day is a grind, every day is work."

"So, I'll get married."

"Who knows whether you'll get married? Besides, you can't rely on someone else to take care of you. You've got to be able to take care of *yourself.*"

"Don't worry about me," I snapped back, "I can take care of myself."

"Oh, you can, eh? Let me ask you something," my dad said. "Do you really believe that you can make a living talking on the telephone and going shopping or sitting on your *tookus* and polishing your nails?" (For

1

those of you who don't know *tookus* or other assorted yiddishisms I tend to use, I've included my own glossary for you in the back.)

More than two decades later I still remember what my father said. I think of it every time I go to work and I smile. Most of you will understand why I smile because most of you know me from my work. For those who haven't seen me on television, let me explain. I'm a host on the QVC network, and for the past eight years I've been sitting in front of a camera and talking over the phone to viewers who want to shop with me. I earn a good living and more importantly, I *love* my job. My work is my pleasure, and I've made a lot of friends through the small screen. People know me, and while I can't speak directly to each and every one, we have a special relationship—we're like an electronic family. My mom says I talk too much about my personal life on the television—total strangers walk up to her in the supermarket and say things like, "Gee, Pat, what are you doing here? Kathy said you were going to Florida." I do talk about my mom a lot, and my dog, Chelsea, too, and other assorted family members, yet I've been far more guarded when it comes to talking about *myself*. Frankly, I never would *say* on television the things I'm writing in this book. Appearing on QVC isn't about *my* adventures, it's about selling products. The only thing I'm "selling" in this book is me, so I have to be honest.

First of all, I was as surprised as the next person when I was asked to write my story, because I don't consider myself a celebrity. I do consider myself one lucky lady, but luck wasn't the only reason I got where I am. Sometimes you have to make your own luck or at least get yourself in a position where a stroke of good fortune can make a difference, and you may have to wait quite a while, too. My good luck didn't surface until I was thirty-four years old. On September 7, 1986, my friend Sandi Donaldson telephoned me.

"Kathy, I'm looking at the Help Wanted section of the *Philadelphia Inquirer,* and there's an advertisement here that's got your name written on it."

"What is it?"

"It's from a new company—some sort of cable television shopping outfit looking for energetic people to staff an up-and-coming industry. This is for you."

A television opportunity for me? I doubted it. At this particular point in my checkered career I was working as a sales manager at the Franklin Plaza, Philadelphia's largest hotel. I had razzle-dazzled my way into the job on the strength of an interview with the manager. I've always been good at interviews—I love the challenge of meeting new people and schmoozing with them. The manager liked me, and I thought he was terrific, too. The day after our meeting I wrote him a thank-you note, put it in a green envelope and mailed it. (I believe in writing thank-you notes after job interviews if for no other reason than it puts you one step ahead of the applicant who doesn't.) I specifically chose the color green because the manager had an Irish name. Sure enough, the manager called be back. "I'm giving you the job, Kathy, not because I think you're experienced enough for a big hotel but because you want it. You're willing to work hard, *and* you sent me a thank-you note in a green envelope."

I started working in promotion and sales. My boss was great and I made some long-term friends, yet once the thrill of getting the position wore off, I found myself doing my job with minimal enthusiasm. You need zeal in sales, and I lacked the necessary ardor. Oh, I got things done and tried to muster up the appropriate excitement for the sake of my clients, but I really didn't try that hard, and eventually I began goofing off. The Franklin Plaza was a short distance from a lovely store named Bonwit Teller, and I wore a path

3

from the hotel to the store. "I know why you chose to work at the Franklin Plaza," my boss said one day. "It's a convenient place for you to store your Bonwit's shopping bags." Before long, I was taking four-hour lunch breaks. I was bored to death, and by the time a new management team came into the hotel, I had lost what little interest I'd had. This was typical Kathy. I'd go after a job with all the eagerness in the world and when I got it, which I usually did, the enthusiasm died. Nothing satisfied me *enough*. I'm service oriented, and my job at the Franklin Plaza, though it highlighted more of my strengths than any other job, still wasn't a perfect fit. After a meeting was booked I'd oversee the preparations from sleeping arrangements to organizing the meeting rooms and getting all the furnishings—chairs, tables, and audio-visual equipment—in place, and making sure that coffee breaks and meals were palatable and efficiently served. Though the work was fun, nothing was dropped into my lap. I had to scour for business, and that's why I didn't do very well. I wasn't lazy, I just hated the hard sell. Mind you, I think the hotel industry is good for women; it's one arena where you have an opportunity to advance. Nevertheless, you have to go out and beat the bushes to drum up sales, and it wasn't for me. So, while I liked being with the Franklin Plaza, I couldn't get focused or extract any real feelings of accomplishment from what I was doing. I used to cry to my mother, "Will I ever find something that I'm suited for? Will I ever get it right?" The fear of not finding myself drove me crazy, and for years I desperately sought some kind of work I could blend into and excel at. I had a million different jobs, yet none of them held my interest long.

While plodding along in my various unbrilliant "careers," I tried to broaden my scope by taking classes—in anything that didn't require intensive study! I studied cooking, wine tasting, Spanish, and acting. One

4

course at the Weist-Baron school, "Auditioning for Commercials," really appealed to me. Classwork consisted of getting in front of the camera and reading actual commercials. My first attempts were sales pitches for Colgate-Palmolive and Breck Shampoo. I stood before the camera, the red light went on, and the minute that little beam shone, something ignited inside me. I fell madly in love with the camera—with television—with performing. I had no hope of actually doing anything on TV, yet I never felt as happy anywhere else as I did standing in front of that Weist-Baron camera with the red light winking at me. My friend Sandi Donaldson knew this, and that's why she phoned me about the cable television advertisement.

"Oh, come on, Sandi," I protested, "I'm not a TV person. You have to be thin. You have to be blond. You have to be really beautiful. I'm not thin, I'm not blond, and I'm not beautiful."

"Yeah, yeah, yeah," answered Sandi, agreeing with me (too quickly, maybe), "but you can do this job."

"Oh, God, they'd never use me. They're probably bringing in their own talent. They've hired Wink Martindale and Vanna White."

"Kathy, stop creating problems for yourself. Get out of your own way. Just ask for an audition." Sandi's pretty tough to argue with, especially when she's convinced that she's right, and in this instance she was certain of her rightness. I agreed to at least take a stab at it and handwrote a letter to the address she gave me. I really wasn't thinking along the lines of performing; I was looking for some kind of secretarial–gal Friday position, anything that would get me into the television industry. I mailed my letter in a white envelope. (Who knew if they were Irish?) I expected nothing, partly—and I can't emphasize this enough—because I didn't have a clue as to what a cable shopping network was, or for that matter, what cable was!

I lived in Philadelphia and at this time we didn't have cable TV in my area. Talk about a pig-in-a-poke.

Sandi showed up at my place the next day and brought the ad from the paper. I took a look at it and began wailing. "Oh no," I cried, "I thought you said Q*B*C. I wrote down the wrong name. They'll think I'm an idiot. They'll never get in touch with me."

Needless to say, I was stunned when QVC actually called me. Imagine, I wrote a stupid note, got the name of the station wrong, and they still telephoned and asked if I would like to come for an interview. I said yes and then called Sandi.

"I'm going for a job interview for that television network."

"Never mind *job*," came the retort, "when you get there ask for an *audition.*"

"Well, I don't think I'm . . ."

"Ask for an AUDITION," ordered Sandi.

I put on a bright red suit (red's a real power color for me) and set off for my interview-audition at the QVC headquarters in West Chester. The building formerly had housed a hospital supply company and was in the process of being renovated. Architecturally speaking, it was then and is now a big brick nothing that stands next to a huge parking lot and fields of green. There are no distinguishing features on the outside of the building, and the inside is completely functional.

Everything happened so fast that afternoon, I have trouble keeping track of things. I do remember quite clearly experiencing an unusual sensation as I walked through the front door of the studio; I was overcome by a feeling that my life was going to be different. A guy named Ron introduced himself and sat me down to chat. "We're doing a shopping show and we're going to be selling products. People are going to be calling in, and we have to have operators waiting to

6

take orders. Would you be interested in being a telephone operator?"

"How much does it pay?" I asked, even though I was completely turned off at the prospect.

"Sixteen thousand a year," Ron answered.

"Well, I'm making twenty-two," I replied respectfully, "so I don't think I'd want to make the change."

"You know, it's a shame," said Ron, "because you really have a very nice look." (See, red really *is* good on me!) "Is there anything else you might want to do for us?"

"Could I have an audition?" I heard the words and looked around to see who had spoken. No one else was there. The request was on my lips before the words formed in my brain.

"Actually," Ron said looking me over, "I'll bet you'd be very good on camera. You have an excellent way about you."

"Who, me?" I said.

"Yes, you. We *are* holding auditions, but it's all by appointment."

"Oh, well . . ." I began, intending to say something to the effect that it was okay and I'd be leaving, when Ron cut me off.

"Let me see what's going on in the other room. I know the guys are back there." He excused himself and went through another door. The crew was on break. They were sitting around eating sandwiches, and Ron asked if they'd be willing to tape an unscheduled audition. Those sweethearts said okay, and Ron returned to get me. I still can't believe how it happened. I swear a mysterious force had taken hold and was propelling me forward. I was there and auditioning—in spite of myself. The audition room was small, and a partition had been set up behind which the crew stood and did what they had to do, leaving a bit of room for me to do what I had to do. "Move over to the center and get in front of the camera," I

7

was told. I did and looked up to see the little red light, my old pal from Weist-Baron, blinking at me. Immediately I was warmed by the glow. I was home.

"Tell us your name, a little bit about yourself, and then sell us a pencil ... and then sell us a telephone." Someone handed a pencil to me. A pencil and a telephone. I thought for a second and decided to start with the telephone.

"Imagine how Alexander Graham Bell's mother felt when he informed her he wasn't going to be a doctor. '*Oy, oy, oy,*' she cried. But aren't we glad he skipped medicine and invented the telephone? Look at all the wonderful things you can do with it. You can call your mother and tell her you're doing fine. You can call for pizza. You can find out the weather. You can make a date for Saturday night...." I went through a litany of possible uses for the telephone without ever describing the product—I simply gave the sizzle. My sales intuition has always been strong, maybe because I come from a long line of retailers. I realized early on that selling is a matter of capturing people's attention and holding it with a good story. I finished the telephone shtick and went on to the pencil.

"If you have long nails and don't want to wreck them, you can use the pencil to push the numbers on your phone. Pencils are incredible because you can erase all your mistakes. And don't forget, if you get angry, you can break a pencil in two; it makes you feel so much better. Then you can give the extra piece to a friend, making you resourceful." To illustrate my point I snapped the pencil I was holding in half and stopped talking. I was met with silence. I didn't hear anything from behind the partition. I figured I bombed.

"Okay." I started to leave. Suddenly I heard these funny gasps, like someone was choking—only it wasn't choking; the man behind the partition was laughing.

"You're funny, you're funny," he told me. Big deal.

I knew I was funny. "We'll get this tape upstairs," he said. Ron took me back to the front entrance and ushered me out the door, saying, "This looks good, Kathy. The guys were crazy about you and they're the toughest audience. You'll be hearing from us." And that was that. As far as I could see, I had come, I had talked, and now I would go back to Philly.

The trip from West Chester takes an hour, and when I returned to the Franklin Plaza, the phone was ringing. I picked it up. "Kathy, this is John Eastman, talent manager at QVC. Could you come back and do another audition?"

"No," I answered, "I have a job. I can't keep running to West Chester."

"We're not trying to hassle you. We want to find out if your tape was an accident. We want to know if you're as good as you seem. Just come back one more time. We won't bother you again, promise." I have to laugh; I was getting a call back and telling them not to "bother" me. First thing I did was telephone Sandi Donaldson.

"This is it," Sandi exclaimed, "this is it! That job is yours. Don't you screw this up. Don't get in your own way. What are you going to wear?" Sandi got me all pumped up. She was the only one who knew what I was doing. I hadn't said anything to my family because I didn't want to get anybody excited. I was excited enough for my entire family, anyway.

I put on another "power" suit—in royal blue—and returned for my second audition. This time I was paired with another applicant, a guy who'd just graduated from college with a degree in communications. He was to do his part first and then I was to come in and join him. I waited on the sidelines and watched him go through his paces; he was poised and pitching pretty well, and suddenly I got scared. I didn't know beans about television, and this guy had a degree in it! I quickly realized that unless I came on strong, he'd

9

dominate. I couldn't let that happen. "This is your chance, Kathy," said a little voice inside me. "Don't give it up. Don't roll over. Stand your ground."

My time came. I walked on and totally eclipsed that young man; I chewed him up and spit him out. Normally I'm not like that—my first instinct is to bolster the other person, but I couldn't afford to be "nice" at that audition; I had to put myself first. Without being obvious or nasty, I rolled through that tryout. I can only compare what I felt then to being on a roller coaster—when it takes off you're on the track and you stay on it no matter how many bumps and jumps. I stayed on track and kept saying to myself, "Don't let go, don't drop this, stick with it." I shmoozed and chattered and laughed and carried on my love affair with the lens and the unseen audience. Even today, when I talk about this moment I get teary—never before had I asserted myself in the way that I did then. I didn't consciously plan to annihilate the other fellow yet I did. I bubbled all over him and when it was over, he never knew what hit him.

I returned to Philly and, sure enough, QVC called again. I was excited but don't think that I was a marshmallow. When John Eastman telephoned and asked me to come back to West Chester, I quickly asserted myself.

"I can't keep shlepping there, I have a job. I'm busy," I told him.

"You don't understand, we really need to talk to you." I figured if they *needed* to talk to me something was bound to happen. I arranged for a third visit.

I arrived at the studio, met with John Eastman again, and was introduced to the director of personnel.

"We'd like to offer you a job," said Mr. Eastman.

"Yeah, and what's it going to pay?"

"We'll give you the same salary you're getting now."

"Well, there's a little matter of an hour commute,"

TV or Not TV

I added. Although I was excited at the prospect of working for the station, I had to do some negotiating. We discussed matters back and forth and I asked for time to think things over. I was thrilled and wary at the same time. They assured me I would be part of a first-class operation and treated well. Realistically speaking, the hotel business was a proven entity, and this TV shopping stuff was "iffy"; who knew it would last? I needed counsel and immediately called Jay Levine, my soon-to-be ex-husband. Although Jay and I were in the process of separating at that point, legally I was still his wife. More important, legally shmeegally, we were still friends. I told Jay what was happening and asked his advice.

"Hey, you always wanted to be a star," he declared.

"I did not!"

"Listen to me, Kathy," Jay said firmly, "you *always* wanted to be a star, you just didn't know it. This is it, Kathy. Go for it."

I couldn't simply accept his and Sandi's opinion—I needed more approval. I called an older gentleman I'd gotten to know at work. This man was a regular guest at the Franklin Plaza, and we'd struck up a friendship. He was in advertising, which, in my thinking, was tied in somehow with television. After explaining the situation to him, I posed the followed question: "If your daughter got a chance to take a job on a new TV venture, what would you advise her to do?"

"I would tell my daughter to run, not walk, for this job. Run. Take it all the way, honey. You're going to be a star."

That's all I needed to hear. I took the job.

Funny, I avoided consulting with my parents. I could have called my father and asked his opinion, but my dad is not a particularly positive man; I knew he'd never give me an encouraging word. I was right, too. When I finally told my father I was leaving the

11

hotel, the first words out of his mouth were, "You're giving up your health insurance benefits? I think you're crazy." I wasn't a kid anymore, so he couldn't argue with me, but he sure thought I was nuts. My mother, on the other hand, wanted to put an ad in *The New York Times*. She was doing cartwheels. Her daughter the star! Mom was thrilled and excited—and *clueless* about what I was going to do. She didn't even have cable! For pete's sake, she didn't see QVC for the first three years we were on air.

I signed with QVC and began an intensive training course. For eight weeks the prospective hosts were put through their paces. Among my original colleagues were John Eastman (the boss), Ellen Langas, Molly Daly, Cindy Briggs-Moore, Diane Gray, Denise Kelly, Bob Bowersox, Amy Bennett, Marty Jacobs, Paul Kelley, Steve Colantuno, Tom Gurick, Jan Ericson, Lou DeMeis, and a few others I can no longer remember. Six weeks after the course began, we were joined by Steve Bryant, Jane Rudolph Treacy, and Jeff Hewson. While Jane and Steve are still going strong, of the *original* group, only *two* remain on air, myself and Bob Bowersox. Bob is the resident chef of QVC, and his program "In the Kitchen with Bob" is a shining star in the repertoire. (In September 1994, Bob went on the air and made history by selling over 150,000 copies of his cookbook, "In the Kitchen with Bob." An inspiration for my book!)

The QVC initiation course met eight hours a day for five days a week and eventually covered over 100 hours of classroom training. It was built around Dale Carnegie's memory training and various related selling techniques. We learned how to remember names by making up little mnemonics. I still recall one that went, "Kathy Levine rhymes with Win!" Maybe this will make things clear for those who don't know that my name is pronounced "Le-*vinn*," with the accent on the second syllable. People sometimes hassle me about the pronunciation. "How come your name is spelled L-e-*v-i-n-e* and you call yourself Levin?" My answer? "That's the way my ex-husband's family pronounced the name, so that's the way I pronounce it." I did toy with the idea of using another surname—not my maiden name, though. *K*athy *K*auffman sounds like you're coughing up a hairball. I seriously considered using my father's *first* name and becoming "Kathy Arnold," but by this time I was known as Kathy Levine and that's the way it stayed. Even if I married a Rockefeller, professionally I'd still use Levine.

I had some problems in the beginning. For the first two years I commuted from Philadelphia to West Chester. It was a drag, especially in the winter when storms rose quickly and made the roads impassable. Sometimes I wouldn't get home till two in the morning, other times, I had to stay overnight at the studio. Finally, I bought a lovely little townhouse not too far from the studio. I wasn't right off the bat crazy about being back in West Chester. I lived there when I was married; and I'd become used to the anonymity of living in a big city. I didn't like the fact that everybody knew everybody else's business in a small town. Also, there was nothing for me to do in West Chester except work. Shopping was nonexistent, and as far as dining, forget it, there was no restaurant, just the D&K Diner, period. (Throughout my training period, I always insisted we go to Philadelphia to shop *and* to eat.) Even more critical, the social ambience was limited. My ex-husband was now remarried, and I did not want to be too close or upset his new life. Despite my concerns, I moved into my townhouse and started my new and I hoped "brilliant" career.

I had big doubts about the memory training course. What was I doing in this situation? I felt like a first grader learning how to read. In my humble estimation the whole thing was B.S. and not too far into the

13

KATHY LEVINE

course I got on my high horse and went to see Diane Berson, one of the producers.

"I don't think I'm cut out for this work," I said to Diane, bluntly. "I've got a fear about this job. I don't think the audience is going to get me."

"What do you mean? Diane asked.

"I mean I'm upscale, Jewish, snotty. I just have a feeling they're never going to understand me in Iowa. I think they're going to hate me."

"Well," Diane replied firmly, "I recommend you either get rid of that attitude or get out now." I didn't expect that answer. I thought I'd get a little TLC. I perked right up when Diane said shape up or ship out. I shaped up and went back into the training with my tail between my legs. Once I settled down I got into the swing of things. We learned a *lot* in those eight weeks. One particular lesson sticks out to this day. We'd been selling products in mock broadcast situations and then the executive producer, Ron Giles, told us that we were to choose, on our own, a product from home and come back the next day prepared to sell the merchandise up, down, and sideways. I selected a clock-radio and made up a spiel about everything from the luminous dial to the A.M.-F.M. possibilities, from the snooze-bar sleep timer to the sleek plastic appearance. I went to bed with that little radio and the next morning I walked into the studio absolutely prepared.

"Okay," Ron said when we trainees sat down, "now I want you all to come up here and put your products on the table." We did what he asked and returned to our seats. "Okay," Ron continued, "who wants to go first? How about you, Kathy?" I leaped from my seat, ran to the table, and grabbed my clock-radio. "Is that your product?" Ron asked. "Yep," I said, ready to roll. "Well, put it down and pick up another one," ordered Ron. "Why don't you take that oversized wooden salad set from Jamaica?" I thought he was

14

kidding; I mean, I spent hours working up a pitch on the clock-radio, and now he was sticking me with a fork and spoon from Jamaica. But he was serious, and the next thing I knew I was standing in front of my peers with a gigantic salad set in my hands. I laughed and began my pitch, which included references to the beauty of the island of Jamaica and the usefulness of having your salad utensils hanging on the wall. I waxed poetic about the salad set and even grew to admire it myself. When I finished, I knew I'd be able to sell anything.

The course was finished, and among those chosen to be QVC hosts was Kathy Levine. Of them all, I felt the most grateful simply because I'd never thought I had a shot at being selected. I didn't go into the program with my eyes closed to the possibility that I might not make it. I really took a big leap of faith when I gave up my hotel job to give television a try, but I felt it was worth the risk. You have to go with the flow sometimes, and this was one of those times. (I should mention that someone had tipped me off that I was within twenty-four hours of being fired from the Franklin Plaza. Sure I took a chance—I had nothing to lose!) The other potential hosts seemed to have some sort of credentials that I lacked—Jane already was in broadcasting and making a lateral move from another station. Steve Colantuno was a biology teacher and very comfortable in imparting knowledge. Steve Bryant was a magician and a computer whiz. John Eastman had sold for the Home Shopping Club. (Also, Big John was six feet five—even if he didn't know anything, who would argue with him?) What I'm saying is, all of the other candidates either had more experience or expertise that I lacked. I think we all wanted to be stars, but I felt *they* knew how to shine and I didn't. I'm happy to say my fears evaporated when we began broadcasting. I had never been on the air before I started with QVC, and I haven't been off it since. The minute I started I knew that everything had fallen into place. After all those years of worrying and wondering that something was wrong with me or that I'd never be able to find success or happiness, I found my niche.

I'm the first to say that my becoming a host was a combination of timing and old-fashioned luck. I was damn fortunate, because at that particular moment of my life, my father's predictions seemed to be coming true—I wasn't going anywhere. Then, thanks to Sandi Donaldson, I hit the jackpot and, via televised home shopping, fell into America's living room.

2
Hair Wins by a Nose

❖ ❖ ❖

Sometimes I think I have the easiest job in the world
and sometimes I think it's the hardest. Easy or hard,
it's always joyous. I was, however, a long, long time
in getting there. Geographically, while West Chester
and Allentown are just an hour's drive from each
other, in terms of life, those two cities are light-years
apart. I'm very fond of Allentown, my hometown—
it's an educational center and a good place to grow
up. There are a number of colleges in the area, including Lehigh University in Bethlehem and Lafayette in
Easton. Muhlenberg, which is in Allentown, always
provided a batch of nice Jewish premed students for
the local Jewish families to bring home for the holi-
days and serve up on the altar of available daughters.
I was one of those girls, but I had a slight problem.
My mom, Pat Kauffman, is tall, slender, and attractive;
her daughter, Kathy, was . . . tall. I was a grungy,
shleppy, overweight kid with a glamorous mother.
During my adolescence and early teens, I most closely
resembled an ostrich—thin legs supporting a bulky
body. Besides being overweight, I had a big, crooked

17

nose and terrible hair. (If some of you think my hair is bad now—and I know some of you do—you should have seen my hair then!) As a child I had thick, weird hair. Puberty arrived and my hair left and now I have *thin*, weird hair, which is a constant source of irritation. (I have Bad Hair Days galore—but more on BHD later.)

My mom was the most glamorous person I ever saw; she was the most glamorous person most anyone in Allentown ever saw. There was no hope for me as a child even to try and enter the stratosphere of sophisticated elegance my mother inhabited. She's still dazzling, and I adore her. She's appeared with me on QVC many times, and the viewers are crazy about her, too. She's been asked to return again and again. There's a twist—my mother following in my footsteps! Although my mother's a super lady and a loving parent, growing up in her shadow wasn't easy and would have been a lot harder if my grandmother Ida Lerner and my Aunt Jeanne Lerner, my mother's sister-in-law, hadn't been around.

You've heard of the Bermuda Triangle. Well, from the ages five to fifteen I inhabited the Kathy Triangle. The apex was yours truly, and my grandmother and aunt were the other two points. They each lived a block away from our house, Nanny to the left and Aunt Jeanne to the right, and I wore a triangular path eating my way from one home to the other. Nanny was a wonderful cook, and Aunt Jeanne baked killer chocolate cake every single day! As a result of my excessive chowing down, I weighed close to 170 pounds before I reached my teens. Fortunately, I had some height. At the age of eleven, I was five-feet six inches tall. I looked over the heads of most of my classmates, including the boys. I was a big girl and while there were advantages—I was a leader because I dominated physically—there were far more drawbacks. Bar mitzvahs were the worst. The boys hadn't begun to grow, and when they danced with me they buried their heads in my chest. I'm pretty sure they weren't as upset as I was about the results of the discrepancy in height. (I'd bet a bundle little Hanky Bishop, for one, thought he'd died and gone to heaven when he celebrated turning thirteen by dancing with his head nestled between Kathy Kauffman's budding boobs.) I prayed for the day when things would even out and the boys would catch up.... That day, alas, was a long time in coming.

What really bugged me during these pubescent years was my nose. I was about ten and a half and playing baseball with my brothers when someone hit a line drive, which I deftly fielded with my face. I passed out and, upon awakening, discovered that my nose had moved to the side. My mother claimed I dreamed up this incident as an excuse to get a nose job, and we had argument after argument about my schnozz. "It's crooked because it was hit," I maintained. "It's crooked because it's crooked. And who cares?" my mother countered. I cared. All my friends were pretty and petite and had beautiful hair and decent noses. I really did stand out like Big Bird in the middle of all these darling little chickadees. I had to wait years before I did something about my nose, so my earliest attempts at making myself more presentable focused on my weight problem.

I have to state right here that my mom never, ever made me feel bad. I had the burden of being the ungainly daughter of a beautiful mother, a mother who taught charm school, yet she never said a harsh word about my size. She tried to bolster me as best she could, and making cracks about my weight would not have been productive. My father was not as supportive; he did not like heavy women and, though he never was out-and-out cruel, he didn't mince words: "You're starting to look fat. You ate like a piggy today. You have to control yourself." Unbelievable as it may

19

sound, on one occasion he said that if I lost 20 pounds he would take me to New York for cheesecake. What an incentive. I should diet so I could eat cheesecake? He should've talked diamonds and it might have worked. Truly, I seemed to do nothing but sleep and eat between the ages of nine and fourteen, and I really packed on the pounds.

If I were looking for concrete reasons for my behavior I'd say one very good one had to be that I was incredibly lonely. I usually came home to an empty house and would proceed to eat myself into a stupor and then take a nap . . . a lethal combination. It seemed that while everyone else had June and/or Ward Cleaver waiting at home, no one supervised me. I was the original latchkey kid. (What's funny to note is that today I'm okay—funny, industrious, successful, and well adjusted—while some of those Cleaver kids are messed up and still looking for themselves.) My dad had gone back to school, and even as he studied for an advanced dental degree, he worked a full-time job at my grandfather's department store. (Dad had started out in dentistry but had to give it up after suffering an injury to his back. During my childhood, he returned to his chosen profession.)

My mother was busy, too. She was involved with her fashion business and a Saturday morning charm school. Twice a year Pat Kauffman's Charm School ran a six-week course in conjunction with the local department store, H. Leh & Company. In those days most women in Allentown, as elsewhere, didn't work; they raised families and were members of the Junior Auxiliary, or the DAR, or the Women's Country Club, or the Jewish Community Center. Many were volunteers; my mother was a professional. She had her own stable of models gleaned from the best of the charm school students and very often ran two fashion shows a day, five days a week. My mom hadn't started out to be a fashion consultant; her goal was Broadway.

Hair Wins by a Nose

She could sing, she could dance, she was gorgeous, and had legs up to her neck. She had it all. In her early twenties she auditioned for the USO, figuring it would get her into the big world of entertainment, the world of the Radio City Rockettes and similar show business institutions. Her father got wind of what she'd done and went to the theater, where he was informed that his daughter was terrific and slated to be hired. "Listen," my grandfather told the USO head honcho, "my daughter belongs home with a husband and a family. Don't encourage her with this kind of life. Tell her she hasn't got the talent. Don't hire her."

They did what my grandfather asked because this was the fifties and men ruled the roost. My mom's potential career was checked by her own father. Many years later he told her what he'd done. (I'm surprised she didn't punch him out; I would have!) By that time she'd married and had children—oh, did she have children! My older brothers, Ron and Bruce, were thirteen months apart, and I came along six years later. So there she was with a husband and kids and still, she had all this energy and talent—somehow it had to come out. First she put her efforts into the community and did volunteer work, then she broadened her scope. She went to Leh's and started doing fashion shows and became an institution—everyone knew Pat Kauffman. She always needed models for her shows and was notorious for walking up to attractive women on the street and saying, "You're very pretty. Have you ever modeled?" It's a wonder she wasn't arrested. My mother used women of all ages and sizes; in fact, she was the first to employ plus size models. Aware that her audience was composed of women in their thirties and forties, she also pioneered the use of older women and was the first to feature a senior model, a woman in her sixties, in fashion shows. My mother traveled all over Pennsylvania doing her thing, and it wasn't just a way of letting off steam, either—the extra

21

money she brought in was necessary to keep us going while my father pursued his career. In fact, if you're a QVC watcher, you know one of my mother's pupils—QVC's very own Pat James Dimentri—is a graduate of my mother's charm school. Pat is one of the ones who "made it"—in the eighties she modeled blue jeans in Japan.

Because of my mom's professional affiliations, I had clothes galore. Usually I'd get a new outfit every week, and believe me, I needed them—I couldn't hold a size for more than seven days. She'd buy a 12 on Monday and the next week I needed a 14. Without making a big deal about it, she tried very hard to camouflage my hugeness. She took me to the preteen section of Lord and Taylor, a haven for young biggies. I wore Jonathan Logan preteen size 15 dresses—huge squares of material that looked like cloth refrigerators. This was the miniskirt era, and I loved to wear my hems high. Like my mom, I had long legs, and they were the one part of my body I was proud of! The dresses were cut "up to Kansas" and I looked like Big Bird. My mother swamped me with clothes, and part of the reason was her enforced absence. She had to be away from home a lot and must have felt guilty. I don't blame her, though—I never have and I never will. She did what she had to do to keep herself going. And, more important, the times we did spend together are some of my dearest and happiest memories. It's unfortunate that parents beat themselves up for the times they weren't there. What really counts is how you enjoy and take advantage of the times you are together. One thing's for sure, part of my propensity for clothing comes out of my being constantly supplied with new outfits; I had a wardrobe before I had a waistline. One day the issue of my weight came to a head. I was lumbering around the bases during a game and was thrown out (I played a lot of kickball as a kid). As I dejectedly walked to the sidelines I heard one of my teammates complain loud and clear, "Kauffman's a loser! She's just too fat." Oh, did that hurt. That evening I waited up for my mother to come home. As I told her what had happened my lips began to quiver at the corners and soon I was bawling.

"What am I going to do, Mom?" I cried. "What can I do?"

"I'll help you," she promised. "We're going to find something or someplace for you." How typical of her to go immediately after a constructive solution rather than beat a dead (fat) horse. She did some research and by gosh came up with a support system, a new program called Weight Watchers. She located the Allentown chapter and drove me to a meeting. I was barely fifteen when yours truly, Kathy Kauffman, became one of the earliest and youngest members of that pioneer organization. The meetings were presided over by a husband-and-wife team, Arnie and Pearl Brooks, two original Weight Watchers participants. Arnie had lost more than 100 pounds, and Pearl wasn't far behind. Arnie was an okay guy, but judging from his belly he enjoyed talking about weight watching more than he enjoyed doing it. I walked into my first meeting with my mom leading me by my crooked nose. The first thing you had to do was get weighed. I stepped onto the scale and watched the needle zero in on the number 169. I had some weight to lose, no question. In those days Weight Watchers suggested a 20-pound loss as the goal.... Forty would have been more like it for me. I joined and immediately became the little star of the class, first because I was so young, and second—I lost more than six pounds in the first week. I was so proud of my achievement that I celebrated by gaining a quarter of a pound the second week and another half pound the third week. After the initial glorious week I began snick-snacking here and there and supplementing my Weight Watchers regimen with cookies and other goodies. Surprise! My

23

weight began to inch back up. Despite my obvious gains, Arnie and Pearl were very forgiving for the next few meetings. They just weighed me and gave me little "suggestions" about keeping on the diet. Then, on my fourth visit, Arnie interrupted his lecture.

"I want to ask the class a question," he announced. "How many of you can open the freezer and take out ice cream without making a noise?" A few hands, including mine, went up.

"Okay," continued Arnie, "how many of you can open up the cookie jar without making any noise?" Again, my hand shot up. "And how many," Arnie asked, "can open a candy bar without having the paper rattle?" Up went Kathy's hand.

"So you can do all that, eh?" Arnie said to me.

"Yes," I said smiling.

"Honey, can I say something?"

"Sure," I answered.

"You look it."

Arnie wasn't exactly following the Weight Watchers credo by letting me have it in front of the class—meetings were not supposed to be run that way. I heard him, though, and the next week I lost six and three-quarters pounds. I was a star again.

Since those WW days, my star and my weight have risen and fallen, and I've had to face the fact that weight gain is a constant in my life—it's a struggle to stay on the sunny side of 160 and I've yoyoed around over the years. My viewers are the first to notice changes in my appearance, and they let me know what they think about it, too. Last year I went up to 164 pounds, and the letters poured in.... "You're putting on weight, Kathy, what's the story?" The story was the old one about eating too much of the wrong foods like the homemade chocolate chip cookies that are served in the green room at QVC. (Green room is a universal term for the place where artists or celebrities await the moment that they go out on stage as a guest or a performer.) QVC bakes the cookies every day, and the aroma is enough to drive anyone—anyone who loves food, that is—crazy. It drove me crazy. In the first four years I worked at QVC I was a cookie monster and ate myself up twenty-two pounds—that's a lot of chocolate chips. The funny thing is, although the cookies are made for the guests, *they* don't eat them, the hosts do. You come off a show all tuckered out and go to sit in the green room and chat with an upcoming guest and bingo! there's a chocolate studded cookie on its way down your gullet, and then another and another and another. None of my colleagues gobbled up the cookies the way I did. I didn't need the viewers to tell me I had ballooned up. For one thing, I was having great difficulty putting on my necklaces. You always put on a necklace with the clasp in front so that you can attach the ends easily and quickly, then you move the clasp around to the back. Well, that's the way you do it when you don't have five chins blocking the way—which I did! Next, my clothing began to show the strain of trying to get around my girth; zippers didn't close, and snaps didn't snap, and all the time that I was gaining I was working with perfect sizes 6, 8, and 10.

Finally, I had enough. There was no thunderbolt, no great meaningful moment or any particular comment by any viewer, I just had enough, and I decided to do something about it. I knew I couldn't lose on my own—or, if I did, I stood a good chance of putting it right back on, so I went to a doctor who was recommended by a friend. This man used acupressure and didn't speak English that well. I remember that he pinched my ear so I wouldn't eat. Typical Kathy—my ear hurt, but I ate. I needed some other pressure, and with the doctor's help I worked out my own regime, which I dubbed the No Thank You Diet. I'm not saying this diet is for everyone—it's very stringent, but it sure worked for me, and it's real simple. First, I said no to sugar, particularly to the three C's—cookies, candies, and cakes. Next, I said no to bread, and that was a nightmare—I love bread. Then I said no to dairy products. Good-bye to cream, cheese, ice cream, the works. As far as protein, I wasn't a meat eater, so it was easy for me to go for the fish. Things moved along at a slow, steady pace, and then I made the big decision to give up pasta. I know lots of people on diets eat pasta, and I would have too except that I can't eat just a portion of spaghetti—I have to have the whole box. (New findings show that some people do not process carbohydrates that well, and I think I am one of them. Pasta is a treat for me, not a staple.) For the next ten months I didn't have a piece of bread or a slice of pizza, but I didn't miss a lunch or a dinner out, and I drank wine with dinners, too. I ate cereal, fruit, fish, and vegetables and I truly ate well. I also learned a few things about weight control by watching the way the celebrities who came to QVC ate. They don't pig out. Those guys watch themselves and eat selectively. I dined with Tova Borgnine on one occasion and noticed that she had two skinny slivers of smoked salmon and two capers on her plate, while I had two bagels, a huge glop of cream cheese, and chunks of smoked salmon on mine. On my No Thank You Diet I took my cue from Ms. Borgnine and dumped the bread and cheese and cut down the fish. Chemicals were out and fresh wholesome food was in, and the effects of eating carefully and well began to show. My skin was radiant, and that was a result of the foods I ate *and* the fabulous Hydron skin products I used. The fat melted, and by God, I became a perfect 10. Everyone noticed the change, from my viewers to my guests. Joan Rivers commented on my appearance and told me I looked fantastic. Well, I felt fantastic, too. It took ten months, but I took off fifteen pounds. Look, I'll never be a reed and that's fine—I don't think you have to be a stick to look good in (or out

26

of) clothes. I have to admit I've become a little lax lately and haven't been saying "No, thank you" as much as I should. I've tried a couple of desserts here and some rolls there and I'm starting to put back weight, but at least I'm aware of it and I'll take the necessary steps to get myself back to "normal."

I'll tell you one thing, no matter what I'm packing on my form I've never forgotten how it feels to be an object of scorn simply because of excess weight. I sell a lot of plus size product on QVC—probably our most popular sizes are 2X and 3X. Those sizes do well because QVC allows big women to shop in the privacy of their own homes and not in public dressing rooms. Even so, the larger woman is never totally protected from comments. A designer will come on to sell his/her clothing and repeatedly says things like, "This outfit will help you look slimmer and this one will make you look five pounds lighter and this one pulls in your tummy and this one makes your hips look smaller." I'm puking tired of that kind of talk. My feeling is, if you weigh 190 and we make you look five pounds lighter, you now look 185—you are still a large woman. It is irrelevant. If you are healthy, take care of yourself, keep yourself neat and clean, and have energy and feel good about getting up every day and participating in an active lifestyle, who cares if you look "trim" or not? People should get off it. Trim is for hedges. On the other hand, if your weight really bugs you and you can't get out and enjoy life because of it, then by all means, make the decision to do what you have to—that's a different story. I'm just real annoyed at every magazine cover promising to reveal the secret of looking ten pounds thinner. What a waste of time. (Now, if they want to tell me how to look ten years *younger,* that's another story. I'm interested in that!)

I have my regime when it comes to food and I also have one concerning exercise—I don't. What I mean is I'm not on any regular program of exercise but again, I'm not recommending my way to anyone. I used to be very active; I took aerobics and played tennis. Years ago I went with my then husband to a resort and while he was in the casino I played tennis. My partners were men, and I killed myself going after everything that came over the net so I wouldn't lose. I didn't lose but I put my back out. I went to see a doctor and he said, "Either you have to give up tennis or learn how to play properly." Ultimately, after several injuries, I did give it up. Since then, I've dabbled in a few forms of physical exercise. I pumped iron three times a week and really loved it. And, while I roller skate, play racquetball, and swim, I don't do any of these things religiously. Bottom line, my exercise consists mostly of walking my dog. I'm sure if I said yes to exercise it would be beneficial to my general health but I'd be a liar if I told you it truly was part of my "diet."

Speaking of which, I've one last word on the subject. I'm often asked what I most *hate* to sell and my standard answer is, I love to sell everything. The truth is there *is* one thing I dislike selling—diet products. As a woman whose weight is always an issue, I like to get away from it and focus on other things once in a while. I'm sure many women feel the same way. There's more to life than the bathroom scale.

A year or so before I began going to Weight Watchers, I had revolutionized my appearance ... that is, a very specific element of my appearance—my fingernails. I bit them something fierce. If I wasn't eating food, I was nibbling on my nails. In the ninth grade I decided I wasn't going to chew them anymore and just like that, I stopped. I mean it, just like that. I don't remember the motivating force, probably I'd seen pictures of beautiful nails or maybe someone commented on my hands. You know, one of those, "Gee, your

hands are so pretty, it's a shame you bite your nails."
(That comment is interchangeable with the classic
"Gee, you have such a pretty face, it's a shame you're
a blimp.") I don't think that nail biting is an addiction;
it's not like craving nicotine or food or liquor. Those
are compulsions that often require discipline to deal
with and in my mind, nail biting had nothing to do
with discipline. I quit and within six months I had
incredible long, strong nails. Everybody noticed them,
and over and over again I heard, "Oh my gosh, look
at those magnificent nails." My mother had a different
perspective. "Those nails are too long," she'd scream.
"Young girls shouldn't have nails like that." Then
she'd grab a scissors and chase me around the house
crying, "Cut them, cut them." The more my mother
hollered the more I loved my nails. Why not? I really
got a lot of attention because of them and despite my
mother's protests, *I* was in control of their length.

While I was never going to win a beauty contest for
my face, I always had attractive hands. My fingers are
long and tapering and really slender for a woman my
size. I wear a 5½ ring, which is small. Anyway, once I
got over nail biting, my hands indeed looked gorgeous.
People now said things like, "Oh Kathy, you've got
model's hands," and I became convinced that my ad-
mirers were right. The question was what to do with
these elegant assets. I called the Wilhelmina and Ford
modeling agencies in New York City, told them I had
beautiful nails, and asked for an audition. "Why
should we bring in someone from Pennsylvania when
we can take any girl and use press-on nails?" was the
reply. I got annoyed. "Why would you want to use
press-on nails when I'm right here with magnificent
hands and ten perfect nails?"

"That's very nice, dear. We don't need you."

I didn't get a job modeling my nails, but it was the
beginning of a lifelong obsession with them ... not
my obsession, other people's. To this day, everyone

29

expends a lot of energy on my nails except me; I don't think about them. Many viewers believe I have a manicure every single day; I don't. I cut my nails when they need to be cut and polish them once a week. I swear I don't baby-sit them, they're just there. Viewers worry that I'll break a nail. Hey, it isn't life or death. Big deal, it'll grow back. I rarely wear a false one, either; the only time I did was on my wedding day. (I had broken a nail and because it was such a special occasion, I put on a fake. The day of the wedding I was so fascinated by the phony I kept picking at it and the entire piece came right off. I got married with nine and a half nails.) I will say that a woman experiences a kind of confidence when she has attractive nails. (A woman who hasn't often tries to hide her hands.) I'm forever urging viewers to give their nails a chance to grow, and I'm real proud that many of them have followed my advice. They tell me they were "inspired" by *my* look, and now they love to show off their hands.

I know of women who make their nail appointments for the day after mine, and whatever color I wear they write and tell me they're going to do it. Hands are terribly important because we show so much jewelry. About two years ago, we female hosts were advised that hot nail polish colors were too distracting. Today I'm one of the few who will wear hot pink and coral or vibrant red. (Just to make sure management's watching, I'll put on a real killer color figuring they'll call or send a memo—they do.)

Hey, it's not just a question of long nails—it's a decision to do something for yourself, something that makes you feel better. I'll never stop encouraging women to do whatever it is to make themselves happy, whether it's growing nails or dying gray hair. Put it this way: If you have always disliked something about yourself and it's a *safe* thing to change, then do it! I don't recommend that people go out and have tummy tucks or the like because that's invasive and dangerous surgery. However, if you don't like your nose, or the bags under your eyes, or the color of your hair, fix it. I'm a good example of doing something for yourself and not just in the nail department, either. It took me years, but I did finally get up the courage to do something about my schnozz.

I really loathed my nose. Every time I looked in a mirror I saw a beak. In my early teens, I told my mother how much I hated it. "If this is bothering you so much, why don't we go for a consultation?" she said. So, we trotted over to an Allentown plastic surgeon for a *free* (an operative word in those days) consult. He examined me, then sat me down and gave me every gruesome statistic relating to rhinoplasty. Noses can fall off; you can hemorrhage to death; you can wind up with a pig nose. The guy terrified me . . . probably on purpose because I was so young. I decided not to proceed. A few years later, I went to another plastic surgeon in the same practice as the first doctor. Once again I was examined, after which the doctor sat me down and asked the big question.

"Why do you want to have your nose fixed, Kathy?"

"Because," I answered, "I'm fat and I don't have boyfriends and I think this would make a difference."

"Well," replied the doctor, "that's the wrong reason. Even if you get a pretty nose, you're still going to be fat." Two strikes. I decided to let the nose go. I got on with my life, got married, had 435 different jobs, and then one morning when I was twenty-seven, I looked in the mirror. There it was again . . . my big nose.

"I want to have my nose done," I told my husband.

"You're out of your mind," he said, "you don't need it. You're fine."

What did he know? I went ahead and made an appointment to see yet another plastic surgeon in Allentown. This time I investigated various doctors and selected a plastic surgeon who specialized in hand reconstruction. That's right—a *hand* specialist. Why did I choose this guy? I chose him because I figured if he saved limbs, he might not be burnt out about cosmetic surgery. I had other criteria. The doctor was married, had five children, and was home oriented. When I went for the interview I specifically asked what he did the night before surgery. "I'm usually in bed by eight o'clock," he answered. I didn't want a single doctor. I didn't want someone eager to party. I didn't want a guy who would come in and look at my face as if I were number two or three of the day and get it over with quickly so he could get out on the golf course or over to a singles bar. I wanted a skilled man dedicated to his craft, and that's why I picked the hand specialist. I'm lucky he didn't reconstruct a thumb between my eyes. Seriously, when it comes to important decisions like choosing a doctor, I'm amazed at how many people just select someone willy-nilly, fork over the money, and hope for the best. Not this woman! Even as a kid, I knew what I wanted and I searched for the person who could give it to me. Hey, you wouldn't buy a car without inspecting it. Well, then, why would you go to a doctor without inquiring into his background?

Once again, my mother came along for the ride and joined me for the consultation. After a thorough examination the surgeon told me that my nose was slightly deviated probably as the result of a former break. "See, Ma," I bellowed triumphantly, "I *did* get smacked in the baseball game."

"What is it that you want done, Kathy, and why?" asked the surgeon.

"Look, Doctor, I'm a happily married woman. I have a lot of friends. I am very well adjusted. I look in the mirror and I see my nose, that's all I see. I want it fixed. There's no hidden agenda, I just want it straightened. I don't think it's going to change anything in my life other than my appearance."

Hair Wins by a Nose

"That's fine," said the doctor. He was won over; my mother still wasn't convinced. She would have loved me if I had a horn jutting out from my head. I returned home and that evening asked my husband to support my decision. He agreed, although he didn't really believe I was going to have surgery; he thought I was going off shopping. A couple of weeks later I entered the hospital in Allentown with my mother by my side. When she called Jay after the operation and said I was fine, he was astounded. "You gotta be kidding," Jay cried. "You mean she did it?" He came down to the hospital to see me and take me home. A week later I went back to the doctor to have the bandages removed and the stitches taken out. At first I was a little skeptical about my new nose. . . . I thought it was too pug and I wasn't happy with the profile, and then, little by little, I grew comfortable with it, and one day, all the energy concerning my nose disappeared. It wasn't 100 percent perfect, they never are, but it was enough better so that I no longer thought in terms of my nose and I could look in the mirror without seeing something I objected to. No miracles occurred, I did not become a beauty queen, I just became more comfortable with my appearance. And that's why I never hesitate to encourage people who really know what's bugging them and want to do something about it, to do something. On the other hand, I feel sorry for women who have repeated surgeries. They are reaching into a large black hole and will rarely find what they need. Most often, it isn't a question of the way you look, it's the way you feel inside. If you're not happy with yourself, how can you expect anyone else to be happy with you? Plastic surgery may work miracles, but those miracles will only be skin deep if you haven't first perfected the inner you—that's what you have to work on. And you do that by making yourself the most interesting, exciting, thoughtful, and super person you can be.

33

3
Little (Ha!) Kathy Kauffman

❖ ❖ ❖

While I was growing up there were two different forces in my home. On one side was my mother, the resident cheerleader and a genuine "upper." On the other side, there was my father, the "downer." Basically, my father's the nicest guy in the world—except to the people he loves. He just wasn't available throughout my childhood, and when he did come around it was to tell me all the things that were wrong. In high school, when I announced that I wanted to be a drum majorette his reaction was, "How the hell do you think you're going to be a majorette? You don't have the figure." In college, I told him that I wanted to be a psychologist. "Psychologist?" he laughed. "You don't have the brains. You've got to have at least a master's or a Ph.D. If you think I'm paying for it, you're crazy." Okay, according to my dad, I didn't have looks or brains. The irony is my father *is* a nice man, he just wasn't a great father, and, too bad for my mother, he wasn't such a terrific husband, either.

No matter what I did or wanted to do, my mother saw me as a potential "great." If I went to her and said, "Ma, I want to be a tightrope walker," she'd say, "You'll be wonderful. I'll order the costumes." My dad, on the other hand, thought I was "average." In those days, I think everything *was* average about me except my weight, my nails, and my sense of humor. My dad's judgment of me was harsh; then again, he'd been through so much himself, he wasn't likely to be hearts and flowers about anything, especially his nudnick daughter. My father trained at Temple University as a dentist and went into the Army Dental Corps. Not long after he got married he began to suffer terrible back and leg pains. It got so bad, he finally went for a complete examination, and tumors were discovered all over his spine. In those days the procedure was simple, cut. Dad had them removed and was in traction for a year. Meanwhile, my mom was taking care of their two infant sons. When my mom got pregnant with the second child, my grandmother went wild. "How could you have another baby so soon?" she admonished her daughter. Actually, my grandmother blamed the whole thing on my father. She called him a "gorilla" and never forgave him for saddling her daughter with two children in less than two years—and what children! Ron and Bruce were devils; their favorite game was peeing on each other through the slats of their cribs. My mother had a helluva time raising those guys; they'd look at each other and start fighting, and she went nuts keeping them separated. She cried daily to my father, "If you really love me you won't leave me here with these two monsters."

My dad recovered from the surgery and in the process he lost a great percentage of his ability to walk and balance. Clearly, he couldn't practice a profession that called on him to remain standing most of the time (sit-down dentistry didn't come in until much later). So my dad went to work in the toy department of my grandfather's store, where he was responsible for everything from buying merchandise to shlepping boxes from the warehouse. There were no malls, no "-marts" in those days, just old-fashioned emporiums like my grandfather's. Lerner's Department Store was on three levels and *the* place to buy everything, from garden tools to girdles, from dresses to school notebooks, from candy bars to shoes. My grandfather himself sold merchandise in every department including bras and girdles and at various times, *everyone* in the family worked in Lerner's. At an early age (I couldn't have been more than seven) I became part of the "sales force." Of course, I stood around more than I sold, but eventually I did sell toys and candy at Christmas. I loved it and I really understood retail before I reached my teens. I got my sales savvy at Lerner's Department Store.

Lerner's was located in Northampton, a tiny Pennsylvania Dutch town ten miles from Allentown, and my grandfather could be found there every work day from seven in the morning till nine at night, and loving every minute of it. George Lerner was a Russian émigré who was called Judge because that's the way he pronounced his first name. (He never said my name correctly, either. He couldn't pronounce the *th* in Kathy and called me Kassy or Kas. My family still calls me Kas.) My grandfather was a workaholic, made good money, and enjoyed an excellent reputation. Yessir, "Judge Loiner" did very well indeed, well enough to subsidize his daughter's marriage. Although he had a steady job, my dad was not in an enviable position. Cut off from being *Doctor* Kauffman the dentist, he also had to accept support from his in-laws. We lived in a beautiful house because my grandfather wanted his daughter's family to have the proper surrounding, not because my dad could afford it. My grandfather paid most of the bills, and my parents were at odds because my mother was living larger than my father's income. My dad was resentful and sad at the same time. Despite his misgivings, my father had a good long run at the department store. Eventually, he saw the handwriting on the wall, and it spelled M-A-L-L. Sure enough, the malls came in and business at Lerner's evaporated.

Way before that happened, though, my dad had arranged to go back to Temple University. Sit-down dentistry was now a reality, and my father wanted to return to his chosen career. He called the dean of students at Temple and told him he wanted to specialize in periodontics (gum surgery). Quietly, without any fuss, my father spent the next two years journeying to Philadelphia to take the necessary courses even as he continued working at Lerner's. His classmates were in their thirties; Arnold Kauffman was in his forties and had a wife and children and a full-time job in Allentown, too! With all the pressure on him it's easy to see he didn't have that much time to spend with his family—that was my mother's job. She went to everything that concerned her children—PTA meetings, confirmations, graduations, assemblies—you name it, my mother was there. My father was just "too busy." Ultimately, that absence affected the marriage.

In 1962, my father finally opened his practice. I've got to hand it to him, the man really knew what he wanted and went after it—all the advice he gave me about finding something and mastering it came out of his own experience. Dad was a typical, old-fashioned kind of dentist. If you didn't have the money to pay for treatment, you could always do a little horse trading. "Sorry, Dr. Kauffman, I'm a little short of cash. How about a nice chicken? or a box of cookies? or a couple of tickets to a movie?" People liked him, he was well respected and had a lovely little practice, but it never was perfect; he was always, always working. He never had vision beyond the point of becoming a periodontist, either; he never knew how to expand his horizons, professionally or personally. My mother said that the whole marriage was reduced to a question and an answer: "What's it going to cost me?" and "We can't do it." We never went anywhere as a family, because he was always working. My mother got more and more into the fashion world, and by the time I was born, she was well established in her profession. Ron and Bruce were adorable as well as rambunctious, and my mother loved them dearly but she'd wanted a girl desperately enough to try one more time. All I can tell you is on the evening of December 31, 1950, the gorilla struck again. My parents were getting ready to go to a New Year's party. She'd showered and had her dress ready to put on when Dad strolled into the bathroom. They had a little time to kill and Dad smiled and asked what she wanted to do. And she smiled back and they were both smiling and sure enough, he nailed her. Just call me New Year's cheer. Nine months later I was born, and my mom couldn't have been happier—she had her precious daughter, and with my brothers at school and somewhat self-sufficient, she could devote herself to me. She decided to give up her fashion career and any other activities that might keep her away from her little girl. She was into the third week of her Stella Dallas routine when she got so bored she threw in the towel. She dressed me up real pretty, tossed me into a basket, and shlepped me off to the Jewish Community Center, where she began running fashion shows. I was exposed to fashion from the cradle.

It was inevitable that my mom would return to work. She was incapable of inactivity—not that she hadn't been doing things all along. Her father had prevented her from being a professional performer, but he expected her to work for the community, especially the Jewish Community Center, where he was very much involved. He'd raised money to build the center and shoveled the first load of dirt at its groundbreaking. He became the center's president, and twenty-five years later, his daughter became the

38

first female president, the only person, male or female, who held the same office as her father. The legacy stopped with my mother. (I'm active in many causes and observe my religion, but I don't want to be president of anything . . . except maybe my own company!)

So Pat Kauffman got her little doll to play with, and everywhere that Mommy went, Kathy was sure to go. "Have Kathy, will travel," was her motto, and she hauled me around in the basket to her various appointments. I may not have been born in a trunk, but I sure was raised in a basket . . . a *shopping* basket. Mother carted and pulled me along until I was old enough to go to school. Then, she hired a college girl, Marianne Reba, to look after me. We got along just fine, and to this day Marianne remains a good friend of the family. She became an anesthetist, and whenever any of us has to go into the hospital for surgery, we always ask for her. At various times, Marianne has been there for my dad, my mother, and for me.

I feel that I grew up in a joyous home. There were laughs aplenty and why not? There wasn't a straight man in the family; we were all comedians. Our house functioned as a gathering place, a control center, especially on Friday evenings. Friday was family night— the other six nights you could fend for yourself, but come the Sabbath, candles were lit, the tablecloth was laid, flowers were everywhere, and the wine flowed— the whole nine yards. And my mother dressed in a hostess gown to match the tablecloth. (Sometimes she even color-coordinated her gown with the Jell-O mold.) We'd go to the temple, and after services, everybody would come back for coffee and cake. Our home was a mecca, and the place was crawling with relations and acquaintances. My brothers would bring their girlfriends over and then disappear with them into the basement—not, I think, to contemplate the beauty of the Sabbath. The house overflowed with

39

people and good spirits and the richness of a *total* family life.

Things changed dramatically when my brothers went off to college. I was eleven years old, and since both my parents worked I was pretty much on my own and very lonely. I really missed my brothers. The younger, Bruce, was always sweet and indulgent. He let me stay up late and took me everywhere. Whenever Bruce went on a date to the amusement park or to the movies, he'd shlep his kid sister along—every date my brother had was a ménage à trois, and I was the "trois." Ron, on the other hand, tried to come up with ways to drive me crazy. He'd sneak up and knock me off my bicycle . . . things like that. I hated him. (That's all changed now that we're grown up. I adore both my big brothers.) When the boys went off to college, it left a terrible void. The activities stopped and nothing much happened around the house. I really looked forward to Thanksgiving and Christmas and their return. Sometimes they'd bring a friend from college and the whole house would reverberate with good spirits and good fun. The suitcases, the excitement, the family, and the food all brought the house to life again. And then they'd go and it was back to square one.

I watched an awful lot of television. I'd come home from school around 3:30, grab some cookies and ice cream, flop down on the sofa, and watch anything and everything that appeared on the little screen. I'd watch right up to the moment that my mother came home. If she were going to be late, there'd be a dinner left to heat up, after which I'd watch television again. If I had a little bit of homework, I did it. If I had a lot of homework, I did a little and went right back into the television. On weekends, my dad and I would watch the "classics." "The Jackie Gleason Show" on Saturday nights and "Bonanza" and the "Ed Sullivan Show" on Sunday nights. When I stayed over at my grandmother's I watched Lawrence Welk, which certainly wasn't my choice, but I wanted to be with my Nanny, and watching the champagne bubble king was part of the deal.

I was the joy of my grandmother's life and vice versa. She was a funny lady and we delighted in each other's company. I rode my bike a few short blocks to Nanny's lovely ranch house almost every day. Roses grew in the backyard, and to this day I have a great fondness for them because the sight and scent of those flowers send me right back to those happy times with her. As I mentioned, my Nanny was a fabulous cook and I eagerly sampled her wares. She made gefilte fish, which took hours to prepare and seconds for me to polish off. She made lamb chops, she made Jell-O, she made corn, she made pound cake, and whatever she prepared I ate. Often I'd have breakfast at my house, then bike over to her place, where she would make me another breakfast—scrambled eggs, a little toast—"Eat, eat." No wonder I had a weight problem! My grandmother shtupped me with food.

I slept over at my grandparent's every weekend other than the times that I stayed with my cousin, Terri. If I couldn't sleep at Nanny's, I threw a tantrum and a half. One time, when I was ten, I practically moved in. My mother was going through a tough period in her life, which we never talked about—maybe it was menopause or maybe my father was just plain busting her stones, who knew? All I knew was she was nasty and snippy to me and I couldn't stand being around her. I ran to my grandmother's. "She's mean, Nanny, mean. I'm going to live with you for a while," I explained. "Don't tell her where I am." Nanny immediately called my mother. "I don't know what your problem is but your kid's here and she's fine." They talked it over and decided to leave the situation status quo. So I hung out with my grandmother for about three days and then my mother called to say we had to have a talk. She came over and the talk consisted of her telling me that she didn't like the way I was acting and me saying I didn't like the way she was acting. We buried the hatchet and I went home. (I remember this incident vividly because it's one of the few times my mother and I were ever at odds.) How lucky I was to have the security of knowing that if trouble arose my Nan was there. It made a big difference.

Life was divided into two headings for my grandmother, "nice" and "bum." Either things were nice or you were a bum. "You should learn to play cards, Kathy, it's nice," she told me. And so she taught me silly games like Go Fish and Old Maid and War. I'm sure my fondness for cards, games, and gambling comes right out of these times with my grandmother. When we weren't playing cards, we were shopping. "I have to go to the supermarket," she'd announce. "You wanna come along, Kathy?" I was delighted to go. I knew she'd buy me treats like chocolate cupcakes. We'd get into her car and go off to the market. My grandmother drove a Cadillac . . . slowly. That Caddy was like a fortress; you barely could hear the outside noises, so while other drivers honked and screamed for her to go faster, Mrs. George Lerner proceeded on her leisurely way. (I grew up thinking that the Cadillac was the ultimate automobile to own and, not surprisingly, I drive one today.) Wherever we drove, to the supermarket or to the department store, my Nanny would buy a little something for her granddaughter. We had a grand time on those expeditions, and I still associate "shopping" with happiness.

My grandmother also allowed me to play with her jewelry, which was a thrill and certainly contributed to my lifelong appreciation of pretty things. She had good stuff, not a lot, but choice pieces—among them fine pearls, a platinum diamond ring, and a beautiful pair of dangling antique earrings. I tried on all of them and admired myself in the mirror while my grand-mother supervised.

"Nanny," I told her, "I love your jewelry."

"Hmphh," she answered, "I'd give it to you in a minute, but you'd make drek from it." She didn't think I'd show the proper respect and in the end she left everything to my mother, who did know how to treat fine things.

Yep, my grandmother was great. Unfortunately, her sunset years weren't that good. Everything went into a decline when my grandfather passed away. She decided that life without him really wasn't worth living and simply gave up. I was twelve when my grandfather died and by the time I was fifteen, my wonderful Nanny had become a sour old lady. One day she put herself to bed, literally, and waited for death to come. The problem was her body wasn't ready. She had a long, slow deterioration until she ultimately reached the point where she really couldn't get out of bed and was taking all kinds of pills. How sad. My grand-mother could have lived a very vital, healthy life, it was in her genes, and yet she spent the decades after her husband's death in a bedridden limbo. I visited her, of course, and sometimes she'd rise to the occasion and show a glimmer of the old feisty Nanny, but it just wasn't the same. The spark had gone.

I can't help thinking that it might have been a lot nicer for my grandmother had she had something like QVC to keep her company all those years. Many of our viewers are people who cannot get out for one reason or another. They tune us in and we keep them company. Sure, our primary objective is to sell mer-chandise, but we're in there for the long haul, too—our viewers are necessary and important to us, and we want them to know that. Also our electronic family usually is far less critical and demanding than flesh-and-blood relatives! Every day of the week, I have wonderful talks with senior citizens who are enthusiastic and delightful conversationalists. You don't have to be young in body to be young in thought, and these viewers are *my* role models for those sunset years.

Over the years I've been receiving my grandmother's jewelry pieces on a regular basis. On my thirty-fifth birthday, my mother presented me with Nanny's pearls. I wanted to modernize the clasp to make it easier to put on; my mother put her foot down. "You're out of your mind. These are heirloom quality, sixty-year-old real pearls. You don't touch anything on them, Kathy." Mom was right; I never did change the clasp. The pearls have real meaning for me and are my favorites of my grandmother's jewelry. They bring good luck, and I wear them for special events. I had them on when QVC went on the air for the first time, and I've kept a video tape of that broadcast. (I don't really keep tapes of myself around—just a few that are important like that premier broadcast.)

When I turned forty, my mom gave me Nanny's slide bracelet. (It's a double-chain charm bracelet, and each individual charm has two holes so you can slide it onto the chains. You keep adding charms and they wind up being mounted rather than hanging.) Slide bracelets are back in vogue now, and I have a magnificent one chockablock with charms, courtesy of my Nan . . . and, of course, my mother. So far, every milestone birthday I've managed to shnor a piece of my grandmother's jewelry. There are still a few remaining, and my mother and I have had in-depth discussions about their future.

"I'd like to take Nanny's watch and mount it on top of a bracelet and wear it as a bangle," I told her during one of these conversations.

"Let's not be in such a hurry," laughed my mother. "You've already got me six feet under and pushing up daisies and you're remounting my mother's jewelry."

I admit to having very strong feelings about my grandmother's things—and why not? I am the one in the family who really spent time with her. As far as my inheritance, what interests me are the pieces that belonged to her and those items that my father bought for my mother. I don't care what happens to anything else. Jewelry is more meaningful when there's a story attached.

When I'm selling pearls over the air, I tell my viewers why pearls have special significance for me. "You know how certain items evoke special memories. . . ." I'll begin. "Well, I forever associate pearls and Estee Lauder's Youth Dew and cashmere with my mom and a particular incident when I was in trouble." Then I talk about the moment when Mom held me in her arms and I nestled against her soft cashmere sweater, felt the coolness of her pearl necklace on my cheek and breathed in the Youth Dew scent. I tell about the warm fuzzy feelings but I've *never* explained *why* I was in trouble, and I'm going to let you in on that little secret right now.

My grades in school were, at best, average. I never relaxed in the classroom, so getting promoted was a big deal. On the last day of seventh grade I was especially thrilled to learn that I'd be moving on to the eighth, and I decided to celebrate by indulging in the rage of the day. I'm not talking about hoop rolling; the rage was nothing less than shoplifting. Yep, all us kids were doing it. We'd walk down the main drag, Hamilton Street, drop into the various department stores, and rip off trinkets, never anything big or expensive, just little tchochkes that were out there waiting to be illegally plucked. Can you believe it . . . Kathy Levine, Shoplifter? The big number of the moment was lucite rings, and Hess's department store had them in a box on the jewelry counter. The rings came in pink, blue, and orange and cost one dollar each. The challenge was to get them without paying the money, and the preferred method was to slip a ring on your finger and then skip off. Bolder kids would put one ring on a finger and another in a pocket and leave with two dollars' worth of stolen goods. I already had visited Hess's with a girlfriend, and we'd each pinched a ring. Mine was blue and hers was pink. I wish I could say I was racked with guilt, but I wasn't; I was thrilled.

On that last day of school in the seventh grade I was going home with another girlfriend, Ginny, who was even more elated than I at being promoted. We decided to mark the momentous occasion by going to Hess's and indulging in a bit of lifting, which Ginny had not yet done. We walked the ten blocks from school, went into the store, walked over to the jewelry counter, surveyed the situation, and began schmoozing over the box of rings. We were talking to each other, but our attention was focused on the contents of the box. I already had a blue so I was in the market for a pink or an orange; Ginny was looking at everything. I picked up a pink ring and ever so stealthily slipped it into my pocket. At the same time, Ginny grabbed two rings and jammed them into her pocket. Mission accomplished we meandered off to another department to look at clothes. Ginny and I were standing over a pile of sweaters when a woman dressed in a coat and carrying a shopping bag came up to us. She looked like an ordinary customer—she wasn't. "Excuse me," said the woman politely, "you have some store merchandise in your pockets. May I see the receipts?" Oh, the fear and trembling that overtook Ginny and me at those words. We were two dopey kids who'd never done anything wrong and now we were caught ripping off cheapo rings. We started fumbling and shaking and the woman said, "Come with me." We fell into step as she led us off the selling floor.

"Don't say a word; don't say anything. Just shut up. We'll get out of this," I cautioned Ginny under my breath. She was shaking all over. We were taken to a

Little (Ha!) Kathy Kauffman

small room with two chairs and directed to sit in them. The woman was joined by a man, and as Ginny and I cowered in our seats, the two of them loomed over us.

"We need to ask you some questions," said the woman. "First, we need to see the merchandise." I reached in and took out my pink ring. "Here," I said as I handed it over, "I only took one little ring. It's only a dollar."

"Listen, young lady, it's not just a dollar. Every ring is worth twenty-five dollars in fines. Have you ever stolen before?"

"No," I lied. I really didn't think that I should mention the other ring at home.

"Then why are you doing it now?" asked the man.

"Everyone's doing it, it's the rage at school."

"Who's doing it?"

What a dumb question. I certainly wasn't going to rat on my friends. "I don't know who's doing it, I just heard about it," I told my interrogators. They finished with me and turned to Ginny. "Let's see what you've got, miss," said the woman. Ginny pulled out her two rings, both of which were blue.

"I took two the same color so really it's just like one," cried Ginny. "It's not fair to count them as two." We were thieves and she was worried about what was fair. It struck me so funny, I got the giggles. Despite my misery, I burst out laughing. At the same time I realized that acting dumb probably would be the best way to pull this thing off. I'd take my cue from Ginny.

"What's your name?" she was asked. What's your mother's name . . . your father's name? What's your mother's maiden name?" queried the man.

"Huh?" said Ginny.

"Your mother's maiden name, what is it?"

"What's a maiden name?" asked Ginny. The minute I heard that response I felt relief. Ginny didn't know her mother's maiden name; okay, I didn't know *my*

47

mother's either. The name Lerner was big in town, and I was petrified to reveal it. If word got out that George Lerner's granddaughter got picked up for shoplifting, I was dead meat.

"A maiden name," explained the man to Ginny, "is what your mother's last name was before she got married."

"I don't know what her name was," cried Ginny.

"What's *your* mother's maiden name?" the lady asked me.

"I don't know," I replied, "I never knew her before she was married."

The man and the woman talked softly to each other and then turned back to us.

"You girls have to go to the courthouse to talk to the probation officer. We're going to send you there on your own. It's six blocks away, and if you don't show up in ten minutes, we'll know you've skipped and we'll send the paddy wagon. You're on your honor to show up."

Ginny and I *raced* all the way to the courthouse and got there in eight minutes. We were terrified. *Courthouse* and *probation officer* were words guaranteed to strike terror into the hearts of preteens. We ran into the courthouse, and the first thing I saw was a straitjacket hanging on a peg. "Oh my God," I thought, "not only am I going to jail, they're going to wrap me up!" The probation officer appeared and gave me and Ginny a good talking-to.

"This is bad business, girls, and your families are going to be mighty embarrassed. Did you know that we print the name of offenders? You happen to be underage, but we're going to enact a law that allows us to identify anyone who steals, regardless of age."

"So, it's not a law yet?" I asked.

"Not yet," said the officer sternly, "but it will be soon."

I felt a flash of pure joy. Soon was not now, and

Little (Ha!) Kathy Kauffman

that meant I was off the hook as far as appearing on a list of felons. Despite my relief at that good news, I was still mighty shook up. Ginny was, too, and cried through the whole scene. We were given a stern lecture and then released. I was shaking in my shoes on the way home because I knew the worst was yet to come. I would have taken the electric chair rather than tell my father; he would kill me. I walked along and envisioned all the punishments that were coming my way. I would be grounded forever; I'd never get out again. I would never attend another social engagement. I was toast.

"Listen, Ginny, I don't know about you, but I'm not telling my father. I'll get killed." Ginny didn't know what she was going to do. She was whimpering the whole time. We went our separate ways and I wound up sitting on the front stoop of my house waiting for my mother to come home. It seemed like hours before her car pulled up and she got out. I remember my mom was wearing an aqua blue round-neck cashmere sweater and matching wool skirt. She had a strand of pearls around her neck, and with her size 10 figure and those gorgeous legs she looked just like an advertisement.

"Hi, honey," she called out, catching sight of me. "How are you doing?" She sat down on the step next to me and I looked at her. Oh God, I thought to myself, she's so beautiful and so nice, and I'm so ugly and so bad. My bottom lip started to tremble uncontrollably. I burst into tears, fell into my mother's arms, and sobbed all over her lovely aqua cashmere. I nestled against her, and as I poured out my tale of dishonor and woe, I was soothed by her presence and enveloped by her scent—Estee Lauder's Youth Dew.

"Oh Ma, Ma," I cried at the end, "I'm so sorry. I'll never do it again. Please don't tell Daddy. He'll kill me."

"You're right," Mother agreed, "he *will* kill you.

49

As long as you've learned your lesson, we'll let this be our secret." My father didn't find out, but there were some close calls. Dad played cards every Monday night with a group of cronies that included Ginny's dad, and that week they were gathering at Ginny's house. My father walked in, and Ginny's mother— who wasn't so crazy about me because she thought I was a bad influence on her daughter, said, "If it isn't the crook's father." Fortunately, she didn't say anything else. Dad figured she was being ornery for some reason or other and didn't respond. (Twenty-five years later I told my father the story. You know something, he got so mad he wanted to send me up to my room, and I didn't even live with him anymore.) I truly was repentant as well as terrified and never, ever stole anything again, and I never forgot that moment when my mother comforted me on the front steps. As I said, though I've told *that* part of the story over the air many times, now you know the reason—the shopping maven was shoplifting. To this day, on those rare occasions when I see pearls and cashmere, and I smell Youth Dew in conjunction with them, I get the urge to pick pockets.

4

"Was It *Bueno* for You?"

❖ ❖ ❖

About the time my grandmother took to her bed, I was wallowing around in my midteens and embarking on a rocky dating career. Good old Muhlenberg College burst at the seams with potential escorts, particularly those Jewish premed students, and Lehigh had its quota of possibilities, too. I had several blind dates from both places, and they were really bright young men. "Bright" wasn't exactly my criterion, though—if a guy asked me out and he was breathing, that was enough. I didn't date as much as my girlfriends, and I truly believed my weight kept me from being popular. My pals were all Junior 5, and I was bursting into a Misses 16.

I went to summer camp for several years and for a couple of them had a crush on one of the counselors. After my camping days were over, I ran into this guy at a reunion. He happened to be a student at Lehigh, and before the evening was over, he'd asked me out. I can't remember his name, but I do recall that he gave me my first French kiss, that sexy exchange about which I'd heard and read but never experienced. The

51

actuality was not all that terrific. I skeeved and gagged
while it was going on; I couldn't believe that's what
all the fuss was about. Sporadic as it was, slowly but
surely, I was initiated into the rites of dating. I learned
one hard-and-fast rule—never accept a blind date on
New Year's Eve. It's a long night, and everyone else
is involved and not interested in what's happening to
you.

One New Year's I got fixed up with a guy who was
a disaster . . . absolutely the nerdiest-looking human
being imaginable. I wouldn't hold that against anyone
today, but when you're young, you're so swayed by
appearances—everybody has to be a movie star. Well,
my New Year's date *was* a movie star . . . Lassie. This
guy had floppy ears, floppy lips, thick glasses, and feet
so huge they entered the room long before he did.
Honestly, I felt sorry for him. Although everything
about him physically was yucky, he was a nice person.
And, oh my, was he ever thrilled to have a date. He
was all over me, and I kept thinking, If this guy kisses
me at midnight I'm going to throw up. I sat there
dreading the arrival of the new year. Everyone else
around us was necking. I kept up an unending flow of
conversation. My performance that New Year's Eve
beats anything I've ever done on QVC. I asked him
if he had any hobbies, if he liked sports, if he liked
movies, and I talked and talked and talked, but when
the clock struck twelve there was nothing I could do
but let the poor sap give me a peck on the lips. The
world's fastest kiss began when the clock struck the
first stroke of midnight and ended when it struck the
second. Of course, he called me the next day and
wanted to go out again. My mother lectured me on
how mean I was and what a nice boy he was and all
that stuff that mothers do and so I went out with him
two more times. (I wish I had a nickel for every time
I went out on a date simply because I didn't want
to hurt somebody else's feelings.) Then I said this is

ridiculous, it's not working and I can't do it anymore, and I stopped seeing him.

I met lots of guys throughout my high school years; one I particularly remember appeared on my horizon when I was sixteen. It seems this Muhlenberg student had been asking around for a nice Allentown girl to meet. He was told that Pat Kauffman, a very beautiful woman, a "Rosalind Russell type," had a daughter and sure enough I received a telephone call.

"Hi, my name is Ted," said the caller. "I'm premed at Muhlenberg College. I understand you have a beautiful mother. I figure where there's a beautiful mother there's got to be a beautiful daughter, and I wondered if you'd like to go out?"

"Perhaps you should ask my mother out," I snapped back. Ted laughed and said something about liking a girl with a sense of humor. I may have a sense of humor, but I wasn't in the best humor at this particular time. I had mononucleosis. The doctor ordered me to bed and told me to dress warmly and, most important, not to get overtired. I followed the doctor's orders and remained inactive in bed—for a while—then I began moving around the house and stuffing my face with food. I blimped up and as big as I was, I augmented my size by piling on the clothing to keep warm. I usually wore a turtleneck, a couple of sweaters, tights under trousers, and a jacket, plus a scarf around my neck. At any given moment, I was thick with clothing.

"I'd love to come and meet you, and we could go out," continued Ted. I explained that I hadn't been well and was recovering and though I couldn't leave the house, he was welcome to come over and get acquainted. He accepted my invitation and an hour later, the doorbell rang. I went to answer it. I remember exactly what I was wearing: a black turtleneck, a black sweater, a bright yellow wool blazer, a black wool skirt, black tights and a pair of boots, and a scarf

53

around my neck. I looked like Nanook of the North. I opened the door and there stood a skinny fellow who couldn't have weighed much more than my clothing and couldn't have been more than three inches above five feet. He looked up at me and his eyes widened like saucers.

"I hope you're her sister," he gulped.

Our meeting lasted a scant thirty-three minutes, but I'll never forget him or his immortal opening line.

My dating career was mostly dismal; however, those ferkakta encounters made for great stories. I had a reputation for having "funny" dates, and my girlfriends would call me in the morning to get the lowdown. That's one of the reasons I never turned down a blind date in those days; they usually made the best stories afterward. I figured a good story was worth a few hours of misery.

The time came for me to start thinking about college, and my father and I discussed my future. He pooh-poohed my desire to be a psychologist, because it would both take too long and cost too much money—and of course he reiterated his belief that I didn't have the brains. "You've got to major in something that you can get into right away," he counseled. "What are you doing in school that you like?" I honestly couldn't think of any subject of interest, so I threw out the first thing that came to me.

"My Spanish teacher's nice."

"Okay, you'll be a Spanish teacher," said my dad.

¡Olé! I became a Spanish major.

In school, I always knew I wasn't *really* brilliant; I also knew I wasn't stupid. I knew I was funny and in a way, I knew I was smart—I just wasn't smart at the times I should have been. Like I wasn't smart in arithmetic then, but I'm smart enough to know how to make money now. I just didn't use my smarts when I should have, when it mattered. Still, I never thought

"Was It *Bueno* for You?"

I was dumb, and I always knew I could talk. You might have thought I was dumb from my grades—they were terrible. I'm sure they were so low because I hated to study. I liked English and reading, and I loathed math, social studies, and chemistry. Sophomore year, I was flunking most everything and had to have a tutor. That didn't work, and I wound up going to summer school.

I loved summer school. The pressure was off, and every day I learned something. Of course, I had to get over the shock of having to go to school in July and August. I did real well that summer. The teachers were great, and I got straight A's, a far cry from my regular marks. Maybe I just needed special attention. Anyway, I realized that my poor showing during the school year had something to do with the quality of the teaching and not just my brain power. I also learned to use my brain along with my humor. The humor took over when the brain lagged. I could get laughs out of almost any situation and truly charmed my way out of a lot of predicaments, including flunking courses. If I were in danger of failing I'd go up to the teacher and do shtick. "Have you met my father? He's Attila the Hun. You've got to cut me a break and pass me in this course. I'll do anything. I will shine your shoes. I will wash your car. I will do your laundry. I will be your personal slave. . . . Just don't fail me." One teacher really laughed at my routine, "That performance *alone* will get you a D," he promised.

People always said that I'd end up doing comedy. Why not? I came from funny people. As far as I'm concerned, my sense of humor is my greatest asset. The jokes were plentiful in my house; the only thing we ran short on was discipline, particularly when it came to my schoolwork. While my friends had special places to do their lessons, I was never told as a child, "You're going to have a desk and a light and a chair where you will do your homework." No, I sat down at the kitchen table where my mother was doing her paperwork and chatting on the phone, or I flopped in front of the TV and, if my father didn't boot me out, did my work there. It's not an excuse, but I didn't have a specific discipline or routine, and I needed one. My brother Bruce didn't need that. He always sat in front of the TV with a quart of milk and a pack of Tastykake cupcakes and did his A-plus honors work while he watched TV. Me? I was dying because I couldn't absorb anything when there was noise. To this day I can't read in front of the television set, it's simply too distracting.

I was an "average" kid in every way except for my sense of humor and ability to express myself. That ability came right from my mother. Her public speaking taught me how to be at ease in front of others. As a child, I wrote very well. I loved to write and I loved to read. My mother encouraged this aspect of my personality and education. I'd be doing homework and I'd call out to her, "How do you spell . . . . ?" and then I'd say a word. The next thing I knew, the dictionary came flying over. "Look it up," she would say. And I did. I learned words and I used them, too. I became very comfortable speaking in public. As I grew older, I opted to work during the summer rather than go to camp. I worked during the school year as well—in places like Lerner's Department Store, Woolworth's, the supermarket, and a shoe store. I worked all through high school on Saturdays and on Thursday nights. I was industrious because of one reason, money. I always knew I had expensive tastes and I always knew I'd have to work to get what I wanted. I swear I knew from "good" before my mother did; I taught *her* how to spend money. We'd go to Simco, a local shoe store where shoes cost $5.99, and I'd turn up my nose.

"Ma," I'd say, "we should go to Chandler's."

"Was It *Bueno* for You?"

"Chandler's is in New York," my mother answered. "Why should we go to New York City to buy thirty-dollar shoes? It's too expensive."

"So what?" I'd say. "You can afford it. It's fun, enjoy it." This is exactly what I tell my viewers today. If you can afford to get something better, why settle for something less?

At the beginning of my senior year in high school, my parents set about finding a college for me—not an easy assignment. I'd already been discouraged from considering further education by the school guidance counselor. "You'll never make it," she told me. "You're not college material, Kathy. You're just average; you don't have the marks." Once again, a naysayer was trying to squelch me. The guidance counselor eagerly branded me "average" and determined that I wasn't college material—and this woman knew nothing about me. She had a folder in front of her and made a snap judgment, which could have colored my entire life. When people are in parental or supervisory roles it's critical for them to know how much impact they have on children. A flip statement like "you'll never make it" or "you're average" can not only hurt but often paralyze someone. People in power positions should be sensitive to children. They should encourage them and make an effort to let the kids know what's good about them rather than what's bad.

True, my grades *were* lousy, and my SAT scores just broke 1000, and most everyone who went to college scored a minimum of 1200. Out of the possible 1600, my brother Bruce scored 1599. He went to Duke. My other brother, Ron, was a little out in left field like me. I don't think he scored as low as I did, but his average was less than Bruce's. Ron went to C.W. Post Long Island and did very well. I wasn't Duke material and probably not C.W. Post material, either, but I wanted to go to college, and my parents figured we

57

had an "in" at the Long Island school. Ron made some phone calls asking if his kid sister who was no Einstein could come for an interview. "Bring her over," he was told, "as long as she doesn't have two heads and she can talk, she's got a shot." An interview was arranged, and I began preparing for it.

Naturally, the big question was what to wear? I wanted to look mature and I wanted to be the chicest thing that ever hit that school. I had spotted this incredible suit in one of the boutiques in town, a simple gray wool with a difference—the collar and cuffs of the short jacket were circled in FOX! (Please note, this was *pre* antifur days.) Plus, I found a pair of gray suede shoes that matched the suit perfectly. I watched that fur-trimmed suit like a hawk waiting for it to go on sale ($350 was way beyond me). Each day I'd drop by and check it out. Meanwhile, every free hour I had, I worked. I babysat, I sold shoes on weekends, I worked as a cashier at Woolworth's, I did anything that would bring me closer to the gray suit. The magic moment came, the suit dropped to half price and was doable. I scooped it up. The shoes cost $70, and I bought them, too. I spent a fortune! I don't think my dad was earning $200 a week at that time—but I wasn't asking him or my mother for help. I worked my tush off to get those clothes and when my parents schlepped me up to the Long Island college, I was farpitzed. I wore the gray suit and the gray shoes, my hair was styled and shiny, my nails were long and gleaming, and my face was fully made up. I walked into the room and the interviewer's mouth fell open— Coco Chanel hits C.W. Post! Knowing what I know now, I'm embarrassed as all get-out. I must have looked like a little girl in her mother's clothes. I wanted to be grown up, though, and I wanted to be in a fur-trimmed suit and in heels and with my nails done. I wanted to be glamorous because that was real important to me. I've always had a penchant for nice

things, and I always worked to get them.... I still
do. Despite my bizarre get-up, the interview at C.W.
Post went fine. I didn't have two heads, I could talk, I
sent a thank-you note to the interviewer, and I was
accepted.

College was okay. I had good roommates, average
grades, and relatively few dates.

In college I was forced to change one of my habits.
All through my adolescence I'd taken naps. I'd stuff
myself with food and then flop down on the sofa and
tune out. I had carried my sleeping habits with me to
C.W. Post and still snoozed a lot of the time. Most
likely it was a way of not dealing with things, and I
napped during the first six months of my freshman
year. One of my roommates was a pretty girl with a
very active social life. She walked in one afternoon,
found me on the bed, and called out, "Get up, Kathy.
You've just had your last nap." She dragged me out
of the bed and took me out to the campus snack shop,
where I spent the rest of the afternoon chatting with
friends. Something clicked. Why should I be hiding in
my bed? I wasn't a child anymore; I didn't need to
get more rest, I needed to get out and socialize. It
was energizing. My roommate was right, that *was* my
last nap. Once again, someone rescued me from myself. I couldn't see that I was hiding out until she made
me aware of it, and once I took a good objective look
at what I was doing—rather, *not* doing—I took action.
From that day on my routine changed drastically,
and I became an active member of the college community—and the big world. I read books. I got into music.
I had friends and I went out—boy, did I go out,
though not necessarily on dates. The drinking age in
New York was eighteen, so my roommates and I could
go to bars. We'd hitchhike into New York City and
hit the theaters and the saloons. Sometimes we'd go
to Maxwell's Plum, a trendy restaurant on First Ave-

nue, and meet young men. Every Friday, we'd hitch into the city. The first time a guy picked us up and lectured us on the dangers of hitchhiking all the way into New York. "You could get killed," he warned. I thanked him for the ride and the next Friday, he picked us up again and then it became a routine. He'd pick us up and warn us not to hitchhike. (Looking back, I realize how right he was. It was unbelievably naive of us to get out on the road. It surely wasn't as dangerous then as it is now; still, for young girls to hop into a car with a total stranger was pretty damn stupid.)

The summer between freshman and sophomore year, three college mates and I took a studio apartment in New York City. We each paid $100 a month for the rent. I was making $90 a week as a receptionist at a Wall Street business firm. The apartment was maybe 20 feet by 30 feet, and when you walked in the door you saw four cots, four hair dryers, four toothbrushes, and 400 pairs of shoes. (The shoes were mine.)

Maxwell's Plum was right near us, and we'd roll into the place almost every night of the week, sit at the bar, and, yes, pick up guys. In 1969, when a bunch of virgins like us went to pick up guys, we expected to have a good time, and then say good-bye . . . hoping that they might use the telephone numbers we gave them. "Picking up" guys today is a whole different ball game. This was innocent group fun.

One night a good-looking fellow sat next to me and introduced himself. His name was Peter; he was from Holland and we began to chat.

"I understand," he told me near the end of the evening, "that American girls don't stand on ceremony and like to have a good time. I find you very attractive and was wondering how many times would we have to go out before I could *be* with you?"

"Oh no," I protested, "you got it wrong. American

girls aren't like that. We like to go out with a guy and get to know him. I mean, you have to see someone at least ... at least ... *twelve* times, before you'd consider doing anything." Where I got the number twelve from I can't tell you; it just seemed like a good figure. So, Peter and I started seeing each other, and he took me to the *best* places—plays, dinners, sports events— it was fantastic and I had a ball. Peter was in the hotel business and worked at a fancy East Side hotel, so he had fabulous connections. We'd had our eleventh date; the momentous twelfth loomed on the horizon, and I was as jumpy as a cat on a hot tin roof. Sure, I liked him, but did I want to hit the sack with him? I hadn't hit the sack with anybody yet, and I wasn't so sure he should be numero uno. Can you believe my good fortune—between dates eleven and twelve, Peter got transferred to another hotel and had to leave immediately for South Africa. The moment of truth was skirted but we sure did have fun. One thing I noticed throughout my dating days: American men didn't ask me out, European men did. The reason? Americans placed a lot of emphasis on physical beauty and a great body, neither of which I had. The Europeans liked a girl with a good family background and a sense of humor. They appreciated family values, they enjoyed going out in groups, and were willing to get to know a person. In my experience the Europeans were interested in front-seat conversation, while the Americans were after backseat tussels.

Junior year was *the* high point of my college days. I was a Spanish major and, though I wasn't a genius in my chosen subject, when an opportunity came to spend a year in Madrid, I was eager to apply.

"What would you think if I went to Spain for the year?" I asked my mom.

"I think it would be great," she answered typically.

"How do you think you'll get the grades to get in?" was my father's reply. Though he talked "grades" I

61

knew he was thinking of the money. I also knew the program would take anybody who *had* the money.

"If I can get accepted to a school in Spain, could I go?"

"What's it going to cost me?" came the inevitable question. (I swear I'm going to put "What's it going to cost?" on my father's tombstone.)

"It's the same tuition as C.W. Post."

"You're not going to get in."

"Daddy, I'm asking you, if I *get* in, can I go?"

"Yeah," he growled. I applied and was accepted and, true to his growl, my father said, "Go."

The day of my departure, my parents took me to Kennedy Airport, where my mother proceeded to sob her eyes out. My brothers already were out in the world, and now the "baby" was on her way across the ocean—the nest was empty. I followed my mother's lead and the two of us cried buckets.

I arrived in Madrid and, along with three other American girls, moved into a flat with a Spanish family, Andres and Teresita Fernandez-Garcia and their children Alicia and Javier. There were 175 students in the program, and my three compatriots and I got the nicest family of anyone. Lots of students got stuck with hosts who were in it strictly for the bucks. These people did things like impose curfews and lock refrigerators. The Fernandez-Garcias were open and generous. You could do what you wanted and eat what you wanted—the exact blueprint for my happiness. I made instant friends with two of the other American pension mates and am still friendly with one of them. I'm picky about my friends, and when I bond it's forever. My roommates and I plunged into the Spanish language. We agreed to look up one new word every day and build up an arsenal of words . . . at least 365 of them, anyway. We vowed to try to speak Spanish together, and the first day was clumsy and comical and full of "por favors" and "graciases." One of the girls was from Texas and spoke Spanish with a Southern accent, if you can imagine that. We all struggled to make ourselves understood, but even though I'd been studying Spanish since the sixth grade, I had to strain to express myself.

My little Spanish "brother" Javier was ten years old, and his sister Alicia was sixteen. They thought I was gorgeous, and why not? I had long nails and dressed like a movie star. One outfit of mine really knocked their eyes out. It was a hot pink polyester pants suit with a tunic top and palazzo pants, which I wore with high platform shoes. I was a Yankee Carmen Miranda! All dolled up in my finery I strutted my stuff around the streets of Madrid and talked to everybody. I didn't realize that American girls were legendary—we had the reputation of being rich and easy—and all the Spanish guys wanted us. So, here I was sashaying through the town, and suddenly I had dates all the time. They were wonderful young men full of fun and genuinely nice, and it was pretty innocent fun, too, because we did everything in groups. In three months I spoke Spanish like I spoke English. I dreamt in it, I thought in it, I could tell people off in it, and I could bargain in it. And, when I spoke Spanish and made somebody laugh, I knew I was home free. My whole life was about making people laugh, and now I could be "me" in another language. I was in heaven.

I did a lot of touristy things and also shared lots of activities with my family. Besides my wardrobe, the Fernandez-Garcias were astounded by me on two other counts; number one, I was left handed and they'd never seen a lefty before—kids always were changed over from the "devil's side" to the right. People were fascinated by my left-handedness, and when I used my hands in public they looked at me like I was a witch.

If the Fernandez-Garcias were surprised at my

being a lefty, they were downright dumbstruck at my being Jewish. They'd never seen a Jew; they thought Jewish people had horns until I breezed into their lives—a left-handed Jew yet. There was a beautiful temple in Madrid, and one Friday night I asked Mamma Teresita if I could take Alicia with me to the services. She said okay, but I could see that she was a bit concerned, I mean, you gotta figure this was the land that gave us the Inquisition, and she must have had a lot of questions about what exactly went on in a Jewish temple. Would Alicia be sacrificed? My Spanish mother trusted me enough to send the kid with me and when we came back Alicia told her it was a lot like church ... boring. Matter of fact, Alicia slept through the whole service.

That year in Spain was not to be believed. I learned the language and some other things as well. I had my first BIG romance, aka my first adult experience with the opposite sex. I was introduced to a Spanish gentleman whom I'll call Pablo. He was thirty-one, eleven years older than I. He was single and well employed and on our first date he picked me up in his Jaguar and took me out for dinner to a fancy restaurant. Although I didn't know much about the cuisine, I had learned a few things about dining out. In those days you drank only bottled water, never tap water. Dining out meant drinking wine or Perrier. Perrier wasn't a status symbol then, it was three cents a bottle and a necessity. The waiter brought us the menus and in my best Spanish, I asked for water. "Agua, por favor."

"Gas?" inquired the waiter.

"No, I'm fine, thank you, just water," I answered in my native tongue. Pablo spoke perfect English and started laughing into his napkin. The waiter went off and Pablo explained that the waiter was inquiring whether I wanted carbonated water and not if I had some physical problem. I laughed and pretended I was just kidding around and then quickly opened the menu.

"What would you like?" Pablo asked.

"I think I'll have the steak tartare," I answered after spotting it on the list. Hey, I figured that steak with tartar sauce had to be good.

"Do you know what steak tartare is, Kathy?" asked Pablo.

"I most certainly do," I lied.

"It's raw meat," Pablo said quietly.

"I knew that," I protested. The minute I heard *raw* and *meat*, I felt like heaving. The waiter reappeared with the water. "May I take your order?" he said to me.

"You know what?" I smiled. "I think I'm in the mood for chicken. Yep, I'll go with the chicken."

Pablo was smooth and sophisticated and I fell madly in love with him. He seemed to like me, too. After a few months of dating, he invited me to fly with him to Paris for a romantic "tryst." I didn't even know what a tryst was but was intrigued by the idea. I wouldn't skip off without discussing my plans with my Spanish mother, though, so I told her the story.

"Could I go to Paris with Pablo? Would it upset you?" Teresita thought for a moment. "It's okay with me, but we'll have to lie to Andres because he'll kill you." (Where had I heard that before!)

"Fine," I said. "Let's say there's a conference in Paris and I'm going to meet my mother."

"That works," said Teresita. And as far as Andres Fernandez-Garcia knew I was flying off to see my mother. Pablo and I got on the plane, and I was so nervous during the flight, I kept running to the toilet. What was little Kathy doing on an airplane flying to Paris for a fling with a Spanish guy who drove a Jaguar? I was terrified, absolutely terrified. I didn't know what I was supposed to do. I didn't know one end from the other. We arrived in Paris, registered in a small Left Bank hotel, and were shown up to a twin-bedded room. Pablo went into the bathroom and came out with his pajamas on. I stood there fully dressed, staring straight ahead.

"Well, which bed?" asked Pablo.

"Huh?"

"Which bed do you want to do battle in?"

"Ohh." I pointed to one. To make a short story shorter, it was over in two minutes and he was asleep and I was positively miserable. All I wanted to do was get out of there. The next morning he said, "I have to attend to business. I'll be gone all day. Why don't you go out shopping and have a good time?" A good time? Would I ever know a good time again? For perhaps the only time in my life, shopping didn't do it for me.

I saw Pablo on and off for a year. Later, I found out that he also was dating the woman he'd eventually marry. I was just a nice American kid who provided an occasional diversion when his *señorita* wasn't around. And it wasn't even the sex—that was minimal. I was so green, it was dreadful. He just threw me a bone now and again by taking me out for a meal or something. I would wait for weeks for the phone to ring, and when it did I would die of excitement. The more I liked Pablo, the more nervous I became. I couldn't eat around him. I couldn't even drink agua with or without bubbles. I worried about how I looked and whether I was dressed right and all that stuff. I desperately wanted his approval. All told, there was too much anxiety on my part for me to fully enjoy my first really close encounter. Years later I escorted a group to Madrid for my aunt Elaine, who owns a very successful travel agency. I telephoned Pablo and told him I was in town; he invited me to have lunch. At that point I was looking pretty damn good. I was in my thirties, my nose was done, and I'd changed my appearance for the better. I wasn't a dumb kid anymore. I'd been married for a while, too, and did know one end from the other. The lunch was my triumph. "Wow," said Pablo when I walked in. "You look beautiful." Pablo was an okay guy, and it pleased me that he could see that I'd grown up rather nicely. I don't know where he is today, but I'm so glad that I had that chance to get reacquainted.

I saw the Fernandez-Garcias again, too. A few years ago I was going to Spain for QVC and asked our guide to call them. Teresita answered.

"Do you remember Kathy?" she was asked.

"Of course we remember Kathy."

"Well, she's on television and she's coming to Madrid. She wants to see you."

"Wonderful." And it was wonderful to see them again and a bit sad too. Andres had lung cancer and was in the hospital; Teresita sat with him all day, but I wasn't permitted to visit. I did get to see Alicia. She met me for dinner at an outdoor café. She was now in her thirties, divorced, and had a ten-year-old son. I would have known her anywhere. She had the same exquisite face, wide high cheekbones and thick, gorgeous black hair. She was a big girl, five foot seven and maybe 190 pounds. *Zaftig.* She wore a navy-and-white polka-dot dress and you could have spotted her for miles. My "little sister" was just a great big beautiful Spanish woman. My Spanish was rusty but in five minutes the two of us were shmoozing away. Now, here's a good example of why I'm crazy about Spain. A guy was sitting next to us and kept looking over at me. Finally, he spoke up.

"You're American and you have such beautiful eyes." I loved it, the guy was hustling me.

"What do you do?" asked Señor Don Juan.

"Oh, it's difficult to explain," I answered, groping for the correct words in Spanish. "I sell products on television."

"Who would ever buy junk on television?" he replied. Alicia lit into him. "Idiot, it's the wave of the future," and, God bless her, she proceeded to jump all over him. She was so cute. She didn't even know what she was talking about yet she immediately came to my defense.

When my visit was over, I promised to stay in touch and even though my schedule became particularly grueling, I've tried. I wrote Alicia recently, and when I go back to Madrid I'll visit again. I have to assume that Andres is gone now, but my affection for him and all the Fernandez-Garcias remains strong. When I think of them, time stands still and I see them as they were all those years ago. I was very fortunate to be with an extraordinarily loving and caring family.

I left Spain at the end of the summer, returned to the States, and finished off my schooling at C.W. Post. By the time I graduated, I had a sense of my own intelligence. I actually had won an achievement award for outstanding ability in spoken Spanish. At last I had a chosen field and only needed to find what was right for me. The problem was I took the job I was offered simply because it *was* offered—that's how I wound up teaching Spanish at Brentwood High School in Long Island. Teaching jobs simply didn't exist, and I was real lucky to get a position. I was, in fact, the only member of the graduating class of Spanish majors to receive an offer. (I had a fantastic interview and, of course, sent the guy a thank-you note. And, it didn't hurt that I spoke flawless Spanish.)

I arrived at Brentwood High full of good intentions, but the minute I stood up in front of the classroom, I blew it. I was twenty-one years old, and the students were sixteen and seventeen, and I committed the cardinal sin for any teacher. I wanted my students to like me, so instead of teaching, I entertained them, and they didn't learn a thing. At the end of the year every one of them failed their Regents (New York

State exams), probably setting a record for the school. Teaching requires preparation—it's not just grading papers, it's creating an interesting curriculum and a lively classroom. It's being available to the kids and being disciplined yourself even as you discipline them. I wasn't disciplined; I just wanted to slide by and have a good time. How could they be stimulated to learn when the lessons weren't inspiring? The kids were bored out of their brains, and most of them were good kids and deserved better. Sometimes I wonder if any of them have tuned in QVC and seen me; maybe it's better if they don't. Anyway, I made it to the end of the year and then was fired.

This was a devastating blow to my ego and my financial future. I felt empty, frightened, and without direction. How would I regroup? If I had stopped to consider my strengths in language, writing, and public speaking and my willingness to relocate, I might have felt more capable of rebounding quickly. As it was, I had no alternate plan, and one should always have a backup. I sure hated being fired, although I couldn't take it personally because I deserved to be fired. Anyway, I learned something very important that year—I was not cut out to be a teacher. I didn't want to give tests and mark papers, but there were aspects I did enjoy. I liked standing before the class and lecturing; in other words, I liked the "public" part of being a teacher, which is very similar to performing. It definitely helped shape what I do today on QVC.

After the initial shock, I refused to let myself get bogged down by my dismissal and chalked it up to another experience. In everything that I've done, I've always tried to take the good parts and strain away the bad. But in all honesty, I have to admit that I might have been a lot more upset about this situation had I not met the man I was going to marry.

5

The Boss and Groom

❖ ❖ ❖

When I meet people and they hear that I'm divorced, they invariably say "Who would divorce you? You're so funny. You're so nice." Why is it that everyone assumes that the woman is dumped? That's the way it is—a wife never leaves a husband. Well, nearly ten years ago, *I* did, but I'm still very close friends with Jay Levine and to this day, he kind of looks after me. For one thing, he takes care of a lot of my financial affairs, which is a real boon. I *spend* money real well; I don't manage it that well. Frankly, I'm so busy working to earn my living I haven't got time to hover over my "hoard." I'm a performer and an idea person and I need people to advise me in financial areas. I can't watch my money like a hawk, but I can't afford to ignore it, either; that's why I have someone like Jay looking out for me. Actually, I do have a lawyer and an accountant and consult with them before I make a move. I know my strengths, and money management isn't one of them. I need help. You have to be very careful that you get the *right* people to help. How many times have you read about a person who's been led down the garden path by a trusted adviser? I've seen those articles, and I don't want that to happen to me. The only way to make sure it doesn't is to stay on top of things, to be aware of what's going on and not to put *blind* trust in anyone—not even a beloved ex-husband. I always go over my own books, I sign my own checks, I do not turn my money over to anyone—I simply have someone oversee the overall picture. Like me, my friends all work hard, earn good livings, and invest their money wisely. Single or married, women need to keep their own accounts, save for the future, and stay out of credit card debt. Although I shop religiously, I am never over my head, and that's always been the case, regardless of my income.

Okay, back to my marriage. For nine years, I was Mrs. Jay Levine, and he was then and is now the nicest man I've ever known. Why did we split? Boiled down, he wanted to be a family man and I wanted a career, or, as Jay put it when the QVC opportunity arose, "You want to be a star." His journey's been quicker than mine; he remarried and had two lovely daughters and I'm still chasing my star.

I met Jay in the fall of 1973. I had started teaching at Brentwood High and as I've already explained, was not in love with my work. One weekend in October I returned to Allentown for a family bar mitzvah and during the reception, a friend of my mother's cornered me.

"Kathy, you look wonderful. Are you dating anyone?"

"No," I replied. "I live in a very remote area. There aren't that many eligible guys."

Her eyes lit up. "Have I got a guy for you! My cousin, Jay."

By this time my dating philosophy had changed and I didn't answer every call anymore. "Forget it," I told Marlene. "I don't take blind dates. The last one I had drooled on me. Better *I* should have been blind. I've

made up my mind. I don't even care about the funny
stories I can tell afterward—no more blind dates."

"Kathy, he owns his own business."

"I don't care if he's a Rockefeller. I'm not interested." Then, without missing a beat—"What does
he do?"

"To tell you the truth, I don't exactly know what
he does. It has something to do with a truck."

"Great, a Jewish truck driver."

"He's not a truck driver. I'll have him call you."

"You do that," I replied. And that was that. I forgot
all about the Jewish truck driver until a month or so
later when I received a phone call.

"Hi, Kathy. You don't know me . . ."

"Oh, yes I do," I interrupted. "You're Marlene's
cousin." No other guys were calling me—it had to be
her cousin.

"That's right. I'm Jay Levine. Marlene told me
about you. I hear you have a beautiful mother."

"Yeah, well, then take her out," I answered, using
the old line from my high school dating days. I was
snippy because, yes, my mother was pretty, and I sure
as hell wasn't, and it was a sensitive spot. Jay rode
right over my remark.

"I'd rather see *you*. Marlene said you were terrific."
I melted a bit after that and we began to chat. I asked
him what he did for a living.

"Why don't we just say I'm in sales," he told me.

"Okay, you're in sales. You must make a lot of
money."

"Not that much."

" 'Bye," I said, in jest.

"No, no," replied Jay, "I do okay."

I found out that he was twenty-nine years old and
lived with his mother in West Chester, Pennsylvania,
about sixty miles from Allentown. Close as it was, I
had never been to West Chester. We continued to

chat and he told me he was leaving for a vacation. "I'm going to Puerto Rico. I like to gamble. Do you?"

"Well, I like to play blackjack."

"Me too. How about if I call you when I come back?"

"Fine," I said. "You do that, and you have a real nice time in Puerto Rico."

"Oh," he added, "if our date works out, will you go out with me on New Year's Eve?"

New Year's Eve? The guy was talking weeks ahead and for New Year's Eve, yet! Oh my God, I thought to myself, if he's lining up his social life with a stranger, he must be a dog. "Look," I replied, "let's take this a day at a time," and I hung up the phone.

I lived in a cute little house near the school with two other teachers and one of them, Pat, had overheard my conversation. She walked by me and said, "You're going to marry that guy." And you know something, she was right. I had a feeling I was going to marry him from the second he called me and from the moment I laid eyes on him, I was certain of it. It was the right time, the right place, and he had all the right credentials. He was Jewish. He came from a good family and had a good history. My mother always told me, "Make sure you pick a guy who'll be at the train station at three o'clock in the morning no matter what. Pick a rock, Kathy, pick a rock." This guy was a rock. I knew he'd go through a hailstorm to be at the train station for me.

Jay called when he returned and we had the best conversation. His stories were lively and fun and we laughed a lot. We arranged for our first meeting. I was going home that weekend to buy a new car—my old one died—and we made plans to rendezvous in Allentown. I took the bus and as it headed into Pennsylvania, the weather started to turn bad; really bad. Snow fell and stuck to the ground, and by the time I reached my destination the storm had turned into a blizzard. I got to my parent's apartment fully expecting to hear that Jay had called to postpone our meeting. Only an idiot would drive sixty miles in a blizzard for a date—an idiot or someone who was eager to see me. Jay couldn't wait; snowstorm or no snowstorm, he had a date with destiny. Later he told me he knew he was going to marry me just the way I knew I would marry him.

I was in a tizzy of preparation. My clothes were wrinkled, my hair was not-to-be-believed bad, my weight was up, and there was nothing left to do but throw a tantrum. While I fumed, my mother took my clothes, ironed them out, and tried to calm me down. I was very excited about meeting Jay Levine. I didn't want the first look at him, though, and decided to hide out in the bedroom.

"Listen, Dad, you take a gander at this guy," I instructed my father. "If he's not nice, if he's not good-looking, you come back and tell me 'cause I'll go over the balcony."

The doorbell rang; I raced into the bedroom and shut myself in. I heard my mother walk across the room, open the door, and say, "Hello. It's so nice to meet you."

Suddenly, my father came into my room and whispered urgently, "Get out now, while you can," he said, motioning toward the window. "Take the balcony. Jump. Make it easy on yourself. This guy is UGLY." I sat on the bed in tears. "I'm not going," I cried, "I'm not going."

"No, no," laughed my dad, "I'm kidding. He's terrific. Don't take the balcony. Trust me. This guy's fine." When he wasn't being negative my dad had a great sense of humor.

My mother came to the bedroom door and called in, "Honey, your date is here." I could tell by the way her voice sounded that she liked him. I walked out, took a look, and knew everything was fine. He was

74

big and comfortable and wonderful and sat his butt down in a chair like he was home. He schmoozed everybody and then got up and said, "Okay, let's go." Twenty-five feet of snow outside didn't deter Jay Levine; he wanted to take me out. We were going to a disco and on the way I lit up a cigarette. "I need you to know, I don't like smoking," he informed me gently.

"Fine," I answered, "you'll get over it." But I did quit smoking shortly thereafter. It wasn't hard for me to give up cigarettes because I wasn't addicted to them—smoking was strictly a social habit for me. I stopped cold turkey, had a headache for a day, and that was it. Even though it was comparatively easy for me, I feel sorry for people who *are* addicted. (Friends of mine tell me how hard it is for them to stop and I can only say that, hard as it may be, it's something I think you have to try to do. There are many support groups and many new techniques like the patch, and I would advise anyone to use whatever methods are necessary to kick the habit.) Like so many who give up smoking, I started eating. I exchanged the cigarette for a slice of cheesecake. Sure, my weight went up. As my lungs cleared, my stomach expanded. Still, I felt a lot healthier and when the time came to diet, I didn't have to worry about substituting cigarettes for food.

We got to the disco and nobody was there; no one else was stupid enough to go out in a blizzard. We sat alone and talked and talked and talked. He didn't smoke and, as I discovered, didn't drink, either. "I don't like the taste of liquor," he explained. Thank God he liked to gamble, otherwise I would have thought I was out with a Puritan Father. We left early and on the way back I said that I hated to see him drive home alone. "Oh, I'm going to stay at Marlene's," he reassured me. He sounded kind of pleased that I would care. We reached my parents' place and he helped me out of the car and saw me to the door.

"I had a wonderful time," he said, and turned to go. He didn't say anything like "It was really nice to meet you," or "I'll give you a call" or, more to the point, "What about New Year's Eve!" I panicked.

"What about New Year's Eve?" I asked.

"Oh, New Year's would be great," he responded enthusiastically. "We're having a party up in West Chester. You've got to come." I made plans to join him on the thirty-first.

After the first date, I left on a vacation to Curaçao with my girlfriends. I'd saved up money for the trip from teaching dancing at an Arthur Murray Studio. I made six dollars an hour and was one lesson ahead of my students. I'm not kidding. I'd go into the studio about an hour before the class and learn what I was supposed to teach. I made money, but it definitely was the hard way. This was the era of platform shoes, and my toes were stomped on over and over again. My feet were bloody, but my dancing booty bought me a nifty little Caribbean jaunt for something like $499 inclusive. I arrived in Curaçao, ate myself into fat city, burnt myself to a crisp, and returned home with blistered lips, peeling skin, and a huge glob of fat around my middle. What a sight.

For New Year's Eve I put on a full-length, sleeveless, rhinestone-studded burgundy T-shirt dress. I looked like a sunburnt side of beef. Wonder of wonders, Jay Levine didn't seem to notice; he was delighted to see me. The party was great and I stayed overnight at his mother's house where he lived. The next day we were eating brunch when he announced that he wanted to take me to his workplace. "It's very important for me to have you see it," he said seriously. By this time he'd told me what he did—sort of. He was a broker for animal skins and bought from the slaughterhouses to supply the tanneries. I didn't have

76

a clue as to what he was talking about. Animal skins? Broker? Go figure. (Please remember, Jay had nothing to do with killing animals; he just bought the by-product from beef cattle.) After lunch we got in his car and drove to a slightly run-down stucco building, half a city block long, in the middle of a residential area. This was his place of business, and it had been his father's and his grandfather's before him. Jay was very young when his father died and, at nineteen, was deferred from the Vietnam draft because he was the indispensable support of his mother and twelve-year-old sister. By the time we met, he had "raised" a family, paid the mortgage, and handled the insurance; he was an "old" man. Jay was used to taking care of things, and I was looking for someone to take care of me ... even if I didn't realize it.

Jay opened the door to the hide house. We walked in and immediately were enveloped in the stench of dead animals. I gasped.

"Smells good in here, 'cause it's cold," Jay explained, adding, "summers can be a little rough." I was dying and he was telling me it could be worse! I put my hand to my mouth, hoping that the perfume on my wrist would help. "It's not so bad," I lied. "I can get used to it." I got used to it all right. I stopped eating meat. We walked in and the first thing I saw were drain gutters full of blood. I was dating Count Dracula! The "Count" explained his business. When animals are killed for meat, the steaks or whatever go off to the supermarkets and the skins are sold to "hide men" like Jay. Jay loaded his truck with the pelts and brought them to the stucco building, where they were stacked and salted. Salt cures skins and drains the liquid, and the end result is a dried, preserved hide. Of course, the liquid has to go someplace, so big troughs were cut into the floor and they were overflowing with a mixture of blood, salt, and water. I stood in the middle of this carnage, dressed to the nines and teetering on my pumps, while Jay explained the business to me. Here we were on our second date and I was getting an on-site course in leather goods. And you wanna know the truth? I loved it. I was thrilled to hear him talk about something that so obviously interested him. Jay had passion and pride in his work. We left the building, and as we walked through the salted stacks on the way to the exit Jay said, "When I see something I want, I get it. And I know what I want, so I'm giving you a year." I heard him, but it didn't quite register. I was too busy trying to get out of the smelly building to catch what he was saying.

"The fact that you didn't die in this building means an awful lot to me," he said as he closed the door behind us.

"Hey," I answered honestly, "I think it's wonderful. I'm fascinated with what you do. This is the coolest job I've ever seen. Not that I'd like to do it."

There was nothing better that I could say to this man than to admire what he did. And I wasn't kidding, I was intrigued. You really had to love the business to be in that smelly, bloody, wet, refrigerated place all the time. When we returned to his home Jay took me to a large closet in the hall and opened the doors. Twelve sheepskin coats—pretty expensive stuff—were hanging in a row.

"These are some of our coats," he told me. "You pick one for yourself."

"Really?" I asked. I knew those coats sold for hundreds of dollars.

"Sure, I always give a coat to girls I date." Much later I was walking in the streets of West Chester and a woman came up to me. "You must be dating Jay Levine," she said. "Yeah, how did you know?" I replied. "The sheepskin coat, honey, it's a dead giveaway," she laughed.

When Jay put me into my new car for the journey home, I gave him a kiss good-bye and said, "I had a great time." He smiled and repeated what he'd said in the hide house. "Remember, when I see something I want, I get it. I'm giving you a year." Three-quarters of the way back to Long Island it dawned on me ... he had proposed marriage.

The next time we saw each other Jay wanted to know how long we'd be dating and how serious we were going to be.

"Look," I explained, "I'm not ready to get married if that's what you're asking. Let's put it aside for a while."

"All right," he said, "I won't bring it up again." He did, though, months later, and again I begged off. As certain as I was that we'd wind up together, I wasn't that eager to make the BIG move.

"I tell you what," Jay offered. "When you want to get married, you let me know."

"Okay," I agreed.

We dated for a year and a half, and a good deal of our courtship took place on the road. One evening, very early in our dating, we were driving between Allentown and West Chester late at night. We were barreling along the moonlit highway on a cold winter evening when all of a sudden, Jay hit the brakes, pulled over to the side of the road, threw the car into reverse, and began backing up into a sea of oncoming automobiles.

"Where are you going?" I asked.

"Didn't you see it?"

"What?"

"Thirty-five dollars on the highway."

"Oh, you just saw thirty-five dollars? And how did you see it? Three tens and a five or perhaps a twenty, a ten and a ... what are you talking about? Where did you see thirty-five dollars?"

"Not in cash. I'm talking about the roadkill."

"You mean that dead animal back there?"

"Yeah, the animal," Jay answered as he pulled up to a dead carcass. "That happens to be a red fox," he said as he opened the door of the car, "and its pelt is worth thirty-five dollars." Even though he had nothing to do with the fur business, an undamaged pelt on the side of the road was found money. Jay got out of the car while I sat there staring straight ahead. He came over to my window and held up the animal by its tail. He opened my door and said, "Push over."

"Are you nuts? Put that thing down. I'm not sitting next to a dead animal."

"This thing's gonna pay for our dinner!" Jay cried. "Now push over."

"I'm not moving," I protested.

"Okay," Jay said amiably, "I'll stick him in the trunk." He went to the back of the car, opened the trunk, and tossed the thing on top of my suitcase. This was a lesson, a test, and one of many I went through during our courtship. I couldn't be squeamish because Jay was so matter-of-fact about such things. In the early seventies, fur was the craze. Pelts were in demand and thanks to Jay I learned all about animals and their hides. For instance, I found out that winter is better than summer because animals develop a thick coat for protection against the cold while in the warm months, their fur is scrawny and not worth as much. Jay was on the lookout for roadkill in the winter, and though he never killed anything himself, if he came across a dead possum or raccoon or fox, anything with a pretty coat that hadn't been splattered, he'd haul it in. He never stopped for deer, though; they were too big to lug around. That night, Jay zeroed in on that poor little red fox and took me out to a beautiful dinner. Not only did Jay treat me to roadkill safaris, he took me around with him to slaughterhouses. That's when I became a vegetarian. No kidding, I still abstain from eating meat.

For the first six months that Jay and I dated, I commuted to Pennsylvania from Long Island. In June, I got fired from my teaching job, returned to Allentown, and moved in with my parents. (They had sold our large house and were now in smaller quarters.) I hung around my parents' place and made no moves except to see Jay, and I sure did a lot of traveling between Allentown and West Chester. In my heart I knew I'd be marrying him, so I didn't feel any pressure to find my own place or to get a job that might challenge or interest me. I was in one of my funks about my future work plans. Now that I'd learned the hard way that teaching was not my bag, what was I suited for? While I was living at home, I picked up a job in personnel, which consisted of finding jobs for other people. We'd put in an ad for a secretary at $90 a week, and 900 girls would show up and I was supposed to place *one* of them. I was drawing a paycheck against commission, which is to say I never drew a paycheck because I never made any money. I didn't feel any pressure, though; I was living at home and my expenses were almost nil. I just hung out, talked on the phone, and shopped. At this particular time, things weren't exactly rosy at the old homestead. My mother was crying a lot and my dad was withdrawn and silent. Marriage to Jay began to look better and better. I figured if I married, I'd be able to get out of my rut and jump-start a new life. Jay arrived for a weekend visit in late spring.

"You know," I said to him, "we met on December twenty-first, a year and a half ago. Well, December twenty-first is about six months from now and it happens to fall on a Sunday. Would you consider having a wedding ceremony on that day?"

"Oh no," he answered. "When I asked you if you wanted to get married, the answer was, 'I'll let you know when I'm ready.' Well, now I'll let you know when *I'm* ready."

"That's fine," I said, "I just thought I'd mention December twenty-first would be a nice day." Truthfully, I wasn't that upset; Jay was playing a bit of tit for tat. I was confident that we'd marry . . . eventually.

KATHY LEVINE

On June 21, Jay and I were on the road to West Chester and we passed a cemetery. I know it was the twenty-first because that always was an important number for us.

"I want to pull in here," Jay said, turning the car through the gates.

"Anybody I know?"

"Actually, my family's here. This is where my grandparents and my father are buried."

We got out of the car and started walking up and down the aisles. I bitched the whole time. "What are we doing in a cemetery?" I complained. "It's gloomy." Jay pointed to different tombstones and called out names like it was old home week. "Hey, there's Stevie's father. Oh, and there's Al's mother."

"Great, great," I mumbled, "I don't want to be here. Let's get out."

"Wait," he said as he stopped at a tombstone inscribed LEVINE. "I want you to meet my father." We stood over the grave and then Jay turned to me. Tears ran down his cheeks as he said, "Will you marry me?"

"I can't believe it," I gasped, "You're proposing to me in a cemetery. Why are you doing this?"

"I couldn't think of a better place. I adored my father and he would have loved you. I wanted you to meet him." He took a pebble and placed it on the tombstone, which is an old Jewish custom, and then leaned over the grave. "Dad, this is Kathy."

"How do you do," I said to the grave. "Okay, I'll marry you," I said to Jay. We met in a blizzard, we spent our second date in a bloody hide house, and now he'd proposed in a cemetery!

Jay wanted to buy me a ring, and I wanted something unusual—a heart-shaped diamond. I also wanted to fashion the setting myself. I had a particular design in mind for years. Jay's cousin, a jeweler, brought three loose heart-shaped stones from which I could choose. One stone was huge, a killer; the next was

82

very nice but very small, and the third was big but slightly misshapen (I told Jay that last heart-shaped diamond needed bypass surgery). Of the two remaining choices, I opted for the killer until Jay's cousin pointed out that the large stone was flawed and slightly yellow. The size had blinded me. Eventually I surrendered to the expert's opinion, selected the flawless 2 carat diamond and designed a bold, wide, crisscross gold band on which to place the stone. A month before our wedding, on November 21, Jay gave me the finished product in a cranberry-colored velvet ring box. It was breathtaking. (Fifteen years later, QVC bought the rights to my design and since then, Kathy's Ring has produced in excess of $7 million! If you think *I* got rich off of this, think again. I sold the rights for a small flat fee. It was a fair deal at the time and I have no regrets. Kathy's Ring has given us all a lot of pleasure.)

Jay and I planned the wedding for December 21 and my dad really hassled me about finances. "I have five thousand dollars to spend," he announced. "You can take the money or you can have a wedding, it's your choice."

"I'll take the wedding," I said.

My mom and I went to Bergdorf Goodman's to look for a wedding dress, and I do mean "look." Money was tight, and we had no intention of purchasing the dress there; we just wanted to choose one, get the style number, and then my mother could order it through her store. The first dress I tried on was $180. It was absolutely positively the simplest white dress you ever saw, no lace, no nothing. (Remember Quiana?) Unadorned as it was, the price was right—my mom could get it for $90. We wrote down the number and as we left the dressing room, I saw another girl trying on a gown. This one had a $1,200 price tag, and it was beautiful—beautiful, with beads and lace and everything. It was to die for and I had a twinge of sadness because I wanted to look like a fairy princess at my wedding but I couldn't touch that price. I had bought the plainest gown in the world and believe me, I only settled for simplicity because of necessity. (Here's a bit of Kathy insight: You could wear a brown paper hat and scuba fins at your wedding and you'd still be just as married as if you wore the most gorgeous dress imaginable.)

When Jay and I began dating, I was eager for him to meet my beloved grandmother, and I took him to see her right after he returned from his vacation in Puerto Rico. Jay was wearing blue velour pants (velour was the rage then) and a loud print shirt. He also sported a big mustache. With his suntan, his mustache, and his outfit, he looked for all the world like a riverboat gambler. As usual, Nanny was heavily medicated and confined to quarters. I brought Jay into her room and we stood by her bed. "Nanny, this is Jay," I said. She turned her glazed eyes and looked at him. "Hmmmph," she grunted and, closing her eyes, she turned away.

After Jay left, I went back to talk to her. Once again she opened her eyes and this time she had something to say. "What kind of bum is that you brought here? What kind of clothes and that mustache!" Nanny was not impressed, and that distressed me. I told my fiancé we had to go for a revisit. We did, a few weeks later, and this time Jay had shaved off the mustache and wore a pair of dark gray slacks and a white shirt. He looked great. We went into Nan's bedroom for an audience, chatted for a while, and then Jay had to leave. As soon as he was gone, Nanny turned to me with a smile. "This one is a nice boy," she said approvingly. "I'm glad you got rid of that bum from before. This is the boy you should marry." I didn't say anything. The last time I saw my grandmother was a month before the wedding. Her condition had deteriorated, and it was obvious that she'd never be able to attend the ceremony. I walked into the bedroom and found her sedated and waiting for death to take her. My God, she'd been waiting for almost twenty years! Her face was very swollen from the medication and her eyes were closed. I stood by her bed and, sensing my presence, she opened one eye slowly and looked at me. She didn't speak for a few moments and then said with a slight smile on her lips, "That was the same guy, wasn't it?"

"Yes," I answered.

"I thought so." She grinned. "He *is* nice, Kathy, he really is a nice boy." I leaned over and gave her a kiss. I was so pleased to have her approval and so relieved that she knew who he was. My grandmother died a few weeks before my wedding. I loved her and she loved me and so we went ahead with the ceremony—she would have wanted it that way.

Bottom line, it was an okay wedding. Of course, I'd gained weight again and the dress was tight. Oh, and whose idea was it to wear those ugly veils? I hated the thing. I sort of wished I'd had a more glamorous gown and all that kind of stuff, but basically everything was lovely. Like all weddings, mine had its crises. My dad and mom had a big fight because my father didn't want to buy a new suit—he didn't want to spend the money. My mother was beside herself. "I'll pay for it!" she told him and dragged him to Philadelphia to a men's store. Dad was a huge guy, a 52 extra long and, like his daughter, resembled Big Bird—spindly legs and a large upper body. He bought a navy double-breasted suit and looked exactly like a refrigerator. My mother was dressed perfectly in fuchsia chiffon and looked gorgeous. I had ordered one pink rose to carry down the aisle instead of a bouquet. The ceremony was about to start and we couldn't find my flower. The florist became hysterical. "Oh my God," he cried, "I forgot the rose." My father ran to all the tables that were set up and began pulling flowers out of the arrangements. He returned with an assortment plus some parsley that he'd stuffed between the blossoms. He wrapped a bow around the mess and handed it to me just as the music began. I clutched it in front of me and we walked down the aisle giggling. Come to think of it, it really *was* a lovely wedding.

Eight weeks before my wedding, I had moved to West Chester, shared an apartment with another woman, and gone to work as a bilingual medical secretary. I had no friends in the area, and knowing that I'd be starting a new life with a new husband, I wanted to make sure that I had something to do, a reason to get up and get out every day. Jay and I took an apartment in West Chester, furnished it from top to bottom, and moved in right after the wedding. Jay was easy about everything. "You can either get busy or you can stay home. Do whatever you want—it's your choice." I made the only choice, I got busy. I think it's sound policy for any newlywed. Don't sit around and wait for your spouse to make it all happen. Do things for yourself.

Jay and I delayed our honeymoon for a couple of months—we wanted to live like married folks for a while. The first few weeks he'd called me from work every day. One morning, I decided that I'd bring lunch to him at the hide house. I made a tuna fish sandwich, cut up some fruit, put the food in a brown bag, and brought it to work with me. At lunchtime I went off to rendezvous with my husband. I walked into the hide house and saw Jay holding up the limp body of a dead raccoon—the roadkill du jour. "Hi, I brought you lunch," I called out as I swung the brown paper bag in his direction. Just at that moment Jay raised an enormous knife and slit open the animal's belly. Guts came spilling out, and I turned and ran out of the room. I stood outside the door and called in to him, "I'll be happy to have lunch with you, honey, but not while you're gutting animals."

The Boss and Groom

" 'Skunning,' honey, that's what we call it."

"Whatever you call it, I don't want to watch it while I'm eating."

Once the luncheon etiquette had been established, I'd take my break, bring a midday meal to my husband, and the two of us would sit among the salted clumps of hides and eat our sandwiches. In February, we took off on our belated honeymoon. We went to Puerto Rico first and then St. Martin. Even though it rained for the seven days we were in Puerto Rico, we had a good time. Jay and I had a good start; we were happy together. Happiness spilled over into other areas of my life. Immediately after my wedding, the financial and emotional burden on my father eased up and our relationship changed dramatically for the better. He *loved* my husband, and many a weekend we traveled to the casinos for dinners and shows and laughs. We saw each other often and next to my husband, my dad was my favorite date.

Jay Levine was one of the country's most respected and knowledgeable men in his field and I picked up a lot of information from him. In fact, I learned everything anyone could want to know about the hide business. He was an excellent teacher. Some of my greatest times were driving in the front seat of Jay's truck and doing absolutely nothing but laughing with my husband. I always enjoyed the simple things with Jay, and it was the simple life that we led. The sophisticated life didn't suit him and the problem was I aspired to it. I loved meeting Jay for lunch and going on truck trips but, except for my job, that was about all I did. My job was interesting and fun. West Chester is the mushroom capital of the world, and a great many Spanish-speaking immigrants pick and pack mushrooms for B&B and other major mushroom companies. When the workers got sick, they'd go to the doctor, and because they couldn't speak English, I would act as interpreter. I got a good feeling from

87

helping the workers by translating their complaints into English. The job was easy, the people were nice, and the pattern was set. At home and in the office, life moved along without any real ups or downs. My husband thought I was the greatest thing since milk chocolate and we were content.

Nine months after we married, in October of 1976, a new X ray machine was delivered to the doctor's office and had just been set up when Jay came by to say hello. He often came to visit me at the office.

"Jay," said the doctor, "I got a new X ray machine and I need to check it out. Want to be my guinea pig?"

"Sure," agreed my husband. The nurse put Jay in place and took a chest X ray. She brought the negative into the doctor and he came out waving the print. "What's the matter with you? Don't you know how to take a picture? This is garbage. Take it again." Jay stood up and the nurse did a retake. She brought the picture into the doctor and once again he came out. He was really angry with her. "It's cloudy. Jay, please, just one more." So, Jay got zapped again. The doctor thanked him for his patience and apologized for taking up his time. Jay left and I went back to work. At the end of the day, I was getting ready to leave when the doctor came out of his office.

"I have to speak to you, Kathy. It's about Jay's X ray. There's something wrong and I'm going to take it to the radiologist next door."

"What are you talking about?" I asked.

"There's a spot on Jay's picture."

"It's probably your equipment."

"It might be," he said, "but I just want you to know I'm consulting another doctor. Please stay here for a few more minutes till I get back."

I sat and waited for him. In all honesty, I wasn't the least bit worried. I was sure the machine was the culprit. It wasn't. The doctor came back and, looking grim, told me the radiologist had confirmed his findings. "There's something wrong with Jay," he said. "Trust me, you've got to get him to a specialist." I went home and told Jay that there was a cloud in his picture that the doctor didn't like. I remember being somewhat apprehensive, still, I wasn't thinking "sick," and neither was Jay. My husband went to a specialist, had X rays taken, and the spot definitely was there. He was advised to go for tests at a teaching institution in Philadelphia. The Philadelphia doctor wanted to do a full exploratory on Jay. "We'll have to open your rib cage and break a few of them and take some tissue samples. It's intrusive surgery and there'll be a convalescence of months."

Both of us were terrified. Jay was numb, I was furious; I couldn't accept the idea of cracking him open like a lobster. I felt that because we were at a teaching institution the doctors wanted to use Jay to demonstrate a procedure for the medical students. No way! I always relied on my father when it came to medicine and got right on the phone with him. "Dad, we have a problem. Jay has a spot on his X ray. We went to Philadelphia and they want to cut him open. It's big, big surgery." My dad asked some questions and I gave whatever answers I could. At the conclusion Dad exclaimed, "Nobody's cutting my boy open. You give me an hour. I'll get back to you." My father was on the staff of St. Luke's Hospital in Bethlehem and immediately called the chief of surgery. Dad described Jay's condition and the surgeon said there was no need for the surgery. "All you do is make a tiny incision, go down, pull up a piece of tissue, and look at it. For pete's sake, we can do it right here." Neither Jay nor I could absorb everything and took off to Vegas for a change of scene. The "denial" ended quickly, though, and on Yom Kippur in 1976, Jay went into the hospital. I know it was the Day of Atonement because my parents were in temple, where I would have been under ordinary circumstances. I took my husband to St. Luke's and after he'd been prepped and wheeled off, I sat alone in his room. Jay was still in recovery when a man walked in and introduced himself as the surgeon and for the life of me I can't recall his name.

"Hello, Mrs. Levine, we haven't got the results back, but I've seen this a thousand times," he said matter-of-factly. "It's Hodgkin's disease."

"What's Hodgkin's disease?" I asked.

"Cancer."

I felt like someone had stabbed me in the gut. Cancer? Jay? It just didn't fit. "Do you die?" I asked.

"Some do, some don't," answered the doctor. "Why, I know a man who was diagnosed with Hodgkin's fourteen years ago and he's doing just fine."

"What do we do?"

"There are a lot of things—radiation, chemotherapy. But that's something we'll have to discuss later."

He said a few more words and then left me. I can't think of the right word to describe how I felt. Stunned is too small. I've never been shocked like that in my life, never. I couldn't breathe. I literally was gasping for air when the phone rang. I picked up the receiver and heard my mother's voice at the other end.

"Hi, honey, I just slipped out of the services. How are things?"

"Um, uh, uh, okay," I mumbled. She knew just by the way I sounded that things weren't okay.

"Hold on. I'm on my way," she said. It's a twenty-minute ride from the temple to the hospital; my mother made it in three. Her wheels never touched the ground. I don't know how she did it but she was with me in a flash. I was bawling and she was trying to comfort me. Then, the elevator door opened and a gurney was pushed out. I recognized Jay's feet coming toward us.

"Oh my God, oh my God," I whispered to my mother, "what am I going to do? What am I going to say?"

The Boss and Groom

"You will put on a smile," ordered my mother, "and you will not let him see you cry. Do you hear me? You will put on a smile, and goddammit, he's going to be fine."

Jay was wheeled into the room. I leaned over him and he opened his eyes.

"I've got it, Boss," he said weakly, "I've got it." Jay often called me Boss because he claimed I bossed him around.

"You're going to be fine," I said firmly.

"I've got cancer, Boss. I might have to 'check out.' "

"Oh no you don't," I laughed. "We haven't even had our first anniversary, and you owe me a present. You ain't checking out, no way!" I went into a typical Kathy routine. I was determined to laugh and tap-dance my way through this, and so was he—I made him smile. "You're gonna be fine. My father knows best. You'll be out of here in thirty days." I kept hammering him with upbeat platitudes until I ran out of material. "I have to go for a minute. I'll be right back," I told him. I went into the hall, found a closet, walked in, and lost it, completely. I cried like a baby.

The minute my father got the news he went to the library and began researching Hodgkin's. "We have a pretty good chance here. I don't think it's bad," he reassured me. "We've caught it at an early stage, it's not in the bones. I'm telling you, Kathy, his chances are really good." Jay had surgery; his spleen was removed and then he had some small biopsy procedures at a major Philadelphia hospital. Now we had to decide on the course of treatment. The doctor wanted to use radiation. "I think he'll be all right with that," was his opinion. Somehow, I did not feel secure. "I *think*" didn't sit well. I wanted to hear "I'm *sure.*" Who knew if radiation was enough? I didn't want to take any chances and began looking for experts in the field. I got the name of a doctor at Jefferson Hospital in Philadelphia and made an appointment for Jay to see him. We drove to Philly and Jay was examined.

"We're starting a new program here," the doctor told us, "and if Jay agrees to be part of it, there's an eighty-five percent chance of recovery. What we do is take all the patient's statistics and feed them into a computer. The computer absorbs the data and prescribes a course of treatment. I have to emphasize that this is something new and therefore still questionable. If you're willing to try, we'll run with it." Jay was very willing. He felt secure with this doctor and so did I. The information was fed to the computer and the suggested treatment was a combination of radiation and chemotherapy. I remember feeling good that I hadn't just accepted the first recommendation. In any situation, especially a life-or-death one, you *must* get a second opinion. Don't just accept the first doctor's say-so. Be demanding when it counts! You can't get another opinion if you're six feet under.

Jay's ordeal began. They radiated his chest for six weeks. During the treatments he was slightly fatigued and had constant heartburn, but it really wasn't that bad. He finished the radiation therapy and after a little time off, went into chemotherapy. Now, everyone has different reactions, I'm sure, but this chemo was horrendous. Anyone who has gone through it or been with someone who's in it knows how devastating the process can be. The stuff they gave him was called MOPP and it made Jay violently ill. He got sicker and sicker as the treatments went on. The sessions were every other week and in between he'd become so psychologically upset that he was physically ill the day before his appointments. He'd throw up on the way to the hospital. He'd get sick in the elevator. It was overwhelming. Sometimes he told me he just wanted to return home and not go through any more of it. I ached for him, yet I would not allow my deep sympathy and concern to surface. I handled the whole awful episode the way I handle any major stress—by carrying on as though it was business as usual.

Jay couldn't keep anything in his stomach. He'd lost a ton of weight and his coloring was gray-green. I rode right over his illness and continued to do things the same. I was cooking like Julia Child. I put all the best (and absolutely worst for him) foods on the table—things like lamb chops, which were way too rich and fatty. He'd eat them and his stomach would turn over. I mean, the guy was not only minus a spleen, he was on chemotherapy, and I was stuffing him with everything wrong just to make him feel everything was right. One time I decided he needed a chocolate milk shake. His eyes lit up. "Oh boy, a chocolate milk shake." I got the ice cream and the milk and made him a shake—only I forgot to read the date on the carton. The milk was bad and within twenty minutes Jay was violently ill. Later, he looked at the date on the container. "You're trying to poison me!" he cried. "Everyone's trying to poison me!" (Since that episode I've made it a practice to read the date on everything . . . no kidding, I read dates on toilet paper.) I felt so guilty because he was so very sick and it really was my fault. To this day if you say "milk shake" to Jay Levine, he'll say, "Did I ever tell you about the time my first wife tried to kill me?"

For the many months of his treatment I drove Jay to the doctors and was with him almost all the time. I tried to jolly him through everything. When they'd come at him with the needles he'd positively collapse and I'd say, "Oh come on, you can do this. You've just got one shot. Come on. We'll go out somewhere, we'll go to a movie." One evening he was taking a bath and called out urgently, "Boss, come here." I raced into the bathroom.

"What?"

"Watch this," he said. He grabbed a hunk of his hair and it came out in his hands.

93

"I can't watch this, but you go ahead and have a good day," I told him as I scooted out of the room. I nearly fainted. I wouldn't talk about what was happening. It wasn't denial, I just felt it was better to try to treat things as though they weren't life threatening. I kept up my banter and my humor, but every so often it would get to me and when I could no longer bear to witness his suffering, I'd call his mother. "You'll have to sit with Jay tonight," I'd inform her. "I can't take it anymore." I'd tell my husband I was going shopping, but then I'd go out and drive around or go to a movie—anything not to have to watch his agony.

In my attempts to help him live as normal a life as possible under the circumstances, I was pretty hard on him. I needed to be heartless because I couldn't stop and think that this man could die on me. I wouldn't let the thought enter my mind. Funny thing is, at times it didn't enter his mind, either. He'd talk to me and say, "You know, Boss, I think they lied to me, I don't think I have cancer." I made him go to work—worse, I made him go to New York on shopping excursions, and he *hated* the City.

One day I told him we were going to Manhattan and he said absolutely no. I lit into him. "You'd do anything to get out of going to New York. You'd even throw up. You're going." We went but he wasn't well; his blood count was all off, and when we got home he had to go into the hospital. My God, I wouldn't even let my poor husband be sick, and he wouldn't let himself be sick. He had a white blood cell count in the millions and would spike a fever of 104 and yet he worked every day, and he was out on the basketball courts, too. He couldn't take jump shots because his feet were heavy and he had terrible cramps from his high white cell count. He needed to know that he was going to make it and to prove it he had to play ball. He'd get up in the morning, put on his jeans and T-shirt, and go off.

94

The Boss and Groom

Jay never whined or complained. He simply was angry because he didn't believe he had this problem and yet it was getting in his way. His hands would go into spasms and he'd get horrible charley horses in his legs. Jay has huge legs; he called them "trees." One day I came home from work and saw him stretched out on the landing floor. I went flying up the stairs convinced that he was dead. He looked at me and whispered, "Cramp," and pointed to his leg. I started laughing, it just struck me funny. Then he started laughing too. Laughter kept us going. For nearly a year, Jay Levine suffered the tortures of the damned but thanks to the treatments and his own indomitable spirit, he triumphed and has been cancer free for twenty years.

I had taken time off from my work at the doctor's office to be with my husband, and when I returned they told me that they were glad to see me but business wasn't all that great. I figured they were trying to unload me so I left. Hey, there were no hard feelings, my having that job probably saved Jay's life. If the new X ray machine hadn't come in and if they hadn't wanted to test it, God knows how long the Hodgkin's disease would have gone undetected.

At the beginning of Jay's treatment, when we knew that he would have to undergo chemotherapy, I told the doctor that we wanted children and asked if the chemo would affect this. He sent us to a genetic counselor and we were assured that to their knowledge chemotherapy did not affect the male reproductive organs. Things didn't turn out the way they were supposed to, though, and for the duration of our marriage, Jay's system shut down; he wasn't producing healthy sperm and we were unable to have children. I got through almost everything connected with Jay's illness relatively unscathed but if I had to name one thing that really upset me I guess it would be the way people dumped on *me* because I didn't get pregnant.

My mother-in-law would say, "If you were home a little more, maybe you could make babies." I didn't tell her that I could have been home all day and night and it wouldn't have made any difference because her son's count was off, not mine. I was hurt that Jay refused to tell the truth to his family. I was held accountable because he was ashamed of the problem. Only his sister knew the truth and staunchly defended me without revealing the reason. To this day my former sister-in-law remains a dear friend.

Years later, the doctor suggested that things might be corrected, and Jay was put on special medication. By then, however, it didn't matter as far as the two of us were concerned. I had decided that much as I loved him, I didn't want to be married to him. I didn't want to stand in the way of his finding happiness, either, and having children was essential for him. Truthfully, it never was as big an issue for me. Don't get me wrong, I love kids and if I'd had them I would have done my best to be a good mother, but I'd be lying if I said that having children was my goal. I was career oriented (even though I didn't know what career yet!). In those days I wasn't as aware of my need and was content to let things fall into my lap. The older I get the more I understand myself and what makes me tick. I've become much more self-sufficient and far less reliant on someone else to take care of me. That's why I'm always after my viewers to look after themselves and to be good to themselves. Ultimately, we're responsible for our own happiness. No big news and yet important to remember.

I didn't decide to leave my marriage until some eight years after Jay's illness. We'd had a good working relationship during those years, and from the outside everything appeared fine. Looking at my marriage now I'd say that we really never had an emotional hook-up; I was a needy kid and he needed to be a daddy. Then his needs turned toward having children and when we were unable to do that, he furthered his efforts to take care of *me*. I no longer wanted to be taken care of; I wanted to get out into the world and do things for myself.

Although Jay and I were soulmates, it wasn't enough. See, we didn't have children to concentrate on. People with children spend all their energy focusing on the kids. You know the kind of stuff, what Johnny did today ... and how he got toilet trained and how he dropped his blocks and how he fell over the piano stool and chipped a tooth and got measles. All that. Your children are your focus and when they grow up and leave, you hope you have a relationship with your spouse to come back to.

I took a look at my life after the first eight years and realized that we were missing the whole middle part. We had no children—and I could see that the rest of my life was going to be exactly the way it was at that very moment. We would be nice to each other. We would go out on Saturday night. We would go to the movies. Once a year we'd fight about a vacation and then go someplace where there was a casino. (Jay only "vacationed" near a casino. My husband loved to gamble, period. He didn't golf, he didn't play tennis. He wasn't the type to sit and chat over dinner. Put it this way—we didn't share many interests.) His preoccupations were work, work, work, and gamble, gamble, gamble. I don't know what mine were but I did worry constantly that our life together would fall into a boring routine and that routine would continue until the day I died. I was in a "Memorex Marriage" and everything was predictable. I could have hit the playback button at any time and heard my everyday routine come back the same, the same, the same. Some people like that kind of existence; it's solid and consistent. It's definitely not for me. I'm left-handed, and there's a certain creativity that comes with the territory. I love change and challenge. I like somebody to call me and say, "Pack your bag, we're flying off to Bermuda tomorrow." Jay wasn't like that; he didn't like to travel, and if I suggested a trip he'd question everything. His stock replies were, *"Where* do you want to go? Why do you want to go there? What am I going to do there? You gotta be kidding!" (Shades of my father!) So we always wound up someplace where there was a casino, or we went our separate ways—I'd go to New York for theater, ballet, or shopping and he stayed close to home and played basketball or cards or whatever. Nothing wrong, just nothing together. When we married he'd been my "protector," and I guess I needed protecting. Then, as I grew older, I didn't need so much "care." Jay babied me and the baby just got too old ... and there weren't any real babies for him to parent.

All along I had been asking myself if I could live in this very calm sea for the next thirty years and be all right with it. And I kept saying, I can. I can accept that it's not fireworks. There weren't going to be any great passionate moments, no highs, or any lows; the coffin was going to close slowly with me in it. I felt there was more to life.

I was tormented by these thoughts and had very low self-esteem. I didn't feel fulfilled in any way. I repeatedly told Jay that I wasn't happy and that things weren't right. "What do you want me to do?" he'd ask. Even though I suggested we see a counselor, deep down I already knew I was going. I began to think that if I left the marriage I'd have a chance to become somebody, and Jay would have a chance to find a more suitable wife and, in the process, a better life. The realization was terrible because it meant I had to hurt someone I cared for, someone who was good and kind, yet I couldn't help but feel that I could create a more meaningful and exciting life for myself. People kept telling me I led a charmed life. From day one my mother told me I was lucky, and I thought because she and the others told me so, it must be so. I kept getting up every day and saying, "I'm lucky" but what I really thought was, "I'm empty."

During this period of frustration and indecision, I wiggled and tap-danced my way into a succession of jobs and, per usual, I didn't pull my weight. I worked for a year as a receptionist-secretary at another doctor's office and once again nearly died of boredom. I was quick and witty and got along great with the clients. I scheduled patients, took money, and filled out the insurance forms. But soon the forms were piling up in the corner and the books were fouled up and the insurance wasn't being done. (I don't like "paper" responsibility. To this day when I have to submit expense sheets to QVC, it's a chore and such hell for me to do I sometimes don't even bother. I lose my plane ticket stubs, my meal stubs, all the receipts they call for. I attribute this to my left-handedness—you know, creative but poor on Math 101 stuff. Which is part of the magic of what I do now—except for those expense sheets, there's no paperwork involved!) The doctor and I had a parting of the ways—I had done all I could do in my capacity as a receptionist, and I wanted something more.

Next I got a realtor's license, but once I got into real estate, I floundered. In real estate, as in everything else, I preferred to entertain rather than pay attention to details, and you cannot "humor" somebody through the purchase of a $100,000 house. I didn't like the sales process. It wasn't simply a matter of showing people houses and saying this is the kitchen and this is the living room—it meant, among other things, that I had to be able to handle all the different kinds of financing once the house was sold. You could look at twenty houses and people could change their minds twenty times. The husband might not get the job offer or the wife preferred a different area—there was no control over the ultimate sale. I was spinning my wheels. Selling houses wasn't a challenge for me. Real estate was at an all-time high and other people were doing really well, but not Kathy. I wasn't cut out for the business and I got out of it. Shortly thereafter, early in 1978, Jay and I went with another couple on vacation to Las Vegas. We were seated at poolside one morning when the guy turned to me and asked, "What are you doing right now?"

"Oh," I replied, "I'm taking some time off."

"Are you having children?"

"I don't think so," I answered.

"So what the hell are you doing? You're not working, you aren't having children. You have no purpose."

I didn't know what to answer so I got up and went into the pool. I completely bought this man's definition of my life and I was devastated. If they aren't reproducing or gainfully employed, many women are put on the defensive just as I was that day. I felt like I didn't deserve to walk this earth because I didn't have a purpose or *the* purposes that were outlined to me by my male pool companion. As I paddled aimlessly in the water I ran down a list of my deficiencies. My husband hates my cooking. I shop. I spend money. I'm self-indulgent. I'm selfish. I can't do anything right. With hindsight, I see that my ready acceptance of another person's evaluation of my life fed into my gross lack of self-esteem. Now I realize that I should have pushed that man into the water.

After the real estate fiasco, I went into the hotel business. I applied for a job at a small local hotel and was hired. I learned an awful lot in the hotel business. I learned how to cater and how to book and run events, which is one reason why I happen to be really good at throwing parties. When it comes to entertaining, I have an eye for seeing things are right. I loved the "entertainment" part of my job. Unfortunately, my boss drove me crazy. She was one of those Jekyll

The Boss and Groom

and Hyde personalities whose mood changed almost by the hour. One minute she was friendly and on a first-name basis and the next minute, she went ice cold and pushed me away. Here's a simple example. Things were slow in the office, and I was going through some old files when she called out, "Oh, Kathy, honey, why don't you take a ten-minute break and go get some coffee." "Okay," I replied, and did as she suggested. I returned to my desk in maybe five minutes and she lit into me with, "Where the hell have you been all this time? Put that coffee away, we've got work to do." Multiply this incident to twenty-five times every day and maybe you get what I mean. She went from good to bad to ugly and I didn't know from one hour to the next which person I was working for, or which person *I* should be, friendly or distant.

The final straw came when I made arrangements for a big meeting without checking with her. I took the initiative, and she couldn't stand losing control. "Who told you to book that meeting?" she demanded. "Well," I replied, "I thought it would be a good thing." "Thought? You're not paid to think, you're paid to type!" That woman stole my self-confidence. I used to come home and cry to my husband and he'd say, "Quit, you don't need this money." (I was making $150 a week.) "I can't quit," I argued, "I have to prove that I can do this. I can't get fired from everything. I need to do this job."

So I continued to work, and basically, I liked it. I learned how to make things happen and in many ways was really good at the job. I loved the clients. I loved planning their weddings and recommending orchestras and working on menus. I learned about different ethnic groups and their tastes. Some like sweet, some like sour, some like lots of bread with butter, some don't want the butter. The problem was my boss's erratic behavior beat me down. All the time, I kept thinking, I can handle this, and I couldn't. I never thought of

101

going for some kind of counseling or therapy. I didn't think in those terms then. I tried to handle the situation by shopping a little more and acting a little more brassy. Hey, we all skirt the real issues in life at some time or other—the bad thing is to keep on avoiding them.

My "office" in the basement really was the phone center with a desk stuck in the middle. There were vending machines outside, and people would come and smack those machines when they didn't work correctly, which was a good deal of the time. The noise of the phones and the banging fists on the machines was enough to drive anyone crazy. Still, I kept on. One day I was in the shower at home and I suddenly realized that tears were mixing with the spray. I was crying. That did it. I'd had enough. I got out of the shower, dressed, and drove over to the hotel. I bypassed my boss and went directly to the owner.

"I'd like to give you my two weeks' notice," I said, adding, "I've found something else."

"Hmmph," he blustered. "Could you at least train the next girl for me?"

"My pleasure," I said. "I'll show you my books and all the weddings coming up." A wedding is planned a year out, and you get attached to the clients and vice versa. I didn't want my customers to feel that I was walking out on them. I didn't want to leave anyone in the lurch. "I'll stay as long as you like, five weeks, six weeks, whatever you need to hire and train someone else."

"Thanks," he said curtly. Our meeting took place on Friday afternoon. Saturday morning the phone rang: it was the owner. "How fast can you get your things out of here?" he asked.

"Well, I guess I could come in today."

"Good," he said, and banged down the phone.

I went to my office and cleaned out everything. I made a pile of all the relevant material for the hotel and put my personal stuff in an envelope. The owner came down to my office and I went over the hotel papers with him and explained the procedures. When we finished, he pointed to the envelope containing my letters.

"What's that folder?" he asked.

"Oh, those are my—"

"I'll decide what's yours and what's mine," he said, grabbing the folder from me. "Now, get out of my hotel." He threw me out and kept my letters. Since I'd been treated like dirt from the first, I should have expected that kind of treatment. I learned my lesson, though, and I vowed that I'd never again be put in that kind of position. I went on to work for a small Philadelphia hotel where the people were very nice to me and I had a good time. I began to get the sense that you don't have to take it. You don't have to have anybody dumping on you—that's not part of the work ethic. Knowing this, I'm tough on women who tell me they won't get out of a bad marriage or a lousy job. I'm tough with them because I know they're at the place I was when I thought taking the abuse was what I had to do. I didn't, and you don't either!

My work situation steadied itself; my marriage continued to deteriorate. It was a constant drain on my energy, my emotions and, almost, my sense of humor. It isn't easy to be with someone you love but have zero in common with. I was suffocating. I had to have breathing room. Jay and I had had months of conversation about our situation. I kept saying I thought I needed to get away, but he didn't understand what I was after. We talked together and we cried together and we even did things together. I accompanied him to a convention in Boca Raton. He was so romantic and so winning and all over me. "Who's going to make you laugh? Who's going to love you like I love you? Who's going to take care of you? Who's going to call you boss? Who's going to be there for you?

103

You can't go. We have so much together." All I could
do was cry. Everything he said was true and yet I
couldn't stay. I wished he had been a bastard, I wished
I hated him, because it would have been a helluva lot
easier. I kept saying I needed to leave for a while and
at last I found an excuse to move on.

"Jay," I said one morning, "my friend Carla's getting married and she's going to Jamaica for a couple
of weeks on her honeymoon. I'm going to house-sit
for her for two weeks." I talked matter-of-factly, trying to convince myself that it might actually be *just*
that simple.

"You need some time to yourself, I understand,"
Jay said. "Go for a couple of weeks, sit the house,
and think about us." I packed my suitcases with only
enough clothes for two weeks. As I walked out the
door, Jay said, "When people leave, they don't come
back. You're never coming back."

Jay was right. I had made up my mind; I wasn't
going to return. After the two weeks of house-sitting
I moved in with another friend. I felt utterly terrible
about what I was doing to Jay, and I went to a psychologist for some help. I'd reached one of those moments when I had to reach out for professional
guidance. A friend recommended a therapist. I went
to see him and per usual interviewed him even as he
interviewed me. I was looking for compassion and for
someone who'd make me feel comfortable, and I
wanted him to be a married man—I was real clear
about that point. This therapist practiced in his home,
and I felt secure knowing his wife and kids were in the
vicinity. I didn't want to sit in anyone's office thinking,
Hmmm, this guy's single and he can really help me.

I marched into the therapist's office and explained
my situation. "Skip the deep psycho-stuff," I ordered
him. "I need ten sessions to get me through this.
Here's the story. I just walked out on a fine human
being: I have just upset my parents; I have disap-

pointed a lot of people who thought I had a good head on my shoulders, and I am terrified. I just want you to tell me that this is going to work and that I'll be all right." I gave the doctor the details and at the end, he told me that in his opinion I didn't have any options. "It's like you jumped out of a boat in the middle of the rapids and you're holding on to a rock. If you let go, you can get ripped to shreds on the rocks. Or, you can have a lovely ride and enjoy it. You made your decision. You've jumped the boat and now let go and enjoy the ride." I felt very comfortable with this man. At last, someone understood my pain and wasn't going to judge me. Friends are wonderful when you want to pour your heart out over a glass of wine, but they shouldn't be used as therapists—when you need *help* you need to go to a professional. Friends, even if they love you, just don't know what to tell you. I walked out of the therapist's office and for the first time in I don't know how long, I felt at peace with myself.

I split with Jay and sides were taken immediately. Everyone waited to see if there was a man "in the wings," and weren't they surprised when no one emerged. Most of our friends had been Jay's local childhood buddies, and it was remarkable to watch how they rallied around him. I was cold-shouldered and had very few people of my own to rely on. Those few each had an opinion and gave it to me. Most said, "You're an idiot. You're a shmuck. You walked out on a good thing." *Once* someone actually said, "Good for you, I can't believe you married him in the first place." Who asked her? I found that comment as offensive as the statements that blamed me. I learned yet another lesson the hard way. If a friend's marriage breaks up, the truth is it ain't your business and unless you're asked, you should keep your opinions to yourself. What you should say is, "I'm sorry and I hope you're all right. If you need anything, call me." Period.

105

(I didn't follow my own advice when someone very close to me at QVC split with his wife ... but more on that later.)

Everyone called Jay to say they were shocked, they were sorry, they couldn't believe it, and, more to the point, when he was ready, they had a nice girl for him. Within two weeks of our separation he was fixed up on a date. Jay hesitated about going out, and his friends let him have it. "Hey, Kathy's not coming back. She's history. She was never there for you anyway." Negative stuff was heaped on me and Jay wouldn't hear it. "You're wrong. You don't know. You saw the Kathy who was out there for you to see, the one who lived to shop and went from job to job. You don't know what she did for me. She made me laugh. She was fun."

"She was a bitch," he was advised.

Jay defended me and he'd defend me to this day, and believe me, I needed defending. Nobody understood why I did what I did. My own parents were in shock. My father loved Jay like a son, and my mother was so devastated she couldn't look straight at me for a year. She cried and cried until I finally said, "Mother, this is ridiculous. I've gotten over my situation and you haven't. You've really got to come to grips with this. Maybe you should get counseling." My mom thought about it and realized I was right—my marriage *was* over and *she* had to get on with things. Jay's mother was tremendously upset as well. Since the day Jay and I began dating she'd told me how much I meant to him. "You're his world. Every Friday when you're coming to visit, he's so excited, he can't wait to see you." Her last words to me before I married him were, "He loves you like the sun. He wakes up every day with a spring in his step because of you. Please don't ever hurt him." *Oy*. What a trip to lay on me. I never wanted to be anybody's sun. Now, I was responsible for an eclipse.

The Boss and Groom

Everyone was so very sad, and yet the Levine family never closed its doors to me, ever. As I mentioned, my sister-in-law and I are still best of friends and, while she was alive, Jay's mother was always kind. You can't pick your mother-in-law and I was fortunate to be blessed with a great one. I adored her. But, oh, when I think of that time, I still get a stomachache. I never felt more awful in my whole life. I know it was a necessary move for me, but I swear I'll never get over the hurt of hurting somebody. Never, never, never.

Jay and I were separated for two years, and during that time he supported me. We were going to divorce and he *still* wanted to care for me—but that's Jay. I hear horror stories from viewers about exes who skip out with everything and never look back. Believe me, there aren't that many Jay Levines around.

I started working at the big hotel in Philadelphia, and when the hourlong commute proved to be too draining, I moved to Philly. Although we weren't legally divorced, to all intents and purposes, I was a "free" woman when I tried out for QVC. I wasn't responsible for anyone but myself, so I decided to go for broke and audition. Because Jay and I wanted an uncontested divorce, I looked for a lawyer who would represent both of us—it wasn't that easy to find someone. One woman wanted to get his financial statements and literally bring him to his knees. I walked out of her office as fast as my feet would take me. Another guy refused outright. "There's no such thing as using one lawyer for a divorce," he advised me. "I'm telling you it never works. We have to negotiate, we have to arbitrate, we have to sue, we have to be mean."

"Thanks very much," I told him and left. Maybe *he* had to negotiate, arbitrate, sue, and be mean; Jay and I sure didn't. I finally found a lawyer who agreed to our terms. This lawyer couldn't get over us. Jay and

KATHY LEVINE

I walked into his office, told him we cared very much about each other but that our marriage wasn't working and we wanted a clean break. "Whatever she wants," said Jay, "I'll give her." We signed the documents and ninety days later I got a postcard from Harrisburg saying "You are divorced." The whole divorce cost $1,200, which is peanuts in terms of legal fees.

While we were waiting for the divorce to become final, Jay made a request. "We've got to get a Get, Kathy," he said. That's not double talk. In the Jewish religion when you marry, you get a certificate called a Ketubah. If things don't work out, then you have to get another document, the Get, which makes your divorce legal under Jewish law. I balked at first; I thought a state divorce was fine—it was uncontested, so what was the big deal? Jay insisted that since we were married under Jewish law, we should be divorced under it, too. It meant something to him, so I didn't argue. We shlepped to New York and appeared before an orthodox rabbi who was a friend of Jay's. The rabbi filled out the Get, and then Jay and I had to go through another ceremony. While he stood, I walked around him three times, saying over and over, "I don't want to be married to you." Jay was crying as I made the circles and repeated my statement. I was crying too. I have to say that was the worst moment, the one time that I was utterly despondent at what I was doing. We signed on the dotted line and the rabbi shook his head and then shook our hands. Jay and I were holding hands when we left the rabbi's office.

We had gone from the Ketubah to the Get, from marriage certificate to divorce papers. I don't care what anyone says, a piece of paper doesn't make a relationship, and canceling that piece of paper doesn't break a relationship. We still had history, we still liked each other, and we still felt connected. Our marriage was legally over, but our relationship wasn't. We had a long ride home and as we approached the Freehold exit, Jay said, "You know, Boss, I do happen to have a horse running today at the Freehold Track. I know this may sound bizarre, but would you want to stop and see him?" (Jay Levine always was involved in a lot of things besides the hide trade and at this point he owned a racehorse.) "Sure," I said. It didn't seem like a strange request to me because even though we'd just been divorced, we still were friends.

"Okay," continued Jay, "I just have to make a telephone call when we get there." I didn't know then that Jay phoned the woman he was seeing to tell her that he really was divorced and everything was fine. He said that I was a little upset so he was going to take me for a bite to eat and give me a pep talk. He didn't mention that the pep talk would take place at the track. We watched the race and, believe it or not, his horse won. The next thing I knew I was having my picture taken with Jay in the winner's circle and he was introducing me to everyone as his wife. I was laughing and crying at the same time. We had a victory-divorce dinner together and then drove back to West Chester.

"Kathy," Jay said on the way, "I have to tell you something. You know I want children, well . . . I want you to know . . . I want you to know that I'm getting married again."

All of a sudden everything clicked. It was real. Jay and I were no longer a couple. I started sobbing. There's chutzpa for you—I drove him out and now I was bawling. Along with the divorce I was awarded a settlement—Jay insisted on it. By then I was doing well enough to tell Jay I didn't want his money. I was the one who was leaving, and he never was unfair to me, so I couldn't see the point of making him liquidate his assets and sell his home to give me half. I didn't need it. I'm not a saint, though—I also told him that if I ever *did* need it, he'd hear from me.

That's the way it was between Jay and me; we

trusted each other and we cared for each other. I didn't want to take him for money. Money was secondary to me. Again, I'm not being a saint, I simply believe he was so good to me for so many years, I don't need his money. I'll always be his friend, I just couldn't be his wife—in fact, I'm not so sure I could be anybody's wife. I felt guilty for years. Now I can look back and tell you with confidence that I was a great wife. I provided my husband with unbelievable amounts of joy, I made him laugh. I had lots of parties. I shlepped with him on that hide truck. I made lunches. For pete's sake, the guy called me twenty-two times a day. We were very respectful of each other, we liked each other. I was a good wife, but I listened to the chatter around me—like the guy at the pool in Vegas—and focused on the cup half empty instead of half full. Because I had no other real job in life and because I wasn't gung ho about having kids, I lost sight of my valid contributions to our partnership. I'm different today; I don't think of myself as a bad person. I *am* self-indulgent . . . but who better to indulge? I love to do nice things for myself and I also like to do nice things for others. And I have very strong attachments to my family. I think if I had children, I would be an excellent mother although it would have been hard. I'm not like *my* mother—she had the energy to be everything: mother, community woman, wife, sister, sister-in-law, grandmother, friend. I couldn't fill her shoes. I didn't remarry, and I've gotten to an age where children really aren't an issue anymore. Put it this way, no man who dates me is looking to have kids.

I was married at twenty-four and made the decision to leave when I was thirty-one, and in spite of all the pain and sadness, I have no regrets. The chips have fallen and I accept the way they fell. Getting divorced from someone as special as Jay was unimaginably tough, yet all these years later I know it was the right choice . . . for both of us.

6

Friendly Fire

❖   ❖   ❖

A funny thing happened about six weeks after I married Jay Levine. My mother called to tell me that she was getting married, too. In case you're wondering what happened to my father, let me explain—it's quite a story.

Long before I was born, when my dad was in the army, his best friend was Lee Seinfeld. Dad brought Lee home and introduced him to my mother. Lee took one look at Pat Kauffman and fell head over heels in love—really, just like that, boom. Fifteen years into his own marriage, Lee and his wife had divorced; he remained single for another fifteen years and became a part of our family. He always was around, and his daughters Ellen, Roni, and Barbara were my best friends. Lots of women were after him, but the truth was, even though my mother was quite content in her marriage and quite unaware of his feelings, Lee needed to be around her if only as a friend.

My parents' marriage had started out just fine. My mother told me that my dad was terrific. He had a great sense of humor and was fun to be with. He was a good student at Temple University and also a pretty good athlete. He was excited about going into dentistry, and the future looked rosy for Pat and Arnie Kauffman. Then my father's physical condition deteriorated; he had to give up his chosen field and also had to live in pain. Not surprisingly, he changed and went from being an outgoing, happy-go-lucky person to a negative loner. His pessimism weighed both of them down. Though they remained married, my parents gradually went their separate ways. When all of us children grew up and left, their home became quiet and empty.

For my mother, the family came first. It was many, many years before she acknowledged that more than a friendship existed between her and Lee. By that time my father had withdrawn, and his relationship with my mother was little more than perfunctory. (Many times, my mother went as a guide for Aunt Elaine's travel agency just to get away from the deadening situation at home. It saved her sanity.) The plain truth was, my mother had a lot more in common with Lee Seinfeld than she did with Arnie Kauffman. Lee and Mom loved the theater and art and dancing and fine dining—the kinds of activities Dad wouldn't do. Still, she stayed with my father.

When my grandfather died, my mother took it very hard. Her father was her champion, and she adored him. My father could not comfort her. There was no warmth from him, no real understanding of loss, so she turned to their best friend. Lee was caring and consoling during this desperate time, and the spark that had been there for so many years was lit. I was twelve when Lee and my mother became involved, and although I sensed this "thing" between them, I didn't understand it because I was a kid. I knew something was cooking, though. Lee would come to dinner at our house and he'd sit on one side of the table and my mother would sit on the other and an electric current passed between them—no kidding, it was like a laser beam of love. The fact that my dad didn't notice shows how out of it he was. I always knew when my mother had been with Lee because she acted differently. Usually she'd call and say, "Hi, honey, got a fashion show at seven-thirty. Dinner's in the fridge. Help yourself. See you later." Other times she'd call and say "Hi, honey, how are you?" I'd say, "You're at Lee's, aren't you?" I could tell by her voice; she sounded so warm and calm and soft. No question, Lee Seinfeld had a very special effect on Pat Kauffman. For years he begged her to leave my dad, but she wouldn't—she couldn't.

Many times my mother would announce: "Lee and I are going to an art show," or, "Lee and I are going to a new musical," or, "Lee's going to take me to dinner." My dad didn't even look up. He just went about his work and when he wasn't working, he got involved in classes. He actually took flying lessons and eventually got his pilot's license. He often took me flying with him. As I've mentioned, my dad was a good man but a distant father. Mom used to say that if Mrs. Schultz next door needed the trash taken out, my father was the first to go over and do it, while our trash sat inside. He always was the nicest guy to everybody else and then clammed up with his family. He simply worked, and everything was gray and hard, and eventually he became the world's most negative man. (Ultimately, that's what alienated my mother, and I guess that's why I try to stay upbeat because I saw a perfect example of what can happen if you don't. I hate that part of me that can be negative.) My dad put a damper on everything, and in the end my mother had to try and find some happiness. She never would have left while her mother was alive, but when my grandmother died, the way was clear. Shortly after my marriage, I got the call.

"Hi, dear," she said cheerily, "I want to talk to you.

KATHY LEVINE

You know, honey, things haven't been good at home for a long time, and I have a chance to get out. There is someone else and I want you to know about him."

"That's great, Mom. I hope you and Lee are very happy," I enthused. Mom drew in her breath. I think she was a little taken aback that I wasn't surprised. As close as we were, she'd never brought her relationship with Lee into our orbit. (I don't know if my brothers were as aware of what was going on because they weren't around as much—and they were men.) I was perfectly happy with my mother's decision. She'd been struggling valiantly for so long, she deserved a break. So my mother and father got divorced and she married Lee and after a little time passed and my father's initial anger wore off, Mom and Lee and Dad continued their friendship. No kidding.

In a funny way I think my dad was relieved. After my mother left, he pursued a warm and lasting relationship with a woman who was more suited to his needs. And so, the players changed roles and went on. My dad and Lee played golf together, they played cards together, and they visited with each other. We all went to family functions as a unit, only now Mom and Lee were the couple. Since Lee had been around for as long as I could remember, the only big difference for me was that my girlfriends became my stepsisters. Everything was civilized, and best of all, my mother did find happiness and, although he never remarried, my father, too, went into a loving relationship. The moral of the story is my mother has been married for over fifty years—most of her life. Each marriage in its own way was a success. I learned that not all marriages are good, and not all divorces are bad. In the end all parties survived, and even thrived, under friendly fire.

For more than ten years my father rented a house in Brigantine, New Jersey, for two weeks every August, and the whole family—my brothers, their kids,

114

myself, everyone stayed with him. My father treasured these visits and really was happiest when he was surrounded by his loved ones. Unfortunately, things didn't work out so well for my dad in the end. About five years ago he suffered a series of strokes. His disease, stroke dementia, is similar to Alzheimer's, and he's in and out, mostly out. I had to put him in a nursing home, and though it isn't easy to deal with now, it was impossible before.

My father still was practicing dentistry when he started displaying very strange behavior. He was getting disoriented and dizzy; however, he's a diabetic and hadn't been watching himself. He wasn't eating properly, and it's no wonder his behavior was bizarre. The dental hygienists in his practice were dismayed by his appearance—he was disheveled and seedy. He didn't always shave, his mouth wasn't clean, and understandably, his patients were losing their patience. I didn't find out how bad things were until one day he called and asked me for a thousand dollars. I was shocked. You must understand—my parents never asked me for anything; they're from the "parents should not be a burden to their children" school. I asked him why he needed the money, and he told me some ferkakta story about winning a car in a contest, only he needed a thousand dollars for the delivery charges. "Great, Dad," I told him, "just show me the papers."

Of course, the contest was one of those scams where you're told you've won a car and it turns out to be a toy or something like that. Anyway, when this happened I got an awful feeling that my father really was off. I decided I'd go over to his apartment and check it out. I walked in and got the shock of my life. My dad always was a pack rat and saved everything, but this was unbelievable. He had stuff from every mail order house in the country strewn around, and what stuff!—water purifiers, health food juicers and blenders, air purifiers, dishes, commemorative plates, you name it, plus magazines piled all over the place. It was total chaos. The phone rang while I was there and I answered it. A man was calling to say they wanted to make delivery on some merchandise and needed a check. I went to my dad's desk and rummaged in the mess for his checkbook. I found it and also found that there were dozens of checks written to dozens of scams.

Meanwhile, my father needed a thousand dollars because he was three months behind in his rent. I further discovered that he was behind at the office as well—his bills were unpaid and his business was way down. I called the credit card companies and was told that he was $67,000 in debt! I was floored. I picked myself up and systematically began to put things in order. First, I paid my dad's back rent and the phone bill and luckily got to the electric company, which was just about to disconnect his service. I paid his insurance, too, and any other essentials, and I cleaned up his apartment as best I could. Then I turned my attention to his debts.

Creditors came out of the woodwork. I was on the phone with those SOB contest salesmen telling them that I was on to their rackets and that I was recording the conversations and would sue them. For the most part, they couldn't have cared less. Those operations usually are so screened you can't get to them. The checks are mailed to some bogus address—a mail center, not a location—and there's almost no way to get hold of these rats and fight back. Someone told me that I was not responsible for my father's bills and someone else advised me to get power of attorney. It wasn't easy, but I got my father to sign the necessary papers. Now I could write letters and assume the responsibility of getting things cleared up for him. For two years his creditors were all over me. Once I received a call from a major credit company. They were looking for Dr. Kauffman because he owed $23,000. I told them that my father didn't have any money.

"We'll make a settlement. We'll cut it in half and make it twelve thousand."

"You can make it twelve dollars. He doesn't have the money," I replied. The company kept calling and calling. Finally I'd had enough. "You gave my father credit nonstop even after he didn't pay his bills. I buy on a credit card and if I'm one day late, I get a finance charge and they threaten to cut my card. You're telling me that you gave this man a twenty-five-thousand-dollar credit line? How could you?"

"Well, ma'am, he's a dentist. We give dentists credit lines." I couldn't believe it. This was a well-known credit company, too, but what they did was irresponsible. Who ever heard of extending credit like that? I couldn't feel sorry for them. Bad as things were, we did not declare bankruptcy—that costs money, and my dad didn't have any. I just continued to stave off his debtors—it wore me down and cost me a fortune.

I took on the responsibility because I felt I was the chosen one among my siblings, not because my brothers tried in any way to shift the burden onto me—they are great guys and always willing to pull their weight—but they're simply not around anymore. Both of them moved out west: Ron is in the computer business and lives in Colorado with his wife, Lisa. He has two kids by his first marriage, Scott, twenty-three, and Brian, nineteen. Bruce lives outside of San Francisco and designs computer systems. He's married to Marti and has two young children, Shelly, eleven, and Michael, nine. Not only are my brothers on the other side of the country, they have families and responsibilities that I, as a single person, don't. That's why I willingly took on the major burden of my dad's finances. My brothers always supported me emotionally and materially to the best of their abilities.

In the middle of this madness, my dad called one day.

"Kathy, I won a car!"

"Yeah, Dad, sure you won a car."

"No, I mean it, I did win a car."

"Where did you win this car?" I asked.

"I put my name in a box at the local bank and I won the drawing."

I got the name of the bank and called—he had won a car! I'd been screaming at him that all contests were scams and my father had won a brand-new $22,000 Chrysler New Yorker. My dad's picture appeared in the newspaper showing him with a big smile on his face standing next to the gleaming automobile. Two weeks later the car was full of dents and missing its side mirrors. He drove worse than my grandmother. He went right up onto curbs, smacked into telephone poles, and parked illegally. The tickets began to mount up. It reached the point where I had to take him to see a doctor. After the examination the doctor suggested that my father be put into a home. As wacky as things had gotten, I was astounded.

"You're out of your mind," I told the doctor.

"I'm telling you," he responded, "your father is suffering from strokes. This man is dangerous to himself. And he's driving a car, which makes him dangerous to others."

Again, I was stunned. Sure, my father's behavior was peculiar, yet I'd never suspected strokes. I didn't know what to do so I called my brother, Ron. Ron accepted the news and immediately told me to get the car away from Dad and to sell it.

"I can't sell it. He'll kill me," I cried. "He'll be helpless without wheels." I couldn't bear to strip my father of what dignity remained to him.

"Get the car and sell it," repeated Ron, "before he kills someone!" My brother had to hang tough, and his strength was my rock during the ordeal. Even

118

though I hated to render my dad helpless by depriving him of his car, I knew Ron was right—it had to be done. I sold the Chrysler to a dealer who bought it for cash, sight unseen, because he'd seen me on QVC. (Even though the car was brand new and only needed body work, I let it go for $14,000. I'm telling you, that dealer got the deal of his life but I wasn't interested in making money on the sale, I just wanted the car out of Dad's hands.) I told my father some cockamamie story about the car being repossessed. He was fit to be tied, but there was nothing he could do.

From then on, things went from bad to worse, and one day the dental hygienist found him on the office floor completely passed out. The next day, the same thing happened. He could not continue. We retired him to his apartment and put his practice up for sale. Within thirty days his life's work was sold. I felt so sorry for him. (For years afterward whenever I'd take my father out for dinner, former patients would come over to shake his hand. Without exception they'd tell me that he was a kind person and a fine dentist. I felt very proud of him. They also told me how proud he was of his daughter.) I hired round-the-clock nurses to look after my father at home. His condition worsened, and the nurses couldn't handle him. He's such a big man they couldn't pick him up. Obviously, my father needed to be in a safe environment, and my brothers and I decided to place him in a nursing home. Since I had power of attorney, I had to sign the papers. I told my mother, and she became completely distraught.

"Oh my God," she cried, "are you sure you're doing the right thing?"

"Please," I begged her, "don't do this to me—it's got to be done."

And so I put him into a nursing home. Many a night I'd go on the air and be happy-go-lucky Kathy just after my father had called and screamed at me for

119

"locking him up." I'd go on and give a stellar performance and then come off the air and sob. That's what you have to do in my job; you have to put everything aside.

Time passed and we thought my dad had recovered enough to return home under supervision. We took him out and now he screamed at me for what I *had* done to him. "How dare you lock me up? Where's my car? Where's my checkbook? You stole my money." (What money?—he was thousands of dollars in debt!) Boy, did he let me have it. I was in tears all the time. Not only did I have a mishugena father raging at me, his creditors were breathing down my neck and I was paying $600 a week in part-time nursing care. But I was making good money, I didn't have kids—I felt it was my duty to take care of my father. Finally my mother stepped in.

"You can't do this," she said. "You can't use up your life savings. What happens to you when your father's gone and you're busted? You simply cannot do this." She was right. Ultimately, we put my father back into the nursing home, where he became so silent and withdrawn the doctors prescribed an antidepressant. After that, he stopped talking altogether. At my request, he was taken off the medication, but he was never the same. To this day he is silent most of the time and says a word or two only occasionally.

"How's dog?" he'll ask—he can't say Chelsea's name.

"Dog's fine," I answer.

"How's Mom?"

"Mom's fine."

"You going to Grandma's?" he'll ask as if she were still around waiting for me to drop by.

That's how it's been for the past couple of years since my father moved into his own world. He's in a wheelchair now, and even though his mind goes further and further into the past I do my best to maintain

Friendly Fire

decent surroundings for him. He's in good hands in a
Jewish nursing home in Bethlehem, and I arranged for
a male nurse to come in three hours every day to
shower him, dress him, and take him out like a gentleman. He gets a haircut; he gets his nails cut; he gets
lunch—whatever he wants.

Bethlehem was close enough to Allentown for my
mother to visit, and she went to see him nearly every
day. Her friends told her she was crazy to take on
the responsibility; after all, she wasn't married to him
anymore. My mother dismissed their comments. "You
don't get it," she said. "Just because our marriage
ended doesn't mean we're not connected. I loved
Arnie Kauffman. We were together for thirty-two
years; he's the father of my children. I still care about
him." And so she continued her visits, and every time
she went to the nursing home, she'd bring my father
a hot fudge sundae. (I don't know what he liked better, seeing her or eating the ice cream.) In his mind
they're still married and this delusion is a blessing—it
gives him a kind of peace and makes it easier on my
mother, especially now. She and Lee recently moved
to Florida, so she won't be able to see my dad on
a regular basis anymore. While he'll miss her visits,
unfortunately I'm sure he won't recognize the time
lapses.

Over the years, I've gotten used to dealing with my
father. We take him out to eat and I say, "Daddy, you
in the mood for meat or fish?" He'll answer something
unintelligible and I pick right up and say, "Is that fish?
Okay." And I tell the waiter, "My dad will have the
snapper and a baked potato." Then we feed him. He'll
drool and slobber but I don't have a problem with
it. However, it's become increasingly difficult for me
physically to handle him. I don't know how much
longer I can get him in and out of the car and the
wheelchair. My brother Ron and I are very much alike
on this, we just handle him. My mother falls apart

121

every time. It kills her. She feels so terrible. Her life is rich and full and his is empty. It breaks her heart—mine too, but I can't think that way. I don't see my dad as often, maybe once a month. We always visit on his birthday and on Father's Day. We round up the uncles and aunts and take him out as a family. The only one who doesn't join us is Lee Seinfeld. My stepfather can't bear to see what's happened, it's too painful. He hasn't laid eyes on his best friend Arnie Kauffman in two years.

My dad always said that he never wanted to be a burden to his children, and knowing how he felt makes the way things turned out even sadder. I wish he'd had a nicer life, a nicer ending, but what can you do? When a child becomes the parent and a parent becomes the child, the decisions are hard, cold, and gut-wrenching and made even more difficult if you don't have help. All children should be aware that parents will get old and that some sort of health care plan should be set in motion before that happens. Everyone should seek strong support when they have to make tough decisions. I wasn't aware; I just woke up one day and had these major obstacles facing me. The strong support of my mother, my brothers, and family meant a lot; still, I was overwhelmed with the paperwork and the responsibility of getting my father into a nursing room. (I remember clearly that my mother had to research where we could put him at the same time that he *had* to be put there.)

Don't get caught at the last minute. Be prepared. It will happen, and it's smart to try and set things up as best as you can for your sake as well as your parents'. You don't want to turn your own life into a living hell. So often viewers will write and tell me about various problems they have with family members who are infirm or hospitalized or suffering from Alzheimer's disease, and I always try to answer those letters with some words of understanding and compassion. I do understand their pain, and now you know why.

7

Thee and Me and QVC

❖ ❖ ❖

Do the words *cubic zirconium* or *Diamonique* mean anything to you? If they don't, then you aren't watching QVC. Cubic zirconium is a created fake diamond; Diamonique is QVC's name for it, and beautiful replicas of fine jewelry can be made with it at a fraction of the cost of the real thing. Although we're often referred to as "QVCZ" or "Cubic Zirconium Network," less than 38 percent of our gross sales is in jewelry, and cubic zirconium itself accounts for less than 5 percent of *all* our sales. We have a great breadth in merchandise and offer our viewers every important brand name of toys, electronics, collectibles, artwork, furnishings, kitchen gadgets, bedding, almost anything you can think of. So why are we called the Cubic Zirconium Network? Very simply, people hooked on to the title—it's good for laughs and has provided abundant material for entertainers like Johnny Carson, who had a field day with C.Z. Calling us the Cubic Zirconium Network is a bit of a putdown and accents the negative. They can call us anything they want; the fact is we provide lovely, relatively *in-*

expensive jewelry for people who can't afford to buy the real McCoy. (Many people who can afford to buy diamonds buy our replicas, too!)

That's the story of Diamonique; however, there's a lot more happening at QVC that has nothing to do with Cubic Zirconium. I'm sure all of you must have wondered at one time or another what really goes on behind the scenes. Well, I'm going to pull the curtain aside a little further and tell you a bit about what it's like to work at America's number one shopping network.

Televised shopping has changed the face of the retail market. QVC is a catalog with pictures, and even more important, we're a "listening" catalog. "Quality, Value, Convenience" isn't just the name of our station; it stands for what we are and what we try to give the viewer. Not only do we provide quality, value, and convenience, we offer another important "C," companionship. We are a talking catalog service and we're there for our viewers twenty-four hours a day. We're your video pals, and we can keep you company when there's no one else around or nothing else to do. QVC has a huge following of people who don't buy—they just watch. They have a good time, and we want them to. Of course, we also want people to buy . . . but *only* if they can afford to. The majority of our viewers use QVC as a service and are as prudent about spending their money with us as they would be in a bona fide store. (Because of my dad's situation, I became acutely aware of the number of vulnerable people out there, especially senior citizens.)

We hosts are there to answer specifically the kinds of questions that printed catalogs deal with in general terms. We at QVC are both knowledgeable and readily available twenty-four hours of the day . . . for you! About the only thing that you could do with the old-fashioned catalogs that you can't do with televised shopping is use them in the outhouse! Demographic studies help us to understand our customers and to target the best times to put certain items on the screen. Whatever the product or whatever the time, we hosts have to be at our very best all the time. Let me tell you about my typical day and you'll get the picture:

9:30 A.M.—get up, walk the dog, run errands, do the laundry, pay the bills. 12 noon to 3 P.M.—arrive at the studio for a meeting, learn new products, iron out any production problems. 3 P.M. to 4:30 P.M.—check the message machine, retrieve all letters and memos from my mailbox, respond to any voice mail requests, stop into the gold office to see new chains, talk to the collectible buyer about Hummel figurines, talk to the set designer about an upcoming gem show, check the computer for e-mail. (Most e-mail messages are reminders about upcoming events, schedule changes, publicity tours, newspaper interviews, or just fun notes from one host to another. They can be left by anyone in-house and each employee has a secret password so no one else can read your mail. We each have a terminal in our homes, too.) 5:00 P.M. to 6:30 P.M.—return home, walk the dog, do hair and makeup, get dressed. 7:00 P.M. to 9:00 P.M.—return to the studio, talk to the producer about the show lineup, review products, meet any guests who will be on air. 9 P.M. to midnight—on air. 12:30 A.M.—return home, walk the dog, read the viewer mail. 1:30 A.M.—drop into bed.

That's pretty much what an average day is like for me and, give or take a few activities, probably what it's like for my cohosts. One thing's true for all of us, whatever goes on during the day and evening, we have to be absolutely on our toes when we're on air. Our basic training back in 1986 set the strategy for the selling techniques we still use today. We learned that while products change, questions are fundamentally the same: Who? Where? When? Why? How? What? and that most demanding query ... So what? We were taught not only to answer specific questions but to *anticipate* questions and respond to them, too.

My first classroom experience at QVC was very similar to my QVC audition with the pencil ... only this time I had to sell a cushion.

"Here's a pillow. Tell me about it," said the instructor, tossing me a sofa cushion.

"Well, pillows add a decorative touch and this one happens to be floral so it matches the sofa over here."

"What kind of material is it?

"It's a cotton."

"So what?"

"Well, cotton's natural, easy to clean, and long-lasting."

"What's inside?" queried the instructor.

"Nonallergic stuffing."

"What do I care?" she came back, so I began talking about allergies. She kept firing queries, and just when I thought I'd said all there was to say, she'd come up with another one. Bam. Bam. Bam. At the end, I was ready to stuff the pillow down her throat. I restrained myself and just fed the answers back to her. Even if your dander is raised you have to rein yourself in—if you show any signs that you aren't capable of working under pressure, then you don't belong as a host. The final shot from the instructor was, "What do *I* need a pillow for? I have one."

"You never know," I answered cheerily. "A pillow can camouflage a stain on an old sofa and give a face lift to a drab room."

126

Thee and Me and QVC

The procedure I've just described is an example of "feature benefit selling technique" and was drilled into us ad nauseam until we got it. To this day it remains my method of operation.

While the purpose of those exercises was to get us to think on our feet, being a host isn't simply a matter of reacting quickly—you also have to prepare. It would be disastrous if people wanted to know something and the host stood there like a lox. You have to have plenty of resources to draw from in order to chat for three and four hours at a clip. When I'm on the screen talking about a product like gems, rest assured I've done my research from amethyst to zirconium and can answer just about anything that might be asked.

There's a lot of repetition in selling, too. How much, for instance, can you say about a herringbone design or a beveled edge? That's the catch, how to take yesterday's tired old herringbone and make it today's new exciting product. I already know a lot about some subjects, especially jewelry, which I've been interested in since I was a little girl playing at my grandmother's. I sure don't know everything, though, and I have to keep up. I always read *Woman's Wear Daily, Vogue, New Woman, Sports Illustrated, Gourmet* magazine—anything to give my sales pitch some spice. Even if you're not buying, my hope is that you learn, you laugh, you enjoy.

As I said, I know quite a bit about jewelry and I know a lot about clothing, too—I'm not Pat Seinfeld's daughter for nothing. Still, there's so much to learn. Preparation is essential, and it takes hours to do properly. Broadcast time is the tip of the iceberg in my work—for every three hours on the air there's four times that in behind-the-scenes activity. Hosts have to know the products inside out and upside down, and we not only do extensive research on our own, we're also sent on "Fam Trips" (familiarization trips) much like the ones travel agents take when they want to find out about

KATHY LEVINE

a place. Recently I went to Brazil to learn about ame-
thysts for an upcoming gem show. I put on a helmet,
grabbed a pick, went into the mines, and dug up my
own amethyst geode! (A geode is the hollow rock surrounding the gem.) I also took a Fam Trip to London
this year when we imported Royal Doulton china and
darling sweaters that had the English double-decker
buses and the distinctive red phone booths embroidered
on them. *Veddy, veddy English.*

The flavor of the country is woven into the presentation and gives the "armchair" traveler the feeling of
really having been there. We do a lot of armchair
traveling on QVC for our viewers and take them all
over the world. Hosts can't always be going on Fam
Trips, so QVC maintains an Information Service department that is a spectacular resource. At least six
library scientists staff the research library and they
find out anything and everything we want to know.
The QVC library is comprehensive and utterly available to us. A host can order any book or publication
and the company will purchase it with no questions
asked. (Hey, maybe I'll order a few thousand copies
of this book!) On an average, I receive 1,000 pages of
information a week from the library, and if you multiply that by 52 it'll give you a good idea of how much
background material goes into a product presentation.

As for the products themselves, QVC has over 100
buyers, and their job is to select the merchandise.
Vendors (aka salesmen) make appointments with the
buyers to show their wares. QVC has to know how
much the product costs, how much is available, how
soon can it be shipped, and even what kind of box
the product is shipped in. That's just for openers. We
also have to know how fast we can reorder if the
product sells out. All of this points up the fact that
an undercapitalized or small company will not be able
to do business with us. (Our hearts go out to the craft-
sperson who makes, let's say, four lovely, handcarved

128

jewelry boxes a month, and we would very much like to put them on QVC. It's just not possible for this to happen because of the magnitude of this retail giant.) After a buyer has seen the product and likes it, he goes to a senior buyer (director) for final approval. Once a week there's a meeting to show outstanding products to all the directors, who then cast a vote for the strongest one(s). If there's solid approval, a large amount of money will be appropriated for a huge quantity, and that product will be pushed hard ... with good reason. One great product can equal 25 percent of our sales value each day. When you have *one* product that will make a quarter of your daily business, it's critical for everyone, including the hosts, to be 100 percent behind it.

Once the product gets the okay from the senior buyer, it is then sent to Quality Assurance. The QA division of QVC has to be *the* toughest bunch of testers in the world. QVC's quality control is so rigorous that often products I would buy in a store without a second thought *fail* our standards. First of all, QA doesn't test "samples," for the simple reason that samples aren't always representative of the final product ... they can be a heck of a lot better. QA grabs large portions of the finished merchandise and proceeds to beat the living daylights out of it. If the merchandise is apparel, QA washes, cleans, and wears every article to death. Fit is extremely important and, since customers always can take things in, QVC clothing is cut fuller; for example, our 12 borders on 13.

QA is fussier than Fort Knox when it comes to gold. Every single piece is weighed, and numerous samples of each item category are melted down and assayed—14 karat gold has to be 14 karat gold or forget it. Early on, one vendor tried to sell "14k" gold to us; it was assayed and discovered to be 13.9k. This guy was banned. By being a pig, he lost out—oh boy, did he lose! QVC is one of the largest consumers of gold chain in the world. I know how rigorously my company investigates product so I can sell anything with absolute confidence and ease. (By the way, I'm sure that goes for all the hosts and not just me.)

Once an article is sold over the air, the next hurdle is the shipping, and QA is on top of that, too. They make sure that what is sent out is going to arrive intact. This can be tricky—some articles are relatively easy to ship, others are a nightmare. For instance we sell a lot of Lladro porcelain, and it's very fragile, so great care has to be taken. First the article is packed and then we test it by dropping the package from a 9-foot platform. As if that weren't enough, the package is then put on a shaker belt (like the ones you used to wrap around your tookus) and the belt shakes the guts out of the package. Only if the article survives this treatment will it be sent out. Sometimes I hate QA because many things I love fail in the testing and we can't offer them. Basically, though, I'm glad QA is there. I take it real personal if anything goes wrong. When I'm out there I have to have complete confidence in my merchandise. I'm not alone in this—anyone selling a product wants to feel she's selling the best. Hosts, particularly the senior ones, will let management know when we feel a product isn't up to snuff (which isn't often), and I think we've had some input in quality control. I have to say, I'm really proud of the merchandise I sell.

In the early days, hosts received "obscenity" training, which was similar to the regular routine except that we learned how to deal with foul mouths rather than facts. The host went through the motions of a regular broadcast and presented merchandise and, once again, the instructor assumed the viewer's role and called in just as it happens on actual broadcasts. Call-ins are an essential part of QVC; they give hosts a chance to interact with viewers, and viewers have fun being "on the air." While waiting on "hold" to chat with a host, many of them throw a tape into their VCR so they can play their phone "appearances" for family and friends later on. It's very exciting to speak live on national television, and how many people get the chance? No wonder the viewers want to tape the big moment. There are, alas, others who are not concerned with discussing the product; they want to make trouble, and we were prepared for such incidents. It's pretty scary stuff, and even though calls are screened beforehand, there's always the chance some nut will get through. Remember, QVC is LIVE—we don't even have a seven-second time delay like they do in radio. Some people wonder why we don't use the delay system, and the answer is simple—not only does it cost a lot to operate, it also takes away from the excitement of live broadcasting. Because of the possibility of something "leaking" through, every one of the hosts has gone through a baptism of fire. I remember my first time; it happened within the first six months and I was selling a silver chain.

"Hi, you're on the air," I announced.

"Am I on the air?" questioned the caller.

"Yes, you are," I replied cheerfully.

"Is this Kathy?"

"Yes, it is," I answered sweetly.

"You're a dumb-assed bitch," said the caller.

"Thank you for calling," I gulped, and moved on to the product.

Fortunately, that call was killed immediately so I didn't get any further abuse. What I did get was an acute attack of the giggles. It struck me funny that I was standing with this big smile on my face and this total stranger bops me. Rather than getting frightened or mad, I got silly. It took a while for me to get control of myself, and then I proceeded to do my stuff per usual. After the show, my boss came down and told me that I had done fine.

Actually, there's only one way hosts are protected, and it isn't a fool proof method by any means. When we're on the air there's no way we can disconnect that telephone line ourselves—that's the responsibility of the control booth. The technique is called "podding," and it's a relatively simple procedure. A slider is attached to the phone in the control booth, and the technician can either raise or lower the volume of any viewer call by pushing the slider up or down. For example, when I say, "Let's go to the phone line," the technician pods up, and the call goes over the air. When I'm finished, the technician pods down and the call goes out. If a technician pods up and then leaves the control booth for whatever reason, and the producer is otherwise occupied, no one is there to take down the call and the host is at the mercy of the caller. (The fastest podder in the East couldn't have saved me from being called a "dumb-assed bitch"—it came too quickly.)

Podding is helpful, but the only true protection is a time delay button that allows the station to hear what's being said before it goes on the air. Now, if QVC had spent a hundred thousand dollars for one of those suckers, I wouldn't have been called names, but it sure would take away from the surprise element. A lot of hosts really have gotten burnt by weird calls, and we have a blooper tape of these occasions—many of which are definitely X-rated. Some fans watch QVC faithfully not necessarily to buy, but in the hope that someone will call in and drop a bombshell. It's bound to happen. Look, we broadcast twenty-four hours a day, 364 days a year—how safe can you be with that much exposure? (FYI: the screen goes blank only on Christmas. QVC leaves the air at 4 P.M. on Christmas Eve and returns on December 26 at 8 A.M. Years ago, I volunteered to do the closing show—hey, I figured the people celebrating the holiday should get time off to be with their families and decorate the tree and get those presents wrapped. I have little to do, so it's become a tradition for me and Chelsea to spend the hours before Christmas Eve with the QVC viewers.)

Along with the pod, there's another essential device for the hosts, the IFB (Interruptive Feed Back) button. In order to maintain some sort of open line with the producer while we're on the air, we wear an IFB in one ear, and that's how the producer is able to communicate with us even as we sell product. Most viewers don't realize that during our broadcasts we hosts have producers buzzing in our brains. I wear my IFB button in my right ear and I'm so used to it being there I don't think I could switch—there's no way I can plug into my left ear. Although it took a bit of getting used to, the IFB is second nature to me now. Even so, a producer sometimes can give directives at a pretty fast pace, and I have to work my butt off to keep up. So, if you're watching QVC and you see a host suddenly smile and reach over to adjust something, whether it's a product that's fallen down or a guest who's got a button hanging loose, you can bet your boots that little ear button has carried the instructions.

On certain occasions, IFB's are used for purposes that aren't strictly business. For example, I'll be on the air with a guest and the producer will kick in and say, "We're ordering Chinese, are you hungry?" I nod my head even as I smile and direct a question to my guest, who, along with the audience, hasn't got a clue as to what I'm hearing. "Okay," says the producer in my ear, "do you want won ton soup or hot and sour?" This is beyond a yes or no, and you have to figure out signals for making yourself understood. You can either sign a W with your finger for the won ton and integrate the move into a gesture toward your guest or the camera, or you can hold up one finger or two, meaning I'll take the first choice or the second. Once in a while, you get scrambled and find yourself talking out loud. You'll turn to the guest and begin to converse.

133

KATHY LEVINE

"So, tell me a little bit about yourself. You started out in—shrimp lo mein—Indianapolis, and then you went on to—moo goo gai pan—Chicago?"

Besides taking food orders, producers have been known to play practical jokes over the IFB. The objective is to make the host break up. A few hosts leave strict rules not to be disturbed because it upsets their concentration. For instance, it can be way too distracting on cooking shows where you have to keep track of ingredients. For myself, I could live with an IFB permanently fixed in my ear; I consider it a pal. During odd hours when there aren't many people around and you're working in a small studio, the IFB is a link to the outside world. I'm in there all by myself except for a cameraman and yearn for some kind of feedback—someone to say "everything's fine" or "you're doing great." I might even have to be told to pick up the pace because the product isn't selling well or that there's going to be an extra few minutes tacked on. Whatever needs to be said, the only way I get the information and encouragement is through my earpiece. No wonder I love my IFB.

Those early days at QVC were hectic and such fun. We were pioneers, and everything was at its simplest level. For example, the so-called QVC "restaurant" was a nine-by-twelve room that contained four vending machines. Today we have a bona fide cafeteria serving up hot and cold meals to thousands of employees. Everybody eats there, telephone operators, hosts, models, technicians, management, you name it. I think it's probably like the commissaries in the old Hollywood studios. At present our biggest problem is our building. We've outgrown it and it's a real dilemma because we've got nowhere to go. Chester County has a rule that you can't build higher than two floors—since we can't go up, we have to go out. To expand we have to take over the adjacent pasture land and move the cows that graze

134

there farther and farther away. And, those cows don't like getting shoved around. They're bossy.

Space wasn't a problem in the beginning—we had lovely offices and they were roomy, too, because there weren't that many people to fill them. If I remember correctly, I was employee number 98. Now there are 98 people to every square foot—space is definitely at a premium. I went into a broom closet recently and grabbed a broom and dustpan. (I had dropped a plant on the floor and wanted to clean it up.) When I returned the dustpan and broom, the closet had been turned into an office and there were sixteen accountants sitting there. Just kidding ... there were only ten. Anyway, they've hired a space engineer, and his job is to find places to put people.

People have been stranded because the "machines" have taken over. Once upon a time the computer was in a little antechamber and now it's in a room that occupies most of the building. There must be 150 people running that machine. It's a massive operation, what with the ordering system, the money processing, the labeling, and the returns ... and it's all computerized. That's the heart of the business, though. The most terrifying horror stories about marketing have to do with companies that make a load of money but go under because they can't keep up with the volume of orders. That's a retailer's worst scenario, but luckily not one QVC has to worry about.

QVC was one huge business to launch and to keep going. In our first year, all of us went into shock because we didn't have the advanced systems that are in use today. Now we can handle up to 5,000 telephone calls at once, and we can *get* that many when we're offering a popular product or a really good value. One time Joan Rivers mentioned a "free" catalog, and the phone lines were jammed within seconds. "Free" is a big word—I feel like calling in myself when *I* hear it used, and I'm in the business. Everything is high tech

135

and computerized whereas in the past we all had to pitch in. When the phones got too busy a red light would flash and anybody who was in the vicinity, from the president of the company to his secretary or a host, would run to the phone station, man the telephones, and take the orders. I remember when we did our first big silver jewelry day. We were selling herringbone chains for twelve dollars and matching bracelets for nine and the phones rang off the wall. We were all pulled in to the studio and asked to answer phones and take orders, I mean buyers, hosts, administrators, everyone! Then, when the ordering was done, we were asked to please go and pack the jewelry. I'm telling you the entire QVC shebang was in there with shirtsleeves rolled up, pitching in. Before we got too big, we had a warehouse right in the studio; today we rent warehouses all over the country.

I vividly remember working in the studio warehouse getting products ready to ship. One picture I'll always have in my mind is of Steve Byrant, my fellow host, going up in a cherry picker to get boxes down from shelves that were 50 feet in the air. Steve had a safety line but wasn't too crazy about heights and there he was, shaking in his boots, hauling down merchandise. We learned about storage the hard way, too. Heat rises, and it got very hot up at the top of the warehouse, and a lot of product got destroyed—cosmetic creams, for example, turn to yuck unless they're refrigerated. Since refrigeration is expensive, instead of storing the merchandise, we'll often have a manufacturer keep his product until the exact day of shipping, then send it to QVC. We check it over and mail it right out. When you buy something *from* QVC, nine times out of ten, it has to go through us. Large items, like treadmills, are often sent directly from the manufacturer to the customer.

Yessir, the beginning was pure fun. You'd be in the warehouse working next to Chairman Joe Segel himself

136

and shmoozing and telling jokes and chewing gum while getting the product out. Many a time I'd finish my broadcast and someone would come racing in to tell me I had to help out. I'd kick off my heels, put on my flats, and start packing merchandise. We use tons of "packing peanuts," and those little suckers are very expensive, so we bought our own peanut-making machine and of course there was some sort of environmental issue and they had to be made differently, which of course cost more money. I did a lot of packing myself until one day I broke a nail and got three paper cuts and decided that packing was hazardous for my health. (Yeah, I know I don't worry about my nails but come on, this was ridiculous.) I pulled a prima donna act. "I'll answer telephones," I told my boss, "but no more packing."

From day one, camaraderie among QVC hosts has been outstanding; indeed, one of the most important support systems we hosts have is each other. When a show goes wrong and the results are off, when a caller tosses in an obscenity or a depressing story that deflates the energy of the show, hosts can let off steam by talking to each other. We have weekly meetings, and the first fifteen minutes before the formal proceedings start are the funniest. My coworkers are the brightest, wittiest story tellers in the business. By recounting on-air incidents, each in his/her own delightful way, the hosts dump their troubles out on the table. We roar with laughter, we cajole, we verbally abuse each other, and as a result, the situations that have occurred become less poignant or disturbing. This tension busting is an essential part of our surviving the stress of a live on-air job. Once I got a letter from a viewer that was so scathing, so unkind that I brought it to the meeting to share with the gang. Bob Bowersox perked up and said he could top it and proceeded to read a letter that was so vicious it made mine seem like a valentine. Then Steve Bryant talked about his letters, Jane Treacy hers, and on and on until it became evident that there always would be someone around who was going to hate us and let us know about it through the mail. This "group therapy" works all the time. I've always supported my peers and been supported by them through troubled times. Moreover, QVC offers its employees the opportunity to complain in a safe environment without fear of losing one's job. We can freely discuss any in-house problems we encounter while on air. Whatever the complaint—whether it's that a model looked sloppy or a program coordinator continually displayed products backward or unfashionably or that a producer was "out of it" and offered no guidance, or that a guest was inarticulate—a justifiable grievance is considered valid and critical to the success of the show. This is very forward thinking of QVC. Just think about all the companies that actually foster fear and manage by intimidation. In such places, complaining to a boss means "squealing" and to seek improvement means overstepping authority. No wonder morale is low. Even sweet Mary Beth has lost her temper at an incompetent technician, and other hosts have stormed off the set to disagree with a producer's call. We hosts also get feedback from other departments and have to take our fair share of "heat." Yours truly has gotten her hackles up and had the "bitch" label pinned on her many, many times, often deservedly so. All things being equal, if you're going to dish it out you better be able to take it. Give and take are the operative words, and all of us hosts like it this way because it works. At QVC, we continue to work in harmony as a host unit because we communicate openly with each other and our departments.

QVC grew and grew and before you knew it, the parking lot was no longer large enough. We went after the cows again and pushed them farther out to pasture so we could blacktop their grassland. Today, the park-

Thee and Me and QVC

ing lot is humongous—something like five football fields. There are 3,000 employees at the studio—luckily we work in shifts or we'd be parking in Philadelphia. The studio has been looking into the problem of more space and I tell you it wouldn't break my heart if we moved to another location. This building is too crowded. One person sneezes and we all get a cold. QVC would be absolutely unlivable if people smoked, but the former president made us a no smoking enterprise. It was a sensitive issue and management handled it beautifully. Classes were given to help people get through the emotional anxiety of not being able to smoke at work. There's a designated smoking area outside of the building called the pagoda and anyone can run out there for a puff. In my opinion, QVC made a wise decision to move the cigarettes out and at the same time give some space to smokers.

In theory, moving to a new building would be great, but I have to admit I have mixed feelings about going elsewhere. I love where I work. It's not the actual physical plant, because the building is inadequate, but I get a warm feeling when I walk through the doorway every day—it's still a magical moment. My mood can be so glum, and the second I enter QVC, my spirits are lifted. It's a tonic. Everybody is friendly and kind and smart—no kidding, QVC has a very special atmosphere, which shouldn't be lost. I'd guess, however, that the ambience is related to the people and not the walls and probably would transfer just fine to another building—a great big gorgeous one!

Here's another bit of inside information for you: Shopping networks are the only ones who *pay* cable operators for airtime. Many viewers are under the impression that if they want home shopping they just have to call up and they'll get it. That's not so. It's really up to the cable operators. We're on a contract basis, and the more cable systems we're on the better. QVC has a tremendous sales force, and they've done a bang-up job on market penetration. The channel placement is very important—the lower the number, the better. QVC tries very hard to get into the first twenty. In West Chester we're channel 8, and in some far-flung areas of the country, we actually are in the first five channels. Our popularity fluctuates and we can be big stuff in one area and bupkis in another.

Wherever we are, people have very strong feelings about the hosts. Did you know, for instance, there's an I Hate Kathy Club in Brockton, Massachusetts? It started when the Kathy Ring was offered and became a best-seller. I got a letter from these women in Brockton who told me my ring was awful and that I had no taste, no talent, and no business designing. The letter ended, "Get out of the design business and stick with what you do. And we don't think you're so hot." Yep, I can get letters attacking me from every which way. Of course, I also get other mail that is helpful and encouraging. Once I talked about having a "hot flash" and a viewer wrote, "At you're age, Kathy, they're not hot flashes, they're power surges." I love my viewers, no joke; they look after me, they worry about me, and they counsel me. I think my greatest compliment and highest praise is the declaration "You make me laugh."

In a funny way I'm a kind of noncelebrity celebrity. I don't know about you, but I think of a celebrity as someone unapproachable, I mean bigger than life— like I wouldn't dare go up to Barbra Streisand and start chatting. So, how can I be a celebrity when everybody comes up to me? It happens all the time. I'll be in the supermarket waiting in line and a woman will lean over and say something like, "What's for dinner?" I'll look at her and rack my brain. Who is this person? Why do we know each other? Did I take a class with her? Does she work with me? And it doesn't dawn on me that she watches me on TV—it never dawns on me. A woman ran over in a shopping mall waving her arm and crying, "Hey, Kathy, this is the bracelet I bought from you. I love it." She loves the bracelet, and I love the fact that she feels she bought it from *me,* yet somehow I don't think she'd be flying over to Cindy Crawford or Demi Moore. I honestly don't expect to be recognized and most of the time I'm not. I can still walk around even in West Chester and get blank stares and yet I might be spotted pretty quickly in Bismarck, South Dakota. Frankly, I prefer the anonymity—there are less demands. Even now when I'm mostly unrecognized, my mother goes bananas because I don't want to wear makeup in public unless I'm working.

"You have to present yourself in the best possible light," she'll argue.

"It's just too much work, Ma," is my answer.

"But you have a persona, Kathy."

"Yes, Mother," I'll answer, "and today my persona is that of a dog!"

8
Here's the (Real) Jeffery

❖   ❖   ❖

If you happened to pick up this book just because you liked the way I looked on the cover but you really don't know who I am, and/or if you aren't interested in steamy, blistering, throbbing, hard-core sensationalism, you can skip on to the next section. If, however, you're a regular longtime QVC watcher, this chapter is the one you've been waiting for—The Inside Story of Kathy and Jeff. So, fasten your seat belts, it's going to be a bumpy ride.

In December of 1986, eight weeks after I was hired, a group of us were standing around chatting in the hosts' lounge. Someone called out my name and I turned to see my boss, John Eastman, coming toward me; another person was walking with him. "Kathy, I want you to meet a new host," said John.

The first thing I noticed was the new host's hair. He had a movie star mane, thick and beautiful, the kind that doesn't quit—the exact opposite of my scraggly locks. Next, I noticed his eyes; they were little and crinkly, very appealing. Then I took in the rest of

My father and my "Mommy Dearest." Doesn't she look like Joan Crawford?

My dad, my brothers and me.

My childhood home in Allentown.

My mom, simply beautiful.

My parents.

LITTLE KATHY KAUFFMAN

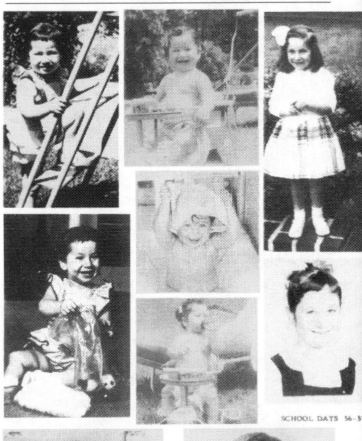

SCHOOL DAYS 56-5?

1951

Confirmation,
1967.

My brothers, Ron and
Bruce.

The original Kauffman family.

Ron Kauffman, age 18, 1962.

Bruce, age 18, 1963.

My dad.

My "nan" at 20. The
year is 1920.

Bruce, Kathy, Mom, Ron.

Ron's 50th birthday. Me, Ron's wife Lisa, Bruce, and my mom.

My mother, Pat, and Lee Seinfeld. (Doesn't he look like Jerry?)

Pat and Lee Seinfeld.

Here comes
the bride,
12/21/75.

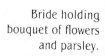

Bride holding
bouquet of flowers
and parsley.

The bride and groom toast their 12/21 wedding (note Kathy's ring on right hand).

My mother and her best men, Bruce and Ron.

The Happy Honeymooners,
St. Maarten.

The Levines, all dolled up.

1976—Jay had just been diagnosed with cancer. We went to
Vegas to forget.

BAD HAIR DAYS

Those college days.

Age 10 months, and already a bad hair day.

Me and my dad. My hair is blonde, blonde, blonde. Most of it fell into the sink.

Preparing to dazzle them in Detroit.

NOT A PRETTY PICTURE

Working out: Do not attempt this unless you are a professional.

I love this one. Rockin' with Richard.

S-s-stretch this! Rancho La Puerto Spa, Mexico, 1989.

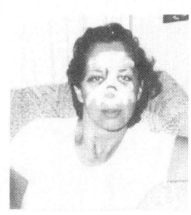

So, you wanna have a nose job?

Bob Mackie, a gentleman and a fine designer.

Bill Blass.

The divine Susan Lucci.

Richard and I on the
Cruise to Lose.

Hello, Dolly—Carol
Channing.

Milton Berle.

My best beau, Richard
Simmons, at Judy and Jeff's
wedding.

Cruising to Lose with
Richard Simmons.

Nolan Miller.

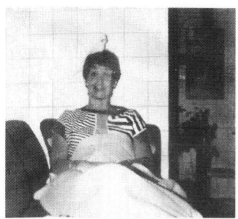

A bird mistakes me
for a nest.

My friend Sandi Donaldson. She
sent me on my way up.

NIMA award, me, and a friend.

Sandi and I.

Kathy and Steve. A
night on the town.

Sandi and I,
party girls.

My Spanish family: Teresita, Andres, and kids Javier and Alicia.

Dan Hughes and I with the QVC Local in Cypress Gardens, Florida.

The NIMA award for best show host. Nick Chavez, best hairdresser, best-looking hunk.

The remaining three
original hosts—Paul
Kelley, me, and Bob
Bowersox—at Mardi Gras,
New Orleans.

A commercial break.

Joan and I share a moment
together.

Joan and I in the green room. Notice Spike and Veronica, too.

X-mas at Joan's, 1994. Tim Conway, Jill Bauer (QVC host), Joan, and me.

My first appearance on Joan's talk show, 1990.

Kathy and Joan; I'm
the taller one.

X-mas at QVC.

ME AND MY BEST FRIEND

MY ONE TRUE LOVE

Alert guard dog; protector of the wardrobe.

Chelsea and Mom napping.

Eat your heart out, Lassie. Chelsea, the world's most beautiful schnauzer.

Steve Bryant and Chelsea.

Mother-daughter sportswear.

him. He was slender and nicely dressed ... and also somewhat stiff. In fact, he looked like he had a pole stuck up his spine. (I later learned that he *did* have a steel bar in his back as a result of a scuba diving accident.)

"Kathy," continued John, "this is Jeff Hewson; Jeff, this is Kathy Levine."

"It's about time you hired a good-looking guy," I said as I grabbed Jeff's hand.

Out of that simple introduction emerged one of QVC's most celebrated partnerships. Kathy and Jeff, or Jeff and Kathy, depending upon which of us was your favorite—or to whom you were related. Whatever the billing, we became the George Burns and Gracie Allen of televised shopping.

Jeff Hewson had been spotted on the Home Shopping Network. QVC was impressed with what it saw and hired him. Once Jeff began on QVC, he became a favorite. Viewers loved his devilish laugh and his boyish charm—women were crazy for him. Jeff and I had an immediate on-air chemistry and it began the first time we had a televised exchange.

One of QVC's policies directs that as one segment is finishing, the host of the impending segment comes onto the set and teases up the next show. These appearances are called "walk-ons." Jeff's hours were before mine, and I'd join him, say a few words about what I was going to sell, and then he'd say something back to me. Jeff didn't know what I was going to be selling and after I announced the product, we'd wing it. Everything was ad-lib, nothing was planned. I had the advantage because I knew what he'd been up to on the air and could josh him about it. He always came right back at me, though, and we played off each other beautifully. Little by little, the humor crept in. Soon we were bantering back and forth, and our repartee captured the imagination of the viewers. Initially

I didn't find our badinage all that funny, but it sure tickled the audience, and eventually, we got real good.

"Hey, Jeff," I called out as I entered the set on one occasion, "I have a terrific vacuum cleaner coming up in the next hour."

"What would you know about vacuuming?"

"I vacuumed once."

"Yeah, when? 1806?"

He teased me about everything. Among other products, Jeff sold kitchenware, which was a laugh, because the guy didn't know anything about cooking—he had one and only one culinary triumph.

"What are you cooking?" I asked him.

"Fried baloney," he answered.

"You eat that?"

"Yeah. How about you? Do you want to cook something for dinner?"

"Are you nuts? I make reservations for dinner."

Jeff's "recipe" for his pièce de résistance was something else. He'd take a piece of white bread, slap on a slice of baloney and a slice of cheese, and drop the thing into a nonstick T-fal pan. Before you could say cholesterol, the concoction would blend together and Jeff would flip the congealed lump onto a plate. He'd munch on his creation while pointing out to the audience that nothing had stuck to the T-fal pan. Fried baloney! Who eats fried baloney? What kind of garbage is fried baloney? But, because he was so cute, he got away with it.

One time I came on and announced that I'd be introducing a new cosmetic product on the next show, a youth cream. "I don't think there's enough of that cosmetic product for you," teased Jeff. "I heard you were born at the turn of the century." Because he was younger than I, he made a big deal about my age and dragged his routine through show after show. We have lucky number drawings at QVC and when Jeff pulled out a figure like 1895, 1901, or 1925 he'd invariably say, "The year of Kathy Levine's birth." I was never offended by his cracks. Hey, it worked to our advantage. (Anyway, Jeff wasn't as young as he claimed; we were more like four years apart rather than the fifteen to twenty he led the audience to believe.)

People began to tune in specifically to hear our walk-ons. If they weren't at home, they taped the exchanges and played them over and over, like bloopers. I can't even tell you what was that funny; all I can say is there was a humorous harmony between Jeff Hewson and me, and before long, I actually began to believe that *my* popularity was tied to him; I thought he was a necessary ingredient for my success. Jeff was a fabulous host—a real showman. For seven years he came on and announced, "My name is Jeff but my really good friends call me Jeffery." When a viewer would call up and say, "Hi, Jeff ... Jeffery," he'd answer, "Thanks for the Jeffery," and that phrase became Jeff Hewson's signature statement. When viewers called me and asked for him, I'd throw in a little jab. "Here's Jeffery," I'd announce, "that's J-e-f-F-R-E-E."

Once a month, Jeff did a four-hour Gold Show of 18 karat imports from Italy. Grecian pillars were lugged onto the set and hung with swag curtains. Candy, the model, sashayed around in an elegant black dress and Jeff really put on the ritz. He wore a tuxedo and for each show he'd put on a different bow tie and cummerbund. Jeff's Gold Show became an institution. I used to tune in just to see what kind of crazy haberdashery Jeff was wearing. He'd come on sporting these outlandish paisleys and rhinestone-studded creations. Truly, Jeffery Hewson made Doc Severinsen look like a conservative dresser.

Viewers thought Jeff and I were cute together and naturally assumed that we were dating. Here's the God's honest truth: Despite an obvious affinity for each other on the air, we never were romantically in-

145

volved, ever. We weren't in love with each other, we were in love with having a good time together on the air—it was professional chemistry, nothing more. Although I'd talk about being available and whine and complain that I couldn't get a date to save my life, the truth was I never was available; I had dated the same person for the first five years Jeffery and I worked together. I wanted America to think that I was free-wheeling and that I really wanted Jeff because we were having fun and clearly so was the audience.

We played up this scenario to the hilt. I'd do all the things that women do when they're after a guy, including altering my appearance every so often.

"Hey, Jeff," I called as I came on the set, "do you notice anything different about me?"

"Nope."

"Jeff, my hair is bright red. It was brown yesterday. I did it for you."

Jeff stared directly into the camera and deadpanned a look as if to say, "This woman is absolutely gonzo." We had a real rapport and though we weren't a romantic item, I was very fond of him; he was my good friend. He too was involved with someone else. Jeff and his girlfriend bought a house together and were with each other for several years. When they parted company, he sold their place and bought a smaller house on my street—about a mile down the road. We were neighbors, sort of, and he was a good neighbor, too. He did lots of favors for me; the most important was his willingness to baby-sit for my dog. If I had to be away, Jeff would take her. That was a big kindness. I love my Chelsea too much to leave her with just anyone; I'd be too worried.

While I got along fine with Jeff, others were not as taken with him. Some found him difficult. No question the man had an ego as large as the QVC network. I knew Jeff's quirks, but, hey, his behavior didn't affect our relationship on the air. In our exchanges, he was

146

the fall guy, the dip. I always roped him in, made him look silly, and then we'd giggle. We were such an oddball combination, the extroverted Jewish girl from the East and the farm boy from Indiana. Jeff played up his roots and talked about chasing hogs and baling hay and shoveling manure. In truth, he did have a touch of the hayseed at the beginning. Later he became extremely polished, yet even though he was as poised as Cary Grant, he'd still pull the "aw shucks" routine. We'd go out to dinner and he'd say, "I can't read the menu. I don't understand it. I'll just have chicken." He was cute, no question, and because of the way he presented himself, he got away with a lot of things simply because he was adorable and the industry tolerates lovable scamps. The smooth sailing between us continued until things started to happen, and soon another side of Jeff was revealed to me.

Jeff wanted to decorate his home and asked me if I liked the person with whom I worked. (Not many stores in my area carry a broad selection of contemporary furniture, and since I didn't have the time to go running around, I was delighted to consult with a decorator whose ideas complemented mine.) "I love my decorator," I told him. "She's easy to deal with and does everything efficiently and quickly." Jeff decided to use her, and I didn't think anything more of it. After a time, though, I sensed that something wasn't right. I talked to my decorator one day and she broke down and told me she was having big trouble. "Jeff ordered curtains made and now he says the fabric's not right and he hates them. He wouldn't take delivery on a sofa because it arrived late." As she spoke, she trembled. She'd never come up against anything like this before. I was stunned. I knew this woman wouldn't rip off a client; she was honest and hardworking. Jeff was way off base. Jeff was never satisfied with the lady who made the curtains and went so far as to leave a long unpleasant message on her answering machine, which she played for several people. Ultimately the curtain lady was so upset that her doctor ordered her to take a six-month hiatus from business. This was my first inkling that Jeff's behavior could be more than quirky.

In 1989, QVC bought the Cable Value Network out of Minnesota and put a few of their best hosts, Mary Beth Roe, Dan Wheeler, and Judy Crowell, on our programs. Judy Crowell, a vivacious and energetic young woman, bought a lovely townhouse in West Chester. (Many hosts live within a five-mile radius of QVC—we have to be close because we're on twenty-four-hour call. If someone, God forbid, drops dead, someone else has to step in immediately, and that someone else better be in the vicinity. Actually, I could walk to QVC if there were an emergency. It might take me all day, but I could do it.) One day at a weekly host meeting, Judy mentioned that she'd bought a gas grill for her patio and was having trouble assembling it. "I'll be happy to put your grill together," volunteered Jeff. True to his word, he showed up at her house and assembled the grill. Later, Judy returned the favor by inviting him to join her at a Phillies ball game. They went to the ball park, watched the game, shared a hot dog, and fell in love. Jeff and Judy embarked on a whirlwind romance and for a while nobody knew about it—not one single person, not even yours truly.

Jeff and I did a lot of photo and catalog shoots together and one day we were on our way to do a commercial spot for QVC when he suddenly turned to me.

"Levine, I'm in love," he announced.

"You? You're the biggest dickweed in the world. Who the hell would go out with you?" While I knew he went out a lot with beauty queens and fancy-shmancy girls with money, I always felt he was playing the field. His statement took me by surprise. Jeff in love? With someone other than himself?

"I'm so in love," he continued, "I can't see straight. This is it, Levine, this is it. I can't wait to get up every morning, I can't wait to go to sleep every night, I can't wait to see this person. I am in love and I am the happiest man in the world."

He convinced me of his sincerity, and I was truly happy for him. "God bless you, Jeff, that's wonderful. Is it anyone I know?"

"Nope," he lied, "you don't know her." Much as I nagged him to identify his girlfriend, he wouldn't.

Now the plot thickens. Judy and I weren't that friendly; I mean, we were compatible working acquaintances but that's as far as it went. When I'm not at work, the friends I socialize with are most often long-term friends and on occasion members of the QVC family. (We hosts spend hours and hours together at work and tend to guard our private time. We don't need to be together twenty-four hours a day!) When I'm at QVC, I'm 100 percent there, and one of the nicest aspects of my workplace is the camaraderie. We all blend; age is irrelevant. I'm in my forties and chummy with kids in their twenties, and it's okay. We do a lot of horsing around in the studio. The models drop by and visit before air time, and we talk about everything and anything and continue the conversations during breaks in air time. Those models you see on QVC aren't just good to look at—they're terrific people. But then, the whole gang is terrific, from the telephone operators to the guys in the technical booth. It's a great place. No kidding.

Anyway, back to my story. Judy and I happened to have the same housekeeper. I'm sloppy—pants hanging off the lamp shade, dust bunnies under the bed, etc. I *need* a housekeeper; Judy doesn't . . . she is the neatest person in the world. She's so meticulous her spices are arranged alphabetically on the rack. How-

KATHY LEVINE

ever, like all of us, she's busy and likes the extra help every few weeks. One day, the housekeeper started telling me about Judy's home.

"She is mighty particular. Everything has to be just so. It's hard enough keeping things in order but now I have to spend all my time clearing out those flowers Jeff keeps sending. Oh, and those cards. That Jeff and Judy, what a romance. Wow."

"Excuse me?" I said. "I don't think I got you. What romance?"

"Oh my God," she cried, "you didn't know? I was sure you must have known."

"Sit down," I ordered the housekeeper. "Sit down and tell me everything."

"Well," she began, "there are dozens and dozens and dozens of roses all over the house. And each bunch has a card and they all say, I can't wait to see you; I can't wait till tomorrow; I love you so much; You've made my whole world; I am so happy; I love you, I love you, I love you ... Jeff, Jeff, Jeff, Jeff, Jeff."

The housekeeper rattled off the messages and I sat there listening with my mouth hanging open. That skunk. I couldn't believe it. All the time Jeff was telling me he's in love and wouldn't say with whom, it was a coworker! I was thrilled. I didn't talk about it, though, I didn't want to upset Jeff's applecart. I sat on my information and kept quiet. Little by little, the situation became known to the others at QVC and finally I confronted him.

"Okay, you rat, it's Judy, and everybody knows."

"This is it, Levine," he burst out, "this is the one."

"A little Christmas engagement ring, maybe?" I inquired.

"Maybe before," he said, "maybe before."

That Thanksgiving, he gave her a killer 3.5 carat emerald-cut diamond ring. Judy's a rather conservative person and a tiny one, too, a size 4 at most. She

150

showed me her ring and after I oohed and aahed, she said, "Do you think it's too big for me?"

"When it comes to diamonds, there's no such thing as too big."

"But ..."

"There's no 'but,' just shut up, it's gorgeous. Enjoy."

Jeff went on the air one evening and at the beginning of his show said he had a big announcement to make and told the viewers to stay tuned until the end of the show to hear it. Typical Jeff, he always was the king of hoopla and build-up. Now he had the audience hanging around to hear what he was going to say. Finally a woman called in and said, "Jeffery, I know what the surprise is."

"You do?" he asked.

"Yes, you're getting married!"

He looked into the camera, crinkled up his face in a big smile, and announced that yes, he was getting "hitched." He never mentioned the name of his intended. The phones started ringing. Everyone wanted to know, but Jeff wasn't telling.

I came on the next day to do my regular show and the viewers started quizzing me.

"It's you, isn't it, Kathy? Jeff's going to marry you, right?"

"Wrong," I answered. And when the audience finally accepted the fact that I wasn't Jeff's fiancée, they began fishing.

"We're so excited, please tell us. Is it Susan Lucci?"

"No, I don't think so," was my answer. "Susan Lucci's been married for twenty years." Short of Jacqueline Onassis, the audience had Jeff paired with every available woman in the country.

Then America began to notice that there was a new ring on a show host's finger; moreover, that host was smiling from ear to ear. Judy Crowell opened up the telephone lines on her broadcast.

151

"Judy, is that an engagement ring you're wearing?"

"Yes it is," Judy answered.

"Are you marrying anyone we know?"

"Yes I am."

That did it. Before you could say "modem," Prodigy went wild. (Prodigy is the on-line pen pal system for personal at-home computers on which people with common interests can type messages to each other. It's an excellent sales marketing tool and, on occasion, a lethal weapon. Prodigy maintains a QVC fan club and when the QVC fans get excited about a show or a person, Prodigy rocks with compliments or complaints.)

"It's Jeff and Judy," Prodigy proclaimed, and within a short period of time, thousands of people were aware that Jeff had given Judy a ring. The happy couple were caught up in media fever at its hottest and soon were giving interview after interview. We were deluged with calls at the station and many came to me on air. "Oh Kathy, I'm so sorry it's not you." "Oh Kathy, we're heartbroken. You and Jeff were made for each other." "Oh Kathy, how could Jeff do this to you?" I took all the messages and made a routine out of it. "Sorry? Don't be sorry, my loss is her loss. She's nuts. She'll see. He's a pain in the rear. He can't cook and how much fried baloney can you eat? He's a prima donna and I don't want him." I had a ball. The letters began to come in and echoed the telephone messages. "We're so sorry for you. We thought it was you. He really loves you. He's misguided. He's making a mistake. You're so good for him," etc., etc.

People were so concerned about me—and I had never even dated Jeff! Nobody got it. Sympathy cards informing me that I was a hundred times better than Judy piled up on my desk. One thing truly bothered me about this "circus"—many viewers were nasty. They were unkind and made all sorts of cracks about Judy not being good enough for Jeff. A few took potshots at him, too. This was one of the very rare times in my career that I felt ashamed of my viewers. Fortunately, there were plenty of well-wishers, and their messages were encouraging and congratulatory.

Looking back, I realize I got into this Jeff and Judy business more than anybody else at the studio. Jeff was my boy, and I had grown to know and like Judy. She's a wonderful person with a lovely personality and a body I'd die for. (She works out religiously and there isn't one ounce of fat on her frame. Judy's like a pumped-up Susan Lucci ... petite but packed.) I was so happy for them. In retrospect, I also see that I was possibly the only person at the station who really felt that this was going to work, that this was really meant to happen. Others were skeptical. They predicted disaster because they knew how difficult two TV egos could be.

Meanwhile, Jeff seemed to be doing everything right. He was a smoker but appeared to curtail his habit for a while. Because of his bad back, he didn't work out but now Judy got him more involved in physical wellness. He learned to ski, and right away he outfited himself for the slopes. The man was the happiest I'd ever seen him and the most social he'd ever been. His reserve melted, and he was at ease in a way that he'd never been before. Judy gave him the boost, she gave him life.

The wedding was planned for April and everyone was caught up in matrimony fever. The pressure on the happy couple began to build up; they had spats. Big deal, every couple fights before a wedding. I got involved in one particular quarrel that had to do with protocol. Traditionally, before a wedding the bride is photographed in her dressing room, in her gown, and with her mother beside her. Jeff wanted to get into that act. He said it was the most important day of his life and he wanted pictures taken of him wearing his 100 percent Egyptian cotton handmade shirt and

153

his fancy tux, with *his* mother beside him. I bumped into him one day and he started complaining.

"Judy and I are just not getting along," he said. "She wants to run this wedding with no regard for me or my wishes," and then he proceeded to tell me the story of the prenuptial photographs.

"I'm going to let you in on something that you're not going to like hearing," I countered. "This is one day in your life where someone else is going to take precedence. The bride is going to be prettier than you."

"This is my wedding, too, and I will not take a backseat," answered Jeff. "I want all the attention I deserve. This is a very important day."

"Of course it is," I replied calmly. "It's a very important day, but there is one important fact, *she's* the bride. I don't know how else to tell you this, Jeff, but you can't be the main attraction, you just can't. It's the bride's day."

Days before the wedding, they were still at it.

"I don't know what to do with her," Jeff complained.

"Everybody goes through this," I advised him. "Just take her out to lunch and then take her home to bed."

"If I could get out of this, I would," Jeff sighed. "She's being very selfish. It's not working. It's just not working."

Judy was in a dither, too. "I'm very unhappy," she told me. "He's not giving. He's trying to run this wedding. He wants it his way. I'm more than willing to compromise but he just won't listen."

I got put in the middle and both sides were hocking me. Sadly, *I* wasn't listening to either of them. I chalked the whole business up to premarital jitters and tried to jolly them through their grievances. The fact is, weddings suck. Weddings shouldn't be allowed. You should get married, live together for a year, and then have a big bang-up party. Maybe if it were done that way, people would get along better.

Jeff and Judy continued to argue over the typical wedding issues and how they were going to fit her stuff into his place. (He had made some changes to accommodate her moving in while she made plans either to sublet her townhouse or sell it outright.)

As I said, I thought the grumbling was a normal case of nerves and blithely went along as though everything was A-OK.

I chose to overlook their obvious differences and even cooked up a little goofball plot. I checked with management and was given permission to present a wedding gift on air the day before the wedding. To appreciate the story, you'll need some background: Jeff owned a huge, 200-pound cement pig he called Cornelia. He got a kick out of the pig and used to put his feet up on her. Judy didn't think the pig was that attractive and gladly would have trashed the stone porker. I found out that someone at QVC had purchased a real Vietnamese potbellied pig and, armed with this information, I sought out the little squealer's owners and did some negotiating.

The night before the wedding, Judy was home, and Jeff was doing his show. I called Judy's family and told them to be sure and have her watch my walk-on with Jeff. Jeff did his thing and I trotted on to the set and went into an elaborate song and dance, which my mother later told me was unintelligible. What I was trying to say went along the lines of, "Jeff's got a pig. Her name's Cornelia and Judy hates Cornelia and Cornelia hates Judy. There's a lot of jealousy here. You see, Cornelia's always been Jeff's girl and she's been holding up his feet for years. Now Cornelia's getting shoved aside. We've either got to move her out or get her a friend, too. So, Jeff and Judy, happy wedding and here's your present ... Hamlet." I turned and signaled the stagehands to bring out the live pig and present it to Jeff. Jeff is great with animals, and when the guys dropped the pig in his arms he just started laughing. The little piggy was squealing to beat the band, and Jeff was laughing so hard, I was afraid he'd drop the poor creature.

Unfortunately, that was the last laugh we had.

Judy's father is a high-ranking army officer, and the ceremony took place at a military installation in Perryville, Maryland. Viewers had begged me to take pictures of everything, so I went to the wedding armed with my camera. I had a zillion requests from viewers. "Make sure you remember what song she walks down the aisle to! Make sure you know what their first dance is. Make sure you know what everyone is wearing and what kind of flowers are there." And on and on. About a hundred people, including all the show hosts, gathered in the little chapel. Even Richard Simmons flew in to wish them well.

Judy was a lovely bride; her dress was magnificent. Her big brown eyes were on fire as she and Jeff exchanged vows. We all cheered, and it seemed that God was in his heaven and all was right with the world. At the reception, Jeff sang to her (he has a beautiful voice) and she danced on the table. I was snapping pictures like a paparazzo because I had promised America that I would show them on air what the wedding really was like. I had the pictures developed immediately and went on the air the next day with the promised photographs: Judy coming down the aisle in her dress; the wedding bands; the other hosts—the whole ball game was captured on film by yours truly. As I showed the photos, I told the audience about the wedding and described everything in detail. Truly, it was memorable and magical.

Jeff and Judy went off on a cruise for fourteen days aboard the Norwegian Cruise Line's splendid ship *Sea Goddess*. It was caviar, champagne, Jacuzzis, and dancing under the stars—everything you could ask of a honeymoon. Soon after the honeymoon, I had emergency surgery on a slipped disc. I had to take seventeen days off from work, and my mother came to look after me. I was in pretty bad shape and recovering at home when Jeff and Judy came to visit. They came over to see me and the minute I looked at them, I knew something was wrong . . . they looked sad.

"I've never seen Kathy's house," Judy told my mom. "Would you mind showing me around?"

My mother gave her the tour and when they were away from me and Jeff, Judy burst into tears and told my mother that Jeff didn't love her anymore. "He actually said that he doesn't love me the way he did before the wedding. I don't know what to do," she cried. "I've been married two months and nothing is going right. He told me he wanted me home when he returned from his six-to-nine shift, so I switched my whole life and dropped my regular activities and stayed home to make dinner for him. He walked in at nine o'clock and said, What are you doing home? Don't you have a life? So the next night I went out with my friends and played my regular tennis match and when I got home he was angry at me for not being there. I'm getting mixed messages and I don't know which way to turn. He told me he loved that I had lots of friends and worked out and played tennis and now he gets furious if I do those things. I don't know what to do."

Meanwhile, Jeff was downstairs with me saying, "We have a day off together tomorrow. What should we do?"

"What do you mean, what should we do?"

"Well, we're experiencing difficulty in finding things to do together." I didn't know what to say. Two months into the marriage and they don't know what to do together? I thought it was peculiar but not necessarily disastrous. My mother was less optimistic.

157

She'd heard an earful from Judy. After they left, my mother shook her head. "There's trouble there, Kathy, real trouble." I told her she was crazy. "They're new-lyweds, Ma, they have to make adjustments." What's that old saying, "A mother is always right"? My mother sure made the right call.

QVC's Joan Rivers show was coming up, and be-cause of my surgery, for the first time, I would be unable to host. Judy was asked to take over the 9 P.M.-to-midnight show. That evening, at five to nine, my phone rang. I picked up the receiver and was sur-prised to hear Judy at the other end. She had only a few minutes to showtime—why was she calling me? I soon found out.

"Kathy, I need a friend and I need one now. My marriage is breaking up. Jeff doesn't love me. Nothing I do is right. I don't know what to do anymore. My life is falling apart and I have to go on the air. I can't do it."

"Judy, you take your life and put it aside and then go on the air," I stated firmly. "Be prepared, Joan's going to tease you about Jeff. She'll probably ask you some silly questions about him, so have answers pre-pared. Don't fall apart. You're a professional and to-night you'll perform your role. Relax and go to work. I promise you, your problems will be waiting when you're finished with the show. They're not going any-where. So, clear the decks and go out and have fun." I leveled with her because she really needed to hear it. Sure enough, not ten seconds into the Joan Rivers Show, Joan said to Judy, "What's the worst thing about being married to Jeff?" Judy didn't have a ready comeback and muttered some non sequitur about "the laundry." Joan's a smart lady and a kind person; she could tell just by the way Judy answered something was wrong and immediately backed off. Ac-tually, Joan previously had expressed doubts to me about the union of Jeff and Judy.

Here's the (Real) Jeffery

The day after Judy appeared with Joan I went down to the seashore to recuperate. Judy called and pleaded to come along. "I have to get away. I'm so upset," she cried. The poor woman was tormented. She couldn't eat, she was throwing up, I couldn't refuse. Having been through a divorce myself, I knew first-hand how people take sides and had sworn I never would. Jeff was my long-term friend and yet seemed to be so unkind to an innocent person, I couldn't find any excuses for his behavior. He was way off base. Out of courtesy she had called to tell him she was going away for the weekend—without saying where—and he answered, "What do you need, my permission?" Later, he called all over town looking for her and was furious that she'd left.

Judy Crowell poured her heart out to me at the seashore. I cannot go into the details because she spoke in confidence. However, I can assure you she never accused Jeff of anything. She just was devastated by his mood swings and his indifference. "He doesn't want to be with me," she cried. "He resents me. I can't cook right, I can't clean right. I can't ever do the laundry right. And he doesn't want to touch me. He won't even help me move my furniture into his place." I didn't want to take sides and yet I felt compelled to offer Judy what solace I could.

Right after our weekend at the seashore, Judy finalized her move back into her own house, which, fortunately, hadn't been leased. (Ironically, because of the swiftness of the events, she had never totally moved into Jeff's place.) Jeff called and told me his marriage was over.

"She left me," he said.

"Jeff," I answered, "I don't think 'left' is the right word. From what I understand, you weren't being real nice to her."

"You don't know the half of it. I'll tell you my side of the story and then you'll know what I've been deal-

159

ing with. I'll see her in court." Jeff didn't want to discuss his wretched behavior toward his wife. He just said she was calling him all sorts of names. I knew she wasn't, but when I tried to tell him, he wouldn't listen. He was determined to take immediate action and got the name of a lawyer from a QVC coworker who was also seeking a divorce. Instead of taking a lesson from the quiet, genteel manner in which that separation was going on, Jeff got on the grandstand and, in my opinion, committed a major error. Their short marriage, public as it was, could have had a short, hassle-free divorce, and with some dignity attached. But Jeff didn't want it that way—he had to turn it into a circus.

The show was about to begin—the main attraction, the Big Tent—take your seats, please.

Judy and Jeff took off their wedding rings and ceased to talk about each other on air. The viewers began to call in and the company answer went something like, "Jeff and Judy have decided to go their separate ways. Please don't make any mention of it." Immediately, the news went out on Prodigy. The *National Enquirer* reads Prodigy, and dispatched a reporter to QVC. We hosts were advised as to what he looked like, what kind of car he was driving, and that he spoke with an English accent. We were cautioned to avoid him at all costs. One evening Judy invited a few of us over for dinner. I was carrying food into her house when I saw a car parked on the street with an out-of-state license plate. A man stood next to the car and as I walked by, he said in a thick English accent, "I wonder if you could help me. I'm looking for my friend and I can't figure out which of these houses she lives in." I ran by him and into Judy's house. Well, now he knew in which house she lived. Somehow the reporter managed to get Judy's phone number, too. He would park outside her house and sit there with a cellular phone in his hand. He sent her a dozen pink roses every day and called on the hour. He hounded her: "This story will be written with or without you. Why don't you cooperate?" Luckily, the answering machine took all the calls. Judy did not reply and maintained her silence. While she fended off the media, Jeff went right out and told his story. In an *Enquirer* article he claimed that Judy had defamed his character by "spreading vicious rumors that he was gay and had a serious drinking problem." The article concluded with Jeff saying that his fans would "definitely see" him again, "a lot happier and with an even more beautiful woman." The whole thing was sickening.

Letters came pouring in to QVC. Jeff couldn't open his mail, it was that devastating. Judy was experiencing the same, only more so. "Don't open those letters," I warned her. "I'll read your mail for you if you want, but you stay away from it." I was also getting letters. People wrote me that Judy was only using Jeff for his money and his position. "I know she's no good because I read about this in the *Enquirer*," wrote one viewer. I took time to answer that letter. "I wonder, when you read in the *Enquirer* about Judy and Jeff, did you also notice the article about a ninety-year-old woman who gave birth to an ape? Did you believe that story, too?"

The way people turned on Judy was unthinkable. It taught me a lesson. The audience loves you as long as you do what's expected of you. If you don't, then people hate you. Viewers love your "persona," and if the real person doesn't act the way the viewer has come to expect, look out. It was a strong lesson. Although both of them got their share of hatred, I think Judy took it on the chin more. That's because QVC is primarily female driven; more women than men watch us. Our audience is closest to the soap opera devotees. Women are more attracted to a man and more apt to dislike a woman who "takes him away" from them. In the minds of many viewers, Judy had done just that. The mail kept coming in, and Judy got sadder and sadder and thinner and thinner. Finally, she got a lawyer.

One thing I must say about Jeff, whenever he was upset with me, he always was forthright about it. He'd speak directly to me and tell me what was bothering him and he did it again during this fracas.

"Levine, my life is falling apart," he told me over the phone. "I'm holding on by a thread and I don't need to hear that you're poor-mouthing me all over town."

"Jeff, I have not done that. That's just not true."

"You don't know the story."

"Jeff, I don't care what the story is. I don't care if she beat you and threw you down the steps. You've been married for six weeks and you have made this into a circus. I was married nine years and when I divorced it was so quiet you could have heard a pin drop. The man you got your lawyer from is getting a divorce and we haven't heard anything about it. Why do you have to grandstand yours? You did a grandstand show on your engagement and your marriage and now you're doing the same thing with the divorce. You're wrong, Jeff, you're flat-out wrong."

"You and I have nothing more to say," Jeff stated angrily.

"Oh yes, we do," I answered, "I have two more words to say." I said those two words—which I won't repeat here—and they weren't "Happy Birthday." They turned out to be the last words I ever spoke to Jeff Hewson. I was angry at myself for getting dragged into the situation. I was angry at having to turn away from an old friend, but I was even angrier with Jeff because his unacceptable behavior had made it impossible to sympathize with him. Like others, my concern went to Judy. Friend or no, I could not condone his behavior.

Here's the (Real) Jeffery

As part of the divorce suit, Jeff claimed that Judy defamed his character. Judy came to me and asked if I would be a character witness for her. "I'm not asking you to testify against him," she said. "I'm just asking if you'll speak on my behalf."

"Judy, I'd be happy to testify on your behalf. I won't say anything against Jeff. I'll just tell the court that you never, ever made any negative references about him. All I heard from you was that he was unkind and that he didn't love you and that's all I'll say."

"That's all I ask," said Judy.

Judy approached another host to act as a witness. The host was very torn because of the on-the-air camaraderie that she had with Jeff. She thought it over and decided that, like me, she would testify only that Judy never said anything bad about Jeff. Jeff got wind of this and called her late at night. He berated her for fifteen minutes and then hung up. She was so shaken up that she began to cry and her husband was ready to go over and knock Jeff's block off. Anyway, this host felt terrible. She started thinking about Jeff and the great times they'd had on the air and how awful it must be for him with everyone siding with Judy. She wrote a letter to him saying that she was not speaking against Jeff, just telling the truth—that Judy never called him any names. She ended the letter by saying that she really hoped that he would understand and that she really liked him as a person and if there was anything she could do, all he had to do was let her know. She left the letter in Jeff's mailbox and went on the air to do her show. In the middle of the broadcast, Jeff came onto the set and stood out of sight of the camera and motioned for the host to look at him. She did, and while she was working, Jeffery held up the letter and ripped it to shreds. She never spoke to him again.

Working with Jeff had been such a joy before—now

163

KATHY LEVINE

it became a nightmare. I dreaded the walk-ons because he was gunning for me and I was vulnerable at this time, too. My weight was up. I was in the 160 range and busting out of 12s into 14s. I was self-conscious about my appearance, and one evening I walked onto Jeff's show wearing a dress that was way too tight. Jeff was wearing a terrible tie. He had some ties that I called $200 Rorschach failures. We joked about this all the time, so I didn't think anything of saying, "Nice tie." He looked at my dress and said, "At least it fits."

Okay, it wasn't the worst thing, but that was just the beginning. Whenever we appeared together, he'd stare straight at the camera when I came on and talk to the little red light. Now, the first rule of television is if there's someone on air with you, you don't talk to the camera, you talk to the other person. I tried to keep my end up. I'd walk on with the stuff I was going to sell and show it to him, and he'd barely acknowledge the product, let alone me. My hands shook. It got worse and worse and became really dirty at the end. He was badgering me and knocking the products.

I didn't say anything to Jeff—I couldn't, I'm not good at personal confrontation. Anyway, he wasn't going to talk to me, he hated me. I didn't blame him for hating me—in his hour of need I was one of the people he thought he could count on, and he was shocked that I didn't support him. But, as fond as I was of the man, I felt obliged to act honorably. Judy needed to be vindicated from the false accusations. Jeff and I had six wonderful years together, and now he was out of control. He didn't step over the line, he jumped over it. The occasional unkindness escalated to the point where I would no longer walk onto his set but waited on the sidelines until he finished. Management called me on it.

"Kathy, why aren't you going out for the walk-ons with Jeff? You have to do it."

164

Here's the (Real) Jeffery

"Fire me," I said. "I'm not comfortable walking on when he's so obviously upset with me." Whatever else I thought of myself, I was a professional. Even if I hated someone's guts, if that person came on camera with me I would treat him with every courtesy because we're there to sell product and to try and make it pleasant. I felt Jeff's behavior was unprofessional.

Ten months after the divorce case was filed, Judy and Jeff went to court. Judy had decided not to call me or the other host as witnesses; she was going to do it on her own and simply tell the truth. She didn't want the ring, she didn't want any money, all she wanted was a divorce. Now get this—after nearly a year of emotional bloodshed, Jeff stood before the judge and declared that he wished to drop the charges. That was the end of it, except for the monumental lawyers' fees. Judy walked out a divorced woman ... and a marked woman. The viewers wouldn't get off her case. My mother was shopping in Allentown and a stranger came up to her.

"You're Kathy's mom, aren't you?"

"Yes," answered my mom. (She's grown used to being accosted.)

"That damn Judy!" cried the woman. "They should have fired her. How dare she take our Jeff and do that to him!"

To those who continue to believe that Judy was cruel and unkind, I can only tell you that you're wrong. I admire Judy Crowell for the way she handled herself all during her torment. She held her head up; she was a lady. She went to work every day and did her best and is still doing it. Jeff is gone. He left QVC for good and I've never seen him again. I'm so sad at what happened. It was out of my hands, yet I remain conflicted about my behavior. I feel I should have been better to someone who'd never been anything but nice to me. My only excuse is, I couldn't do it

165

because I truly believed an innocent person was being maligned. There was no reason for a court case. Twelve weeks married, ten *months* to divorce? It could have been quick and far less painful. My mother always says there are three sides to every story—his side, her side, and the truth. So where was the truth? Go figure.

To this day, people call and ask me how Jeff's doing, and letters still arrive saying, "We miss the two of you together." I miss those good times, too. I've learned, however, that while we were great as a team, I could do just fine without him; my popularity wasn't dependent upon him. I'm sure that Jeff will be back on television someday; he's simply too talented not to be on the air. At his best, he was the best, and what fun we had! So, wherever you are, thanks for the memories and thanks (for the) Jeffery.

9

The Happy Hawker

❖ ❖ ❖

Okay—so I never was involved romantically with Jeff.
I guess it's time to talk about the guys I did hook up
with—my bona fide romances. I'll begin at the beginning at the predawn era.

In the twelfth grade, I fell madly in love with one
of my teachers . . . madly. He taught psychology, which
was new to the school and offered as an elective for
seniors. I took the course and was singled out by the
teacher; by that I mean, he showed a genuine interest
in me and what I was doing. This was a novelty, and
I responded like a puppy being petted for the first
time. My teacher liked my sense of humor and really
enjoyed talking to me and I found him thoroughly
fascinating. Soon my days began to revolve around
the times that I'd see him. I'd get up at 5:30 in the
morning, shower, wash my hair, trowel on my makeup,
get dressed like I was going to Cinderella's ball, and
race off to school, where I'd drop into the teacher's
room and chat with him until classes began. I craved
attention and since I wasn't getting it at home, I
dumped my need at this man's door . . . and not be-

cause he was any kind of good looker, either—the reason was simple; he *noticed* me.

I was a good kid, happy and pleasant and willing to accept the fact that my parents were caught up in their own efforts to make a go of things and unable to give me their full attention. I was capable of taking independent action and pretty much called my own shots. Under similar circumstances, kids often go bad—not Kathy. I wasn't interested in sex or drugs or booze, or any of those avenues; I napped and ate my way through my distress and stress with a smile on my lips ... and no one knew I really was in trouble. Nowadays kids *demand* attention and go wild if they don't get it. I never thought of exhibiting any antisocial behavior; I was just a good kid who was being kind of ignored so I moseyed around doing my own thing going over to relatives or hanging out with my friends. The West End of Allentown was heavily Jewish upper-middle-class, and we all lived within a few blocks of each other.

Then the psychology teacher appeared, and things changed for me. I was totally energized by this man's presence, and my own pattern of behavior altered. Instead of lying supine in my bed until the very last second, I got up way early in the morning, prepared myself like some movie actress on early call, and trotted off to school. Two months into the routine, my mother got wind that something was up. Why was her daughter getting into full makeup and elaborate dress and racing off to school in the predawn hours?

I had once written the teacher a note and he answered me back. The correspondence was innocent, just comments about everyday occurrences, and I kept his letter in my purse. Now, my mother had a bad habit of going through my purse, which I considered a nasty violation of my privacy. She didn't do it on the sly, either, she'd dump out the contents right in front of me. "Your purse is a mess," she'd cry, "and

The Happy Hawker

I'm going to clean it out." So saying, she'd tip the bag over and go through the clutter. There always was a generous supply of previously chewed gum wrapped in paper, assorted lipsticks, and other gems of that order. One day, *not* in my presence, she did purse inspection and the teacher's letter came sailing forth. She read it (!) and voiced her concern to my father. The idea that I had a personal relationship with a male teacher was very disturbing to them. My parents discussed the matter and without letting me know, called the teacher in question. He was ordered not to write or telephone me and to keep his relationship with their daughter on a strictly classroom basis. In effect, they took away the one thing that was giving me the attention I craved.

Despite my parents' admonitions, I remained friendly with that teacher for years—all through college, in fact, and when I came back to Allentown, we would meet for drinks or dinner. While I had been too naive and young to recognize anything about my teacher during the early stages of our friendship, it gradually dawned on me that this man was gay. Had he been straight and not a good person, he probably could have taken advantage of me just as my parents feared. He could have taken me out to lunch or dinner and I undoubtedly would have ended up making my big first foray into the sexual world with him. In that sense, my parents were appropriately concerned about their teenage daughter. Well, they need not have worried, and how ironic it is that depriving me of my friend was one of the few occasions Mother and Dad gave me the attention I so hungered for. Because of the extenuating circumstance, I guess you couldn't call this liaison a "true" romance. Nevertheless, I really was crazy about that man and he really was very important to me, though not an actual lover. My introduction to physical intimacy came a bit later, but you already know that story. Sí?

*   *   *

169

KATHY LEVINE

Here are two big lessons I've learned. One: Never take a job where you have to *eat* dirt, and two: Never have a romance or relationship where you *feel* like dirt. In 1985, I got myself into *both* situations. I had recently split from my husband and in my very raw state had concentrated all my energies into work. I was in the hotel field then and went through three jobs in three different hotels. For six weeks prior to my stay at the Franklin Plaza Hotel in Philly, I worked in a small hotel on the outskirts of town. In little hotels like that one you don't make money on meetings or dinners or weddings, you make it on people putting their heads on your pillows—in other words, you're looking for occupancy. Our little hotel was running mighty low on heads, and I was told to do something about it. We were located across the street from a Marriott hotel and I noticed that a group of about thirty-five orthopedists was scheduled to arrive there in a few weeks. Thirty-five people to the Marriott chain was a drop in the bucket; thirty-five people to my small hotel was a cast of thousands. So I did something unkosher and unprofessional—I stole some business. I offer no excuses even as I tell you what I did; I know it was wrong and there's no way I would ever do such a thing again. I called the Marriott and made up some bogus story about needing to know the name of the contact person for the orthopedic group. I found out the name of the coordinator and called him at his office in New Jersey. His name was Dr. Burt Kramer (and if you think that's the real name, then I have a bridge connecting Manhattan and Brooklyn I want to sell you). The doctor came on the line and I fed him a line.

"Hi, Dr. Kramer, this is Kathy Levine and I've heard through the grapevine that your orthopedic group is holding a meeting in Philadelphia. I don't know what the hotel you've booked is offering you, I only know that if you move your group to my hotel, which is right across the street, I can offer you a lower rate, free breakfast, and a free drink at check-in."

"Sounds great to me," the doctor replied, and we plunged into negotiations. He gave me his list of attendees, and I called every one of them with the same proposal: Instead of $99 a night, they'd pay $79 and get breakfast and the drink as well. None of them knew I was hustling and none of them turned me down. I booked the group into my hotel and honestly didn't feel anything but relief that we had *occupancy*.

The day the doctors arrived, I was sitting in my office. It was around five in the afternoon, and I was winding down for the day. I planned to meet my friend Sandi Donaldson for dinner and beyond that nothing special was on my agenda. Someone knocked at the door and I called out, "Come in." A man entered the room and said, "Are you Kathy Levine?"

"Yes," I answered, "and you must be Dr. Kramer."

"Right." He smiled. "I just had to meet you." The words were scarcely spoken when he pulled out his wallet and showed me a picture of his beautiful wife and son. I admired them even as I felt a strong sense of disappointment. I was instantly intrigued by this man and the sight of his family burst my little bubble. We chatted for a few minutes and he told me how much he appreciated the discounts and so forth and then said, "Would you have a drink with me?"

"I'm not permitted to drink in this hotel," I explained, "but I'd be happy to join you at another place."

"Well, perhaps we could go out somewhere. Matter of fact, perhaps you'd like to have dinner?"

"I'd love to," I answered quickly. "I know terrific restaurants in Philly and we're only eight miles from the center of town."

"Great," he replied enthusiastically. "How about if I pick you up here in thirty minutes?"

"I'll be ready." I smiled. He walked out the door and I picked up the phone to call Sandi.

"I'm canceling dinner, Sandi; I've just met someone who's going to change my life. You're my best friend, you'll understand." Sandi did understand, although I don't think I mentioned that the man who was going to change my life was married; maybe if I had, she might not have understood. Why I did this after seeing a photograph of the guy's family, I don't know. My reasoning was self-serving; I was unattached and if he wasn't that was his problem, not mine.

A half hour later he picked me up and brought me to his gorgeous racing-style car with a personalized license plate. As we drove along I looked out of the corner of my eye at the good doctor. He had everything, the M.D. after his name, the fancy car, he was tall, trim, gray at the temples with blue eyes, and he was Jewish. Wow, I thought to myself, this is what I was raised for! I'm amazed at how quickly I assumed the role of a Jezebel.

We drove to trendy South Street in Philadelphia. South Street is a Greenwich Village–SoHo type place. We walked around a bit and then went to a new hot Chinese restaurant. We ordered everything on the menu and had enough food put before us to feed the province of Canton. You know what? I couldn't eat a bite. I couldn't put a green bean to my mouth. I, who could eat the leg off a table, couldn't put one noodle, one wonton, one anything near my lips. He didn't eat either. We were mesmerized by each other's presence and caught up in conversation. It was as though we were in a bubble and floating over the world. Nothing else existed, not even moo goo gai pan.

Dinner over, we returned to his car. As we left the restaurant, he offered me his arm, and I swear I was stepping three feet above the pavement as we walked along. Burt dropped me off at the hotel. I don't think he kissed me good night, he didn't have to .. in my imagination we'd left kissing far behind. The next day he dropped by the office with a little gift, a bottle of body lotion. "I had such a lovely time last night. I was over at Saks buying presents for my son, and I thought you might like some of this." We chatted some more and then he was gone. Burt returned to New Jersey and soon thereafter I took my "big" hotel job in Philadelphia. Months passed and Burt occasionally would call. Eventually, he confessed that he and his wife were estranged. "I didn't want to tell you before," he explained, "but I have a feeling that she's preparing to leave me. When I showed you her photo, I was pretending to myself that things were okay at home. I was really attracted to you, and I was trying to distance myself by putting a wife and child between us." I accepted his explanation at the time, though later I thought it was more self-serving than he admitted. Burt was a snake. But I should talk . . . I was a snakee.

Burt phoned several times after that and finally announced that his wife indeed had left him and he wanted to see me. We arranged to rendezvous at a small harbor town on the Jersey shore. Okay, we met, had the "honeymoon," and the fact is, it was mediocre probably because I was so worried about how I was doing things and whether or not I looked right. I found myself visually sitting on a chair watching me make my moves. Am I good enough? Am I pretty enough? Is my hair right? Are my thighs flapping? I was my own judge and jury and found myself guilty on every count. Despite my feelings of inadequacy, though, I really fell for the guy. I saw him infrequently but whenever I did, I always got caught up in a whirlwind of anticipation and activity. I had started work at QVC, and thank heaven I had something to occupy my time; otherwise I'd have spent all my hours mooning over the doctor. I went on an involuntary diet. I couldn't eat, I couldn't sleep, and was working on sheer adrenaline. Talk about high gear . . . I could

173

KATHY LEVINE

have sent an Apollo rocket to the moon. I talked non-stop to my girlfriends on the phone, boring them about the love of my life. This was it! My ship had come in. Had I looked up I would have seen *Titanic* written on the prow.

In preparation for an upcoming rendezvous with Burt, I bought an outfit for too much money—a red sweater with black trim and a short black skirt—and off I went. (I tended to spend too much money on my clothes to reduce my feelings of inadequacy—sound familiar?) This time everything was so romantic, I went completely overboard. I was experiencing a severe case of lovesickness, what the French call a "coup de foudre," a bolt from the blue. I wanted to marry this man. I wanted to move to New Jersey. I wanted to be the stepmother to his son. I was completely gone.

Burt, I discovered later, wasn't quite on the same ecstatic wavelength as Kathy. I turned myself inside out and upside down for this man. I melted off nearly twenty pounds, I spent a fortune on clothing and on various beauty treatments . . . all for him. "I love short hair," he said one evening after I'd had a bob cut, "but I really love blond hair." I went out and had a double process and just about lost my damn hair; it turned snow white. The only thing to go with the color of my hair was blue-blue eyes because Burt liked blue eyes, not gray-green eyes like mine. I don't wear glasses; however, these were the days when everyone was wearing fashion lenses as opposed to corrective ones, so I trotted over to the opticians and spent 150 bucks on a pair of rich turquoise contacts—the color of the ocean, not of a human being's eyes. Okay, I had white hair and android-blue eyes, and to complement my new hues, I wore a hot pink lipstick.

What the hell I was doing to myself, I don't know. I only knew I had to please this guy. I'd seen pictures of his wife and knew she was a beauty queen. There was no way I could compete with her in the looks

174

department so I went through all these ridiculous alterations to the basic me hoping that he'd take notice. After a time he drew back and allowed as how things might not be quite right. "We're both newly separated and maybe it's a little risky to get so involved," he told me over dinner. "I think we should slow down and take things step by step. I mean, I like you but I am dating other women."

I was stunned to hear that Burt was seeing others. Would I ever learn? I kept on assuming that since he and his wife had separated just as Jay and I had, he must feel the same way as I. Rebounds are the pits. No one should be allowed out for six months after a breakup. The law should say that after a divorce you have to be locked up and your hormones put in a jar on the shelf while you chill out. The fact is, your heart is right out there, you put it on a plate and let someone carve it up for you.

As I've written, right after I split with Jay I went into therapy in order to make myself feel better about leaving my husband. Well, I met Burt around the second session of that therapy and by the eighth or ninth, he had already begun to reject me. The therapist was very compassionate and told me that I was at a very crucial time of my life. Although I left a nice husband for reasons that were right for me, I still felt guilty, and now I'd fallen head over heels for a man who'd just been left by his spouse, and I was too blinded to see that he was all wrong for me. Actually, both of us were walking wounded.

I accepted the awful fact that Burt was dating others and held on to the hope that he'd eventually concentrate solely on me. He didn't and this nonsense continued for over eighteen months. At one point he stopped calling altogether. I was numb. Months later he called to say he'd be in Philly and would like to see me. Here we go again! At this point I was just beginning at QVC and feeling very focused and together. Still, I couldn't stay away from this man. We had a date one evening and I'd bought a gorgeous beige silk pants outfit and was so looking forward to seeing him I could barely think straight. QVC was on the air by this time and I was going to work that evening and planned to see him the next day. He called about five o'clock that afternoon and said something had come up and he wouldn't be able to make it. I didn't even have time to indulge my desolation because I had to get to work. I was co-hosting with Steve Bryant at that time and went straight from home to the set. I was so off at the beginning, the producer came over to me at the first break.

"I know you have a problem tonight. I can tell you're suffering. You're not yourself. You're not Kathy. But, you're a professional, you're a trouper. This job has to be done and done with priority. So whatever's bothering you, set it aside. In three hours you can take it back and you can carry it out of the building with you. Right now, Kathy, I need you on!" I responded immediately, did a complete flip, and went on to do the show just fine. Afterward, Steve came up to me. "Kathy, I have to talk to you about what went on at the beginning of our show. I don't know what you're doing, I don't know who you're dating. I don't know who's hurting you but the guy's obviously not good for you and I'm sorry. *But,* don't you ever pull that crap with me on the air again. You're either here or you're not!"

Steve was right. I was shocked to hear that my private anguish had invaded my public performance, and it was a real eye-opener. I was so sad and so hurt and so madly in love and I knew I was getting dumped and the whole horrible episode had affected my work. This was the initiation by fire into the further intricacies of male-female relationships. It's so very difficult to be involved with someone and try to do a job. I

176

think a lot of professional women are single because they can't be 100 percent on all fronts.

My roller-coaster romance continued. Burt invited me to his home, which had been vacated by his wife and child. I was thrilled to death. I put on a pair of white trousers, a white blouse, and a blue blazer and drove like Mario Andretti to his place. I had to stop and pee at least five times, I was so nervous. My stomach was in my throat. Was my hair all right? I wondered. Even if it wasn't all right, it was all white, in fact it was as white as it could be before falling out of my head. Plus, I could just about see out of my contact lenses, which were killing me. (I never did adjust to the damn things and eventually scrapped them.) In my eagerness to please a man, I'd overhauled myself to the point where I didn't know what I looked like. Thank God, Burt thought I had nice hands; otherwise I would have cut them off for him.

I drove up to his house and got out of the car. I rang the bell and Burt came to the door. He'd just come out of a shower and smelled and looked absolutely beautifully clean. He'd put on a pale blue (the color of his eyes) oxford shirt and was buttoning the front over his damp, glistening body. He looked like something out of an advertisement.

"Hi," he said, "how are you?"

I walked into the house saying, "Fine, fine."

"It's great to see you," he continued. "You look good. Well, maybe your hair could be a little blonder."

That comment took a bit of the wind out of my sails. No matter what I did, it wasn't enough, and yet I kept plowing through.

"I've made lunch. We'll have it by the pool and then take a dip."

"Wonderful," I said, and I meant it. We sat down for lunch, a green salad topped with blue cheese dressing. I despise blue cheese dressing. Burt never asked me what I liked to eat, though, he just presented me

177

with what I would eat—and I did. I'd have swallowed razor blades. I tell you true, today's Kathy wouldn't put up with that kind of treatment for one single second. The 1995 Kathy would have told him up front, "The salad's lovely but I prefer oil and vinegar for dressing."

The minute I came into the house I could see that his wife had good taste. Most of the furniture was gone, but you could tell from what remained that the place had been elegantly appointed. The lunch was lovely, except for the dressing, and, after we ate, I went into the kitchen to help him clean. I was drying a dish when Burt spoke.

"You know, Kathy, I think you ought to consider moving down here. I think we should be together."

I dropped the dish and it bounced on the floor.

"You can give up that little job you have up there and find something to do down here," he continued. I picked up the dish and said, "Wow, let me think about that." I was ready to accept the proposal until he mentioned giving up my "little job." That gave me pause. Still, it didn't interfere with the next activity. We went swimming in the pool and then made love. Later, as we sat on the patio, he gave me a daffodil. It was heaven. My career, my little job, was growing dimmer and then Burt spoke again.

"What time are you leaving?" he asked.

"I don't know," I answered truthfully. The fact is, I'd cleared my *year* of engagements.

"Well, I have a date at five o'clock and I have to pick her up. We're going to a formal ball and I'm in charge of it."

"Oh," I answered. "Oh . . . fine . . . okay, I'll be out of your way."

"I'm running a little late today," he explained. "I have this crazy neighbor who knows that my wife's split. She keeps coming over to see if I'm okay and if

178

The Happy Hawker

I need anything. I really feel sorry for her. She was over this morning before you got here."

At this point I was about to go over the edge, and I don't mean the edge of the swimming pool. This man had sandwiched me in between two lays of the day. He had already had breakfast, I was lunch, and dinner was at five. I left and drove back to West Chester sobbing at the wheel like something out of an old movie. I put my tail between my legs and went back to work.

Steve Bryant couldn't have been dearer. "Look, Kathy, I don't know who this man is but I do know that you are the most wonderful person. You're good and kind and you're falling into some horrible trap. I just wish I could do something. If I met that guy, I'd deck him." Steve was thoughtful and compassionate just like a big brother. I couldn't think of him or any other man as anything but a "brother" because my entire being revolved around that miserable M.D. I continued to be at that mumzer doctor's beck and call. The calls became fewer and fewer. Then he phoned and asked me if I wanted to go with him for a weekend at the seashore. We would be together with no distractions. Nobody else coming and going or calling, just the two of us. I was thrilled to hear from him and eager to be with him. He took me to a charming bed-and-breakfast. I was so excited. Everything went back to square one—or did it?

We checked into our room on Friday evening and Burt explained the nature of our stay to me. "Look, Kathy, I'm seeing a psychiatrist and he's recommended that I try to appreciate women for who they are and not as sexual objects." I did not need an interpreter to tell me that Burt was saying he wasn't going to touch me. The next morning he had another bombshell to deliver. "Kathy, if you don't mind I'd like to cut the weekend short. I really think I have to get back; I want to see my son."

179

I was crushed. I got into my car and cried all the way home and then I cried through all the phone calls I made to my girlfriends and to my mother. My mom dismissed this affair as a flight of fancy. She still was hopeful that I'd go back to Jay Levine, whom she adored. "Do whatever you want with this man and then get rid of him. I don't know this wiseguy but he's awful for you, he's not nice to you and you cannot settle for this. Get it out of your system," she advised. "You're hyper and teary-eyed and you're just not my Kathy." I didn't listen, I didn't hear a word. I just continued to cry. And while I cried, I hovered over the phone waiting for the cause of my tears to throw me a crumb. I kept hoping *this* would be the day. I never made any plans, on the off chance that he'd want to see me. My calendar was as clear as a cubic zirconium. I thought of him morning, noon, and night. I was obsessed beyond obsession. This was without doubt the most degrading time of my life. Only later did I figure out that my obsession had nothing to do with love; this was a *need*. I needed to have somebody interested in me. Burt was my programmed Prince Charming, and I never stopped to look at him objectively. Had I done so, I'd have admitted to myself that he was more of a frog than a prince. He wasn't that nice or that much fun or that interesting. Actually, he was dull. He was self-centered and not all that great in the sack, either. He was someone I just got caught up in. I'd never experienced anything like that before and I hope to God I never do again!

I received fewer and fewer phone calls from Burt. So I took the initiative and began to call him. His reactions were the same. "Hi, how are you? Good to hear from you. Gotta go now. Gotta date." He always had a date, always. Finally, I pinned him down to seeing me one specific Saturday night. Two days before we were to meet he telephoned. "Look, Kathy, I'm going to be honest with you. I've been seeing someone

180

else all the while I've been seeing you. She and I bicker a lot, but last night her daughter came down with a very high fever and we spent the night nursing that child back to health. I realized there was something special there, something I really want to work on. I'm not going to see you again. I am so sorry if I have ever hurt you. You are a wonderful person and I do love you. Good-bye."

That did it. I crashed, I burned, I cried. I called everyone including my mother and wailed for months until I had no more tears left. Everyone told me that time would take care of things and the hurt would go away.

I jumped into my work and tried to stay away from all potential hurt. I began dating another man (whom I'll identify soon), and we had a nice, easy relationship. My "little" job grew to be a big job and I grew, too—my career took off. I never felt good enough around Burt and I now prayed that he would see me on television so that he'd know I had accomplished something. Gradually, Burt faded away to a rarely noticed dull ache. Then one morning I picked up my mail at QVC and right on top of the pile was a letter with Burt Kramer's return address in the corner. My hands shook and my palms sweated as I opened the letter. Burt wrote that he'd been watching a football game with his son and during a break, he'd gone into the kitchen for a beer. "My son switched the channels and suddenly I heard that sweet voice. I came back into the room and saw those beautiful hands on the screen and I knew that was my Kathy. I wish you tons of happiness. Love, Burt." I wrote a quick reply saying that "life was fabulous and I was enjoying sunshine." I sent it off and that was that, I thought—my little closure to the most degrading chapter of my life. Ha!

Three years ago, I was having lunch with a group of girlfriends and another woman and her boyfriend stopped by the table. She introduced us to her friend, who turned out to be from the same place in New Jersey as Burt Kramer. Real casual-like, I told him that I used to date a guy from his hometown and asked if he knew Burt. "Oh yes, I've run into him around town. He just got married." We exchanged a few more words and the couple moved off. To the amazement of my luncheon companions, I pitched forward into my tuna salad and cried. My girlfriends thought I'd flipped my lid. I had, but for the very last time. Put it this way: Just once in your life everyone should hit rock bottom. That way there's no question about what direction you should be going! I hung on to memories way too long but they did serve as a good lesson; I will never let anybody walk on me again. I must admit that Burt helped teach me how not to repeat my mistake. He once told me that the Kathy he met was vital, lively, and feisty. "The second you became interested in me, you gave all that up," Burt explained. "You deferred to me. You were boring to me. You just didn't have a spark anymore. I liked the person I met—I didn't like the person you chose to become." The bottom line is, if someone is attracted to me on Monday, why should I become what I think they want on Tuesday? Especially since they might not want me on Wednesday.

I realize that my relationship with Burt was all out of whack from the beginning. The worst thing that could have happened would have been for me to wind up with him. I never would have survived, and I would have lost everything, my career, my self-respect, the whole ball game. I'm really grateful that he dumped me. It's scary to think how many women are called upon to "give up" things for someone. I don't think it's a matter of "giving up," rather it's what you gain by doing something together. I wouldn't give up anything for any man; he'd have to compromise with me and we'd have to have an even-steven deal. I am who I am, and you like it or don't. I'm not changing. No

coup de foudre is going to strike this girl twice. Since
I made the decision to be myself, I've had more fun
and better relationships than ever. I don't date drunks,
druggies, abusers, or womanizers. There are nice people in this world—I have found them and so can you.
They may not have vanity license plates, muscular ab-
domens, or M.D. titles, but they do have N.G.—Nice
Guy—after their names, and that's a title every woman's entitled to.

Lest you be reduced to tears by the sad tale of Burt,
let me perk you up a bit by letting you in on a little
secret, or, if you're a dyed-in-the-wool Kathy Levine
watcher, a *big* secret. First, let's backtrack. In November 1986, QVC went on the air for three hours a day.
(Mind you, we were *always* working even though the
station only broadcast during a small portion of the
day.) We went from three hours to twelve hours and
finally reached twenty-four about six months after we
started. The process took time, because we had to get
up to speed and we needed enough hosts and camera-
men and crew to man three separate shifts for each
four-hour segment. In those early days, QVC's
founder, Joe Segel, watched attentively and sometime
after the first of the year, he decided it was boring to
watch one host for three hours at a time. He thought
it would be better to have *two* hosts go on for two
hours, come off for two hours, and go on again for
two. Essentially this meant two hours of preparation
and six hours of work even though you weren't working in the middle. This schedule made for a huge, long
day of work and, no surprise, the policy lasted all of
two weeks. We hosts simply burned out.

During those two weeks, though, I was paired with
Steve Bryant. Steve had been helping me through my
rough times. Steve was a rock and a good buddy and
we worked together real well as a team. He had an
electronics background, so when I had a product that
had an on-off switch, he was there to help me. And

I'd give him an assist when it came to things like fashion . . . and he sure could use it. Steve's partially color blind and he'd come to me with various articles of clothing and say things like, "Levine, I have to sell this green shirt tonight. Help me out." I'd tell him the shirt was brown and give him some fashion pointers. Steve and I alternated selling. I sold a product and then he sold one. We did three minutes on and three minutes off. When QVC went on round-the-clock, we worked crazy hours.

One night during the time that Mr. Segel's two hours on, two hours off, two hours on regimen was in force, Steve and I were standing together waiting to go on air and chatting.

"Do you like this job, Levine?" Steve asked.

"I really do," I replied, "except that I miss the night life I used to have. I miss going out with my friends. I miss having dinner. I miss having a glass of wine. It seems like I'm always working and getting ready for the next show before I've finished the last. Oh, boy," I sighed, "I just wish I could have a Saturday night out like a normal person."

"I've got an idea," Steve said. "let's have a 'night out' right here. I'll bring the wine if you bring the food."

"How about chicken salad?" I offered.

"Great!"

Steve later told me he hated chicken salad. He didn't want to give me a hard time, though, so he went along with it. We picked an evening and arranged to have our dinner between the two-hour stints on air. We were scheduled to work from 6 to 8 and be off from 8 to 10 and back on from 10 to midnight. I don't think I thought of this plan as a "date," per se—I was still getting dumped by that slime bucket Burt; it was simply an opportunity to have some fun.

On the appointed evening, I made a chicken salad, fancied it up with grapes and cashews, and toted it over to the station. Steve arrived with wine, candles, fine silver, china, stem glasses, and a pair of cloth napkins. We stored the stuff while we went out and did our first shift. At 8 P.M. we stepped off the front wedge of the QVC pie set and moved around to the kitchen set at the back end, which was not going to be seen on camera. Steve set up the round butcher block table with the china, silver, and stemware. He lit the candles, and we sat down for our Saturday night out. We were damn lucky we weren't fired. We were brand new on a brand-new job, and there we were playing "night out" on the set. The funny thing is nobody seemed to notice or care. People went by and said hello and we answered hello. They didn't even notice that we were drinking wine. To this day, it cracks me up to think about that rendezvous. While the on-air hosts were selling their guts out on the front of the set, Steve and I were dining in the back. If that turntable ever had been activated, we would have revolved into the red light and America would have been treated to the picture of hosts Kathy Levine and Steve Bryant dining at Chez QVC. It was one of the most delightful dinners I've ever had and during the course of the meal, I learned what an interesting and versatile guy Steve was. He was an accomplished magician and an excellent guitarist and completely self-taught, to boot.

Steve and I frequently did the midnight to 5 A.M. shift, and when we were finished we would go out for breakfast together. We'd sit in Denny's and Steve would tell me a little bit about himself and I'd tell him too much about myself and my crummy affair with Burt until one day Steve said, "I don't want hear about this anymore, Levine. It sounds like a lousy relationship to me. You've got better things to talk about." Sure enough, I did have other things to talk about. We got to know each other and he was easy and relaxed to be with, the exact opposite of Dr. Wrong.

One Denny's morning, Steve and I were talking and laughing and all of a sudden he stopped laughing and said, "Levine, I like you. I would really like to go out with you." My first thought was, "Oh jeez, no." He was such a nice guy, but I didn't want to go out. Breakfast was okay, a mock night out on the QVC set was okay, I just didn't want to get serious. On the other hand, he *was* a nice guy, and I didn't want to spurn him. "Why don't you come over for dinner?" I asked. I wasn't in the least self-conscious about inviting him to my home . . . we were friends. Steve accepted. I made a simple meal of grilled tuna, baked potatoes and salad, and he showed up with a cute stuffed animal, "Alf," as a present. It was comfortable to be with him and I had a good time.

The next day, Steve said, "I know a wonderful vineyard where you can have dinner and pick out your own bottle from the wine bodega. Would you like to join me?" "Sounds great," I said enthusiastically. The next thing I knew, we were dating as well as working together and before long, Steve Bryant and Kathy Levine were in a "relationship."

That's right, dear viewers, the alliance about which you constantly questioned me was with Steve Bryant. I never said it on the air because television is my workplace and there are rules about business and pleasure. For all of you who guessed correctly, congratulations. Those of you who thought I was dating Jeff Hewson were dead wrong. And, those of you who thought I was seeing Jeff, Steve, Paul, the CEO, or the twin electricians were more than dead wrong. I'm monogamous, I only see one man at a time, and Steve was it for a long time—five years.

Everybody at QVC knew Steve and I were an item. We had to go public because ordinarily, two hosts cannot be on vacation at the same time, so we had to get special permission when we went off together. Steve and I had a good time with each other. There was, however, a basic problem: we were both working at the same place and doing essentially the same job, and a relationship is difficult to carry on when your business is involved. We lived and breathed QVC twenty-four hours a day. Opportunities began to arise for me, and for Steve, too, and the competitive spirit was there . . . for both of us. If he saw me going into the boss's office, he'd question me as to what went on. Is everything okay, did you get a raise?—stuff like that. Which is understandable, yet it made me uncomfortable. I didn't get a raise every time I walked into the office, but if I did and he didn't, or vice versa, it became a point of contention.

We brought our work home with us and out with us. Eventually QVC was the only safe topic we could discuss, and then it became a hostile subject and our relationship went the way of many that are work based—it didn't last. We were always cordial and respectful to each other and still remain so. I don't attempt to make an enemy out of anyone I dated or liked, I don't see the point. Just because I don't choose to spend my life with someone doesn't mean that I don't like the person or don't want to be friendly. I'm certain Steve feels the same way. Although we no longer work as partners on the air, occasionally we do work together and it's fine. Professionally we still get along very nicely; romantically, we've both moved on.

I've been with a man for a while now and I met him at QVC. (He doesn't work at the station, though; he's an outside rep.) He'd come around and chat with me and we got along real well. I liked him right away, though I wasn't looking for romance. I fixed him up on a blind date with a girlfriend. The day after they went out he called me.

"How'd it go?" I asked.

"It was okay," he replied, "but the truth is, Kathy, I don't want you to fix me up. I want *you* to go out with me." So I did—and we've been seeing each other for two years now. On the whole, I feel much more secure being with someone who understands what I do and does not do what I do. I can't go out a great many Friday and Saturday nights, so I have to plan midweek dates. This is a drawback and any man I date has to make the concession. It is not an option; the doctrine is Job First.

As I said, I only date one man at a time. There is, however, one constant love of my life who's been with me for the past six years. Bottom line, my greatest love is my dog, Chelsea, and Steve Bryant played a major role in getting me and my dog together.

During our relationship, Steve was gentle and nurturing and brought me back to center from the outfield where the bad doctor had left me. Steve knew how much I loved animals in general and of my great love for dogs in particular. I desperately wanted a dog and talked about getting one for years, especially when I began working regularly at QVC. My mother went ape telling me that I shouldn't. "You're never home. It would be unkind and cruel to have a pet that you can't take care of." The funny thing is, I *was* home a lot in those days. I didn't work quite as hard as I do today because we weren't involved in meetings and we weren't working with celebrities and we didn't go on Fam Trips. We had one meeting a week and I was doing a shift in the evening—in essence, I had the whole day free. I could get up at eight in the morning and not go to work until eight at night. "It's a perfect setup," Steve said to me. "I'm working days and you're working nights. We can take turns with the puppy." The groundwork had been laid; I was now in the market for a dog.

Just as I am incapable of walking by a jewelry store,

The Happy Hawker

I cannot walk by a pet store without ogling everything in the window—dogs, cats, birds, ducks, rabbits, weasels. You name it, I love them, especially dogs. I can stand in front of the window for ages watching the animals inside and making up scenarios for them. I feel sorry for them being in cages and hope that they're well taken care of and that there are homes waiting for them. By the time I finish my window gazing, I'm usually in tears and ready to buy the lot just to keep them from being homeless. There's a pet store in Cherry Hill, New Jersey, which I was forever dropping into and once I decided that a dog was in my future, I headed right for it. One afternoon in the summer of 1989, I went into the pet shop and took a look around. I did the same thing a few days later and by this time I knew the "stock." I noticed a silly-looking black dog in a cage in the rear. This pup didn't bark. She was totally self-absorbed and played by herself while all the other dogs were going crazy. I watched her for a good forty-five minutes and in all that time she kept to herself and did not appear in the least needy. I wasn't looking for a needy animal, and her self-sufficiency appealed to me. I came back another day and watched her again. Steve and his mother came along, too. I went back a third time and took the black pup out of her cage to play. She didn't have a whole lot of interest in me. She just walked around. She wasn't wild. She was a sweet little bitty thing with no tail. You couldn't even tell if she liked you because she had nothing to wag. She was funny and kind of silly looking. They told me she was a miniature schnauzer and her black coat was rare; most schnauzers are gray.

"So how much is she?" I asked.

"Four hundred fifty. She's got papers."

Papers? I didn't care whether she had the Declaration of Independence or the Constitution of the

United States of America, $450 was too much for me. I complained to Steve.

"I think you should buy her," he said. "You need to have that dog. You like that dog. I like that dog. My mother likes that dog." Steve called the pet store. "Look, we like that black schnauzer; what can you do about the price?" They said they'd get back to us. A short time later they did, and over my speaker phone the owner said, "We can let you have her for three seventy-five." Before I got a word out, Steve said, "Sold." The pet store was open until nine, and I said I'd drive over that evening after dinner to pick up my purchase. West Chester is about an hour's drive from Cherry Hill. Steve and I had dinner and while he went off to do whatever he had on his agenda, I got into my car and drove to New Jersey. On the way I had an attack of buyer's remorse. What the hell was I doing? What would I do if my job became more comprehensive and I had to travel a lot? How was I going to take care of anything else? I could just about take care of myself, etc., etc. While I was going through all this analysis I made a wrong turn, and in Cherry Hill that's lethal. Things go in circles in that city and if you move off the path, you've had it. I was good and lost and was circling and circling. It was five minutes to nine and I was nowhere near the pet shop. I finally got there about five minutes after nine. I parked my car and went over to the door. It was locked. I looked in and saw the black puppy in her cage and a young woman sweeping the floor. Okay, that was it—it wasn't meant to be. I turned and began to walk away. Meanwhile, the girl in the shop had spotted me. She dropped the broom, unlocked the door, opened it, and called out, "Are you here for the little black schnauzer?"

I hesitated for one second. "I guess so," I sighed.

"Oh, she's been waiting for you. We're so glad you're here. We were hoping that you'd come." I went back into the shop and paid for the dog. The girl gave me the papers and took the pup out of the cage. Wouldn't you know, now that I owned her the first thing that hound did was pee on the floor. I bought a little leash and a little bowl and the next thing I knew I was on the way home with a miniature schnauzer named Chelsea sitting beside me. I knew her name was going to be Chelsea from the second I saw her. When I was a kid my dear friend Barb Barker had a Chelsea, not a schnauzer but a Chelsea nonetheless, and I loved the name. "Someday," I vowed to myself, "I'm going to have a Chelsea." I always knew, long before the president of the United States thought about having one, that I would have a Chelsea—only mine would be on four legs.

Speaking of which, I once ran into a snag over the name. I was singing the praises of my pup on the air and a viewer brought up Chelsea Clinton. "Oh, my Chelsea's better," I bragged, "she's just as pretty and she has a better bite and nicer hair." Oh boy! Did I get criticized. Did I get mail. Hey, I think Chelsea Clinton is a great kid. I didn't mean to insult her. I don't know her. I *know* my Chelsea. I *love* my doggie, and I still think she's the prettiest Chelsea in the whole wide world.

Although my Chelsea looked like a Chelsea, there was a hitch. I went to register her with the American Kennel Club and discovered that there were 50 million Chelseas. She had to have a more formal name. Steve and I dubbed her something like Chelsea Von Doobee III. Chelsea moved in and began eating everything she could get her teeth on. She ate every pair of shoes I owned. She ate Steve's magic tricks. She ate books (good books ... she had a penchant for mysteries), and it was two years of hell. Steve was dedicated to Chelsea. He baby-sat for her and took her to dog obedience school—the classes were held at night and I was working. Truly, the reason Chelsea is well be-

191

haved, well mannered, and such a good dog today is that Steve Bryant supervised her upbringing.

My mom was right; having a dog *is* a huge responsibility and I'd never recommend it for anybody unless they knew what they were in for! Chelsea goes everywhere with me and she's great in the car—the only thing she can't do is drive. My schedule is hectic and when I do have to leave her it's most often with my friend Andrea next door. I also have a corps of dog walkers to call upon just in case. Chelsea is the world's most beautiful schnauzer and, truly, *the love of my life*. So, now you know!

10

Diller Meets Diva

❖ ❖ ❖

In 1992, QVC hit the entertainment big time because
of one man, Barry Diller. B.D. (Before Diller), QVC
was kind of a mom-and-pop operation. We'd been
going for almost seven years and, despite all the jokes
about Diamonique and cubic zirconium, we were the
fastest-growing company in America. We grossed a
billion dollars a year and yet QVC remained a "family" operation. We didn't advertise, there was no fan-
fare or celebrity status for anybody, and we didn't
spend money. That's why we made money, we never
spent it! We had the same set from the first day and
except for a once-a-year cleaning, it wasn't touched.
In a way, the set was just like the home you bought
thirty years ago; you live in it and occasionally, maybe,
you go out and buy a new pillow for the sofa, or
maybe an area rug for the hall, but basically it's your
place as you know and love it.

Longtime viewers may remember that the QVC set
was *very* basic—round, and divided into four sections
like a pie. The pie could rotate, giving you four different possibilities for viewing—one in each wedge.

193

KATHY LEVINE

There was a kitchen set, a living room–dining room set, a "store" set with countertops, and a cozy outdoor patio set. Our happy home rotated and locked in on the screen according to the product. If I were doing outdoor items or toys for the children, for example, I'd probably be on the patio set. Dinnerware would be shown in the dining room or living room set. And so on and so on. The important thing was the product. The product was the star and continued to be.

In general, "change" wasn't an operative word at QVC—even management shifts were on the rare side. Since our set never altered, if you closed your eyes and opened them again, you didn't know from one year to the next what year you were in. Occasionally a new plastic plant or tchochke might appear and sometimes, when the hosts and viewers went bananas and complained, they'd change a picture on the wall. I remember this crazy brass deer that for some unknown decorative reason sat for six years on the mantelpiece of the living room set. The hosts used to get together and kvetch about the deer. We hated the damn thing and you'd get "points" if, by accident, you knocked "Bambi" off the mantel. We were sick to death of the set, but our feelings didn't count for anything. Management had no interest in making it look good, why would they? It wasn't a priority. They weren't trying to keep up with any of the fancy talk and news shows on the major networks; all QVC cared about was product. It's the bargain-basement concept brought to the little screen; gimme those good deals and I'll forget the pipes on the ceiling. Our job was to sell and there's a real smart message in that philosophy: Don't forget the business you're in—if selling is what you do, then do it.

Although the viewers actually were very interested in hosts, the media wasn't; we were a billion-dollar joke. The Cubic Zirconium Network was déclassé—nobody wanted to interview us and nobody famous

194

wanted to come on the show. When celebrities *were* approached, they'd snicker, "You gotta be kidding. Why would I get off my throne and dilute my power to sell crap on QVC?"

This situation was similar to one that occurred during the early years of television. Big movie stars were prevented by their studios from appearing on the small screen because it was considered beneath their dignity. Television eventually gained respect as a theatrical medium and then it was okay. Well, we were not a theatrical medium, we were a talking bargain basement and snubbed by the big timers. The minute that televised shopping became a legitimate vehicle for making money, however, snobbery flew out the window. And interest really went into high gear when Barry Diller was named CEO.

If any one person could be said to have brought on the Barry Diller era at QVC it would have to be Diane von Furstenberg. Diller and von Furstenberg have been very close friends for years and years. Diane von Furstenberg is a legend in the retail world—furthermore, she's one of those lucky ladies who's got everything—looks, brains, money. As if that weren't enough, she also had a title, which she got by marrying Prince Egon von Furstenberg. The marriage dissolved years ago and I guess being a princess goes by the boards when you get a divorce.

Anyway, Diane von Furstenberg doesn't need that kind of frosting on her cake. I mean, the woman's got the classic kind of European looks you'd give your eyeteeth to see reflecting back at you from a mirror, plus there's the rest of the package, smarts and real talent. Back in the seventies, she created a wraparound dress that revolutionized women's wear. The dress was cotton and, just as it said, you wrapped it around you—no matter what size you were—tied the attached strings, and presto change-o, you were ready for anything. That dress not only *fit* every imaginable

195

figure, it was flattering as well. The wraparound was so popular that if you didn't have one in your wardrobe, you weren't considered dressed. When I got my first job and was making what to me was real money ($150 a week), the minute I had enough cash, I went out and bought a Diane von Furstenberg wraparound. As far as I was concerned, I had arrived. My mother had one, too—every woman in her right fashion mind had one—the dress was a classic.

Following the wraparound bonanza, von Furstenberg continued to flourish professionally, though not perhaps as flamboyantly. She began to license her name and by the end of the eighties there was a lot of DVF merchandise out there over which she had no control. She wanted to regain that control as well as her design power, and when the licenses ended, she devised a new plan to put her back in the hands-on position she'd relinquished. In 1992 she came to QVC with a proposal; she wanted to do another line of the wraparounds—at the *same* 1970s price—$99. This is the kind of retail miracle only Diane von Furstenberg could pull off. The network liked the idea and six months later von Furstenberg made her first appearance on the air. (It always takes a good half year of preparation to get a product up to speed in all quantities and sizes.) She presented her merchandise under Jane Treacy's guidance, and in the process took to television like a duck to water. The show was a hit. The dresses sold like hotcakes, and Ms. von Furstenberg was the belle of the television shopping ball. *Newsweek* magazine had her on its cover posing in an original wraparound dress and in the nineties version. Nearly twenty years later and the lady hadn't changed a smidgeon, still chic, and still with a shape to die for.

Diane von Furstenberg is really a very nice lady, although I have to say she's a bit easier to get along with *off* the set. It's kind of the reverse of what you expect from a celebrity. A star usually puts her best foot forward when she's before the public and saves the other kind of behavior for the private moments. With few exceptions, celebrities come across as extra nice, and this makes viewers assume that they're not seeing the *real* person on television. That's why they always ask what so-and-so is really like? Diane is kind of tough to work with on the air because she's aggressive and tends to take over. She has no qualms about stepping on the host's lines. Hey, she didn't get where she is by being a pussycat. Come to think of it, though, "cat" is a good word for her; there is something very feline about her, even her movements are catlike, very sensuous and lissome, like some graceful panther. For all her business savvy, however, she still had to learn about being on camera. Initially, she was pretty nervous; she's calmed down a lot yet still has a terrible habit of playing with her hair, which drives those of us working with her crazy. We've threatened to glue her hands to the chair. So far the warning hasn't worked; she's still tugging at her locks.

Diane von Furstenberg was very impressed with how well her line did and how much money she made. She called her friend Barry Diller and suggested there might be something in this for him. Diller was between jobs—not that the man needs work. Much like his friend Diane in the merchandising world, Barry Diller was a legend in the entertainment world. Among other master strokes, he'd sold the networks the concept of the miniseries, which became television's bread and butter. As head of Paramount Studios, Diller was instrumental in getting one of its biggest hits, *The Bad News Bears,* on the screen. After Paramount, Diller went to Fox Television, where he backed a little show called "The Simpsons." And so on, and so forth. Everything the man touched turned to gold and he raked in the Oscars, Tonys, Emmys, whatever. (This year he was elected to the Television Academy's Hall of Fame.)

197

KATHY LEVINE

At Diane's suggestion, Barry Diller came to the studio and stood by watching attentively as she presented her clothing line. The merchandise pulled in over $2 million and creative fireworks must have started going off in Diller's brain. This was the place for him to be. He could take his vision and couple it with the knowledge of the people who ran QVC and together they could get a jump on what was being called the "superhighway of interactive television." In simple terms that means that some day in the future you'll be able to sit in your own home with your own little computer terminal and not only watch television but order merchandise by just tapping into the terminal.

The possibilities are endless. A viewer could watch a sitcom like "Murphy Brown" and fall in love with an outfit worn by the leading character and be able to punch in for information. Faster than you can say Candice Bergen, the price of the jacket would flash on the screen. Another button would reveal the size and color and, if everything was A-OK, yet another button would allow the viewer to order the jacket and then be free to sit back and enjoy the rest of the show secure in the knowledge that within a short space of time she'd be wearing the same clothes as Murphy Brown. The sky's the limit for interaction. Who knows, it eventually may come to the point where your television set will open up and deliver the goods right then and there. Realistically, the idea of combining entertainment with computer shopping for a superhighway of interactive television is not in the near future—it's far off into the future.

Once word got out that Barry Diller was interested in us, we were besieged, and yet for the longest time we had no idea what was happening. This megadeal was going on right under our noses, but I found out about it like the rest of the world—by reading the newspapers. Articles appeared every day, and press people who all along had denied us interviews were

198

now banging on the door, and we didn't even have a publicity department to deal with all the commotion. The minute I heard the news about the new CEO, I called my mother.

"Ma, you won't believe it. Guess who's going to be running QVC ... Barry Diller."

"Who's that?" asked my mother. I gave her a quick rundown on the new CEO. After hearing his credentials, she paused and, in the great tradition of Jewish mothers, asked, "Is he single?" Bless her, my mom never could be accused of selling her daughter short. Barry Diller hadn't even walked in the door and she already was setting up the wedding canopy.

Events moved quickly; one day Joe Segel became chairman emeritus and off he went, and the next day Barry Diller arrived and the media went berserk. Suddenly, the wallflower QVC was a contender in the glamorous world of the rich and famous. I'd pick up the papers and read how Barry Diller was going to do this, and Barry Diller was going to do that, and Barry Diller, and Barry Diller, and sandwiched in between the Barry and the Diller there would be sporadic, casual reference to something called QVC. It got my dander up. My pride was wounded. Hey, QVC had been doing damn well for a long time and I resented the fact that after the short shrift we'd been receiving, suddenly we were on the map and playing second fiddle to the new CEO. I'd helped in building a billion-dollar company and now some dude showed up and was getting all the credit. Mr. Diller was being cast as Rumpelstiltskin and damn it, we weren't hay. I was "EJA"—Envious, Jealous, and Angry—over the treatment QVC was getting. So, along with my desire to meet Barry Diller, I also was piling a bunch of chips on my shoulder to fling at him.

I read in the program schedule that Diane von Furstenberg was making an appearance and decided to drop in and say hello. I had been meaning to introduce myself for quite a while (I always want to meet the celebrities—all the hosts do—like you, we're human). I walked down the hall and knocked on the door of her dressing room. "Come in," called Ms. von Furstenberg. Diane was sitting at the mirror and doing her hair. She wore a black body stocking; she tends to wear them under her clothes (and what a body was stuffed into that stocking).

"Hi," I said, "I'm Kathy Levine, one of the hosts, and I just wanted to tell you I think your line is great. Matter of fact, your wrap dress was the first thing I ever put on that made me feel I had arrived into the big world." She smiled and said something gracious. I muttered a few more words and turned to leave. "Well, it was nice meeting you and good luck on your show," I said as I walked out the door. Then it happened. Where the hell was I going? This was *the* moment, and I decided to seize it. I made a U-turn and marched right back.

"Listen," I began, "I just have to tell you something that's been bugging me. I want you to know that although your friend Mr. Diller is very important and we're glad he's here, we're not chopped liver. You tell your friend we were a billion-dollar company before he arrived on the scene. We're not overnight glamorous and I am annoyed at all the press and all the attention going to him. I hope HE knows that WE built this company."

I got everything off my chest and was met with complete silence. Diane stared at me and didn't utter a word. I don't know what I was expecting, but it wasn't silence. I had blurted out my feelings and was ready to receive some sort of response. It didn't come and I beat it out of there. " 'Bye," I said, and once again left the room.

Ms. von Furstenberg came right after me. She bounced out of that dressing room in her black body stocking, rushed up behind me, and called out, "HEY, wait a minute!" I turned and there was Diane von Furstenberg in my face, wagging her finger at my nose and backing me down the corridor.

"Let me tell you something," she said very strongly and firmly. "Don't think for one minute that Barry doesn't know how important you all are. You people are definitely what made this company grow and he appreciates everything you've done. He knows who you are and don't you forget that!" My mouth was hanging open and I kept turning my head to make sure I wasn't going into the wall. When she finished, I managed a weak smile, said, "Okay, I'll remember," and turned and ran.

Later I thought about what I'd done and got a bit nervous. You big-mouthed jerk, I said to myself, why can't you keep your yap shut? You're making waves and you're going to get thrown out of the boat.

The next day at the host meeting it was announced that Barry Diller would be making an appearance at our next session. We were told to dress up and be on our best behavior. My immediate vision was the entrance of Mr. Diller and the subsequent exit of Ms. Big-Mouth Levine. At the next meeting all of us were fairly subdued and putting our collective best foot forward. Usually we hosts can get pretty vocal, and it's quite a scene when you have twenty articulate, bright, and funny people going at it. Mr. Diller came into the strangely quiet room. My first impression was of a handsome man with the most beautiful, piercing green eyes; you could sense the power in them. This guy definitely had an aura. He's about five nine or ten and dresses beautifully in colors like olive and brown that are complementary to his eyes. He's quite trim and obviously works out. Diller smiled at all of us and proceeded to speak. I expected to hear something along the lines of, "Nice to meet you all except for that woman sitting over there who will no longer be with us . . ." and was relieved to hear something quite

201

different. "I just wanted to tell you what a grand opportunity this is for me and how eager I am to work with all of you. I know you people are the best at what you do and I'm in awe of what you do," he began.

Obviously, from the way Barry Diller was speaking he'd heard about my rendezvous with Diane von Furstenberg. It also was obvious that she was an okay lady. I could have been sealing my own QVC death warrant when I spoke to her as I did. She did not use everything I said against me; she was fair enough and wise enough to recognize the importance of my remarks and passed them on to her friend in a constructive rather than destructive manner. Diane von Furstenberg is a class act.

Diller opened the meeting up to questions and was immediately asked what he intended to do, where did he see us going? He replied there were very good people at QVC and that we needed more good people, so he planned to begin hiring. Once we heard that hiring and not firing was the operative word, we relaxed. He intended, he continued, to learn the business inside out and would go from the maintenance room to the phone room to the cafeteria and to the set, from the top to the bottom, until he had a sound knowledge of the business. That done, he would overhaul whatever he felt needed to be adjusted. Nothing, he assured us, would be done until he felt secure in his knowledge. "If there's a show you don't like or there's something you find that's not proper, I want to hear about it," said the new CEO.

"Try doing four hours of linens sometime," I growled under my breath.

"Excuse me?" Mr. Diller heard my mutter and picked right up on it. I had to say something. If I backed down I'd lose face with my cohorts and besides I was doing what the boss wanted—giving my opinion.

"I do a linens show, Mr. Diller, on which I sell

202

sheets and pillowcases and comforters for four solid hours."

"How do you feel about it?" he asked.

"How much can you say about linens for four hours? A sheet's a sheet."

"Do you like the show?" he asked.

"I hate it," I replied. Hey, I wasn't going to play Ms. Nice Guy. The man asked a question and I told him the truth. Funny thing about Barry Diller, he asks a million questions and it seems like he isn't necessarily listening to your answers. While you're responding he's on to the next question. It's rapid-fire investigation, and at a certain point I got annoyed because I didn't think he was paying attention. (How wrong I was. The next day I was taken off the linen show and given another assignment. For me it was a sure sign that the man was serious.) The meeting went very well. Barry Diller made all of us feel good about ourselves and our work. At the close, he reiterated the bit about telling him if we felt something wasn't right. "My door is always open and if you have anything on your mind, come on in to my office and tell me."

QVC has a number of special occasion days during the year and we make a big fuss over them. One of those programs is our annual Gold Rush show (actually there are two Gold Rush shows; one honors the California search and the other commemorates the Klondike rush). As part of the former, we do a whole Western number, from wearing period costumes to working in sets that are replicas of the frontier. We prospect and "pan" for gold and come up with chains and bracelets and other jewelry. People get a kick out of seeing us all dolled up, and we hosts enjoy it too except for one particular point of contention—the costumes. From day one we complained about the get-ups we were forced to wear; they were old, they were smelly, and they didn't fit—especially on me. The buttons on the blouse popped, the armpits cut into me, and the skirt was 3 inches shy of circling my waist. I was hot enough in this crummy outfit and then the studio lights went on and the temperature shot up to about 105 degrees. I had just finished a segment on the Gold Rush when Barry Diller walked in.

"Well," said the boss, "how do you like wearing these costumes?"

"It's fine if you want to keep your job and you don't mind looking like a sideshow Miss Kitty," I snapped. "How the hell would you like wearing a stinky-pitted get-up that somebody else wore for fourteen years?" He asked, I answered—boy, did I answer. I couldn't help it. I'd been standing around in that miserable costume working my tail off and was in no mood to pretend. Boss or no boss, there was no way I could smile demurely and say everything was hunky-dory. Diller looked at me and burst out laughing. This was a triumph—I made Barry Diller laugh and he's not an easy guy to get going. He's Jewish, and he doesn't have a Jewish sense of humor. (Joan Rivers once said that Barry didn't laugh at what she said and therefore she knew she was dead.) When my boss, the Hollywood Jewish WASP (yes, there is such a thing!), started laughing, it kind of broke the ice; we started chatting.

I knew that Diller had "moved" to West Chester to be near the studio and was staying at our local hotel, which is a sweet little place but no Ritz; there are cows grazing in meadows next door, not celebrities in night clubs. I asked him how he liked living in West Chester. He told me he hadn't seen much of the surroundings because his activities were confined to the studio and the hotel. Here was my opportunity. I offered to take him out to dinner at one of our "better" restaurants. He said that would be fine and told me to call and set up a date. I was elated. All too often women don't assert themselves in the workplace because they're afraid of appearing "aggressive." Not

Diller Meets Diva

me. I wanted to know this man and to find out what made him tick. Maybe I was a little pushy, but he responded in a positive way. I took a chance. My feeling is that if you don't take chances you might lose advances.

I called Diller's office and told his secretary that I was inviting him to dinner. She gave him the message and phoned me right back to say that he'd be available the next Tuesday at 7 P.M. I died. I panicked. Barry Diller was going to have dinner with me and although I was bursting to share my big news, I didn't want to tell anybody. I wanted to keep it quiet until afterward, then, even if someone else invited him to something, I had done it first. As it is, I don't think that anyone else thought of taking him to dinner except for me.

I had to tell someone, so I called my mother. First things first with Pat Seinfeld, fashion expert. "Oh my God," she cried, "what are you going to wear?" The next day I ran wild getting myself ready for the big encounter. I zipped into Nan Duskin's, an exclusive specialty shop in Philadelphia, and bought a very simple, very basic, very, *very* expensive Michael Kors outfit—long palazzo pants in beige silk with a beautiful matching top, all solid, simple, and neutral, really classic and classy. I regarded the purchase as a business expense, a necessity; I had to look my best. I made appointments at the beauty parlor for a manicure on Monday. I couldn't make up my mind whether to have a French manicure or red nails and whether to cut my hair short or dye it. I spent a week agonizing over the dinner.

I arrived at the station on the momentous Tuesday and received a call saying Mr. Diller was running late.

"Oh, okay," I said. "What time shall I pick him up?"

"Oh," said the secretary, "Mr. Diller will be driving his own car and if you come by around eight o'clock, he'll follow you." Already my evening was taking unexpected turns. The secretary continued, "And where are you going and how far away is it?"

"We're going to a lovely place about forty minutes away."

"That's too far. Mr. Diller only has an hour."

An hour? This was beginning to sound like the most costly sixty minutes of my life. "No problem," I answered, and flipped into another plan. "There's a lovely little French-Thai restaurant five minutes from his hotel."

The French-Thai place was strictly a bring-your-own-bottle establishment. I didn't know whether Mr. Diller preferred a red or white, although I was certain that he drank something like Chateau Mouton-Rothschild and/or Dom Perignon. I wasn't going to take any chances. I got into my car and chased over to the liquor store. Pennsylvania is a controlled state, so liquor stores are like an early Howard Johnson's, one or two flavors. They don't carry esoteric wines; as a matter of fact they don't carry most great wines, just an assortment of Californians like Gallo, Inglenook, and an occasional Mondavi. I've always enjoyed good wine and learned about them in one of those classes I took. My brother in Colorado usually sends me cases, and I almost always have a good selection at home. Of course, at this crucial juncture, my cellar was bare. I got to the liquor store, went to the shelves, and selected the best available red and white, a cabernet and a sauvignon blanc. I had them pack the bottles and put them in the back of the car. Mission accomplished, I headed back to the studio. I had a meeting late that afternoon with a senior buyer and after that I planned to go home, shower, do my hair, and put on my beautiful outfit.

The best-laid plans of mice and Kathy definitely went astray. My meeting went on and on. I looked at my watch and saw that it was twenty after seven. I was dying. The only thing that kept me from collapsing was the knowledge that Barry Diller was in his own meeting behind closed doors; he wasn't going anywhere, either. My meeting ended at seven-thirty, and I traveled faster than the speed of light to the exit. I had one foot out the door when I realized that ten tons of rain were falling from the sky. A tornado had dropped into town, literally. Power lines were down, trees were falling, lightning was jumping around. It was torrential, horrendous, and there was no way I was getting home to change. I'd be lucky if the storm subsided enough to get out of the building. I resigned myself to go just as I was and called Mr. Diller's office to make final arrangements. The secretary informed me that he still was in the meeting and asked for directions to the restaurant. I gave them and then went to the door. The storm abated somewhat. I ran to the car, drove over to the restaurant and ran inside, hurdling puddles and clutching the clanking wine bottles. My hair was down, my makeup was running, my shoes were squishing. At least I wasn't wearing my elegant Michael Kors pants suit. A very young man stood in the reception area. I dropped the two bottles of wine in his arms. "I'm going to be here with Mr. Barry Diller tonight. He's coming right behind me. I want the best table," I barked.

"Huh?" The boy looked at me perplexed.

"Don't huh me," I cried. I grabbed the kid's lapels and pulled him toward me. "Listen, this is a very important person to you and to me. Put the white wine on ice and the red wine on the table and I want you here the second this man walks in the door to take any order he has. Don't you leave us for a minute. You stand right by me. If you screw up this dinner, I will kill you."

The kid looked absolutely blank. There wasn't an iota of comprehension on his face. He turned and disappeared into the kitchen while I scooted over and plunked myself down at the nearest table. Barry Diller walked in, spotted me, came over, and said, hello, and sat down.

"I have a red and a white wine," I said. "What would you like?"

"I don't drink," he answered. "There's something in wine that gives me a vicious headache. I'll just have a club soda."

My damp underwear clung to me like a wet bathing suit. I was dying, dying. Nothing was going right. My gorgeous outfit was in the closet, my hair and my face were shot, and now my wine meant bupkis. There was no bar in the joint, and I wasn't so sure they'd even have soda water. Our "rocket" waiter came over and, hallelujah, they had it! Once the water arrived and the orders were given, I settled down and, despite my continuing dampness, actually had an amazingly good time. I asked Barry Diller how he was doing and for quite some time that was the last question that came from my side of the table. He began firing questions at me.

"Tell me about your boss," he said. "What do you think of him?" Thank God I thought well of my boss and was pleased to say so.

"Do you think the hosts could be better?"

That was a tough one; I didn't want to implicate any of my fellow workers, so I served up a small portion of humble pie and mumbled something about, "I'm sure everyone could do better, myself included."

He ran down the list of managerial personnel and asked me what I thought of each one. I had to be very careful. I didn't want to put the finger on anyone. I'd been working with some of these people for six years; they were family. On the other hand, I didn't want to lie. He needed to know the score and obviously had decided I was a person with good insight. Still, I had to be very guarded.

"Who do you think is the weakest link in the chain?"

That was a heavy question. I gave my honest opinion. "I agree," he answered. The food was served and we continued talking as we ate.

"What do you think of the set?"

"I don't give a damn what the set looks like," I responded bluntly. "Just get me Donna Karan at fifty percent." Maybe I shouldn't have been so forthright; however, I was incredibly at ease, and why not? I knew more about my business than he did. Diller recognized that I was good at my job and was trying to get a sense of how I and the rest of the gang worked. Because I was comfortable, I could speak truthfully. He looked at me and nodded his head. "Yes, I see, I get your point . . . and I will get you Donna Karan at fifty percent . . . but don't you feel that when you turn on the TV in the morning and you see 'Good Morning America' or the 'Today' show or a CBS morning show or any of the news-talk shows, don't you think they come across better when the sets are attractive?"

I didn't want to tell him that I really didn't watch television and I didn't know one show from another. I did know my business, though. "I can see *your* point," I replied, "but don't forget, our business is to sell product."

"Yes," he answered, "but why can't we do both? Why can't we have great products at great prices in a great set? Why should QVC look like a joke? Even the building is ugly. There isn't a flower anywhere. Frankly, I've never seen such a cold place in my life!" I had to laugh, he hit that one right on the button. "My mission," enthused the CEO, "is to make the show *look* good at the same time that we're selling the product." Barry Diller wanted an esthetic balance and, listening to him talk, I was sure he'd get it. I was incredibly flattered that he was talking to me on a genuine one-to-one level. I reveled in his questions and his proposals. There's nothing better than an exciting interchange, and I was smack in the middle of one, at least it seemed that way.

I offered up an idea I'd had for a while. "There's nothing glamorous doing in the wee hours. It's down time. I've always thought that a terrific overnight person should be hired and that a good product be featured. There's a world that shops late at night, and we don't offer them the same glitz as we do in the daytime."

"That's an excellent point you've got there," he said. I plutzed. Barry Diller thought Kathy Levine had an excellent point.

"How did you get your job at QVC?" he asked. I gave him an edited version of my story. He listened attentively and when I finished, he said, "There's no denying that you have a real gift. You've got a special 'I want-to-watch-more-of-her quality' that's captivating."

I grinned from ear to ear. "Thank you. Thank you," I bubbled. "It's great to hear you say that." And it was!

All in all, that dinner was one of the magical moments of my life. Sitting there soaked to my skin with Mr. Barry Diller telling me *I* was good was heaven. If there's a moral that could be taken from our brief encounter, I guess it would run along the lines of the expensive outfit wasn't necessary, the semi-fancy wines weren't necessary, and getting my hair and nails done wasn't necessary. Nothing mattered except that I had a really lovely meeting with a genuinely nice man who honored his word, gave me a chance to speak with him, and used the opportunity to be kind, thoughtful, and encouraging. I felt extremely flattered by his attention. I did notice that we were in and out of the restaurant within an hour—he'd said sixty minutes and kept his word on that, too. Anyway, I'd never again "worry" so much about having dinner with someone. Sure, I'd want to look nice and probably would buy an outfit, but only because I look for any excuse to shop and not because I'm trying to impress anyone.

The next day I got to the studio and discovered that QVC had experienced a little touch of Barry overnight. He had told me he couldn't stand the fact that there were no flowers or plants in the building, and now the studio was loaded with dracenas, ficas, and ferns and the like. I swear, thousands of plants were delivered that morning. Barry Diller wanted flora and by golly he got it. You couldn't see the people for the shrubbery—a vast wasteland had become a rain forest. One of the telephone girls grabbed me by the arm. "Kathy, go down the hall and take a look at Mr. Diller's office. He's not here now, so don't worry. Wait till you see that place, you won't believe it!" I scurried right over and stuck my head into the office; what I saw was awesome. The room was awash with orchids. Thanks to Barry Diller, Glamour with a capital G had come to West Chester, PA. Oh, and as further evidence of his ability to effect change, a memo was issued that day that stated that from then on during any future gold or silver rush shows, all costumes would be custom made and every host would have his or her own costume personally fitted.

QVC continued to flourish, and we became the darling of the press. Every magazine in America was beating at our door, and our so-called "publicity" department struggled to keep up. That particular division had been an insignificant part of the company and functioned simply to field phone calls from free-lancers who wanted to write sarcastic articles about us. It was easy to get laughs writing about a network that had absolutely no pretensions to anything other than selling merchandise. It was snobbery, pure snobbery, and because of that attitude, we avoided media coverage. Joe Segel's theory was, "I don't want any press unless it's good press." As a result, 95 percent of the interviews requested were turned down because all they wanted to do was poke fun at the Cubic Zirconium Kids. A.D. (After Diller), the press came to praise QVC, not bury it, and to a large extent that interest was due to the charisma of the new CEO. Mr. Diller had the kind of clout to pull people in. We had everybody there, including Liz Smith, who came to do book reviews. Ms. Smith honestly admitted that she didn't know QVC until Barry got there.

Barry Diller gave up his plan to move into the studio, took over the hotel suite, and called upon his friend Diane to help spruce it up. Now he divided his time among three cities, New York, Los Angeles, and West Chester. You know the old saying, you can't make a silk purse out of a sow's ear? Well, they could jazz up the hotel suite all they wanted, it still was situated in Nowhere, PA. When you have Hollywood in your blood and New York in your veins, it's very difficult to love the kind of country where QVC is situated. There's no aura, no sparkle. There's no picking up the phone and saying, "I'm Barry Diller, I'd like ..." There's no Morton's, there's no Ivy, there's no Le Cirque, nothing. Nobody's there except the cow next door, and she doesn't give a moo who's living beside her. I can just imagine Barry Diller looking out his window and instead of seeing Park Avenue or the Paramount lot, catching sight of Bossie chewing cud. Wow.

However boring we might have been, my company had a lot of money, and because the powers that be felt that he was going to do something very good for the company, Barry Diller had a pretty free rein. He was going and doing and wheeling and dealing and spending money. All the big television programs wanted to interview him *and* see us. On a "Good Morning America" Sunday broadcast, Jane Treacy went on live satellite feed from QVC. The interviewers kept asking questions like "How much profit does

Diller Meets Diva

Joan Rivers make?" and Jane smiled her wonderful smile and completely ignored the question. Instead, she cheerfully talked about the purpose and value of televised shopping. Jane handled herself like a real pro . . . and a real lady. Remember, we weren't trained to meet the press nor were we prepared to be on mainstream media. I'm sure if I'd been the host selected to talk and I was asked loaded questions, I'd have come right back, rudely. Jane Treacy refused to go on the offensive or the defensive, she just talked about QVC and what a terrific service we provided. Very classy. It was like we weren't working for QVC anymore; we were working for Barry Diller and every one of us was a *star*. Yessir, the man definitely put us on the map and I was proud to tell everybody that I worked for him.

One day I came off the air for a sixty-second break and Barry was standing there with two men who looked sort of familiar. Barry put his arm around me, gave me a light hug, and said, "Kathy, I'd like you to meet David Geffen and Calvin Klein." I have a vague memory of my jaw falling open and a high-pitched squeal passing through my lips. I hope I'm remembering wrong and that I had the aplomb to say something a little more respectable like "Nice to meet you" before I dashed back onto the set. A friend of mine was standing nearby and overheard Diller tell his guests as I rushed off, "Kathy's great. One of our best show hosts." When that was reported to me I no longer was sitting in a studio set, I was sitting on top of the world.

Diller continued his campaign to bring QVC into the glitzy world of marketing. Taking his cue from the Broadway stage and Hollywood, he hired a bunch of superb set designers, people who knew what they were doing, and before long the old pie wedges were replaced by elegant and elaborate slices of decor. At present, we have sets for approximately fifty different events, including a Western scene with a waterfall for our beloved Gold Rush days. Any regular guest like Diane or Kenneth Jay Lane or Joan Rivers gets his or her own signature set, too. These sets are paid for by the companies the stars represent, not by QVC, and are at the ready for the celebrity's appearances. They're put up when the time comes and then dismantled and stored in the warehouse for the next visit. Barry Diller was waving his magic wand and our pumpkin was turning into a palace.

In my estimation, one of Mr. Diller's most effective moves was to hire more senior management people and to promote the outstanding members of the existing team. We never had enough manpower in that area and being light on management caused endless inane situations. For instance, if you had a problem with the air conditioner, you called the president of the company. If you were thinking of buying a new copier, you called the president of the company; if you had a problem with your salary, you called the president; if a light bulb needed to be changed, you called the president of the company. There was nobody to talk to at the middle level because there was no middle level. It was buyers, hosts, programmers, and then, president ... and nobody in between. You can't grow if everybody there is already overwhelmed with what they're doing, which we were.

Barry Diller filled in the gaps by hiring a senior executive for every department, from gems to garden tools. He brought in people from New York and L.A.—Bloomingdale's and Neiman-Marcus types who had solid retailing experience. Diller really built up a force, and at last there was some meat on the company's bones. He also recognized that the hosts were overworked in many areas. It used to be that whatever had to be done the cry was, "Get the host!" Among other chores, we had to do our own voice-overs, which meant shlepping up to the booth after our regular broadcasts to read copy for upcoming shows. We

214

hated the imposition; it was just one more unnecessary drain on our time and energy. Barry Diller said, "I don't want any show hosts doing voice-overs. I want professionals." They were hired. And so Diller infused new life into us by swelling our ranks with knowledgeable and talented people and by doing so, he energized QVC.

In one of my early conversations with Mr. Diller, he asked me about contracts.

"Contracts," I queried, "what contracts?"

"You know, the contracts you hosts signed with QVC."

"We don't have any contracts," I replied. Mr. Diller began to sputter, "What do you mean you don't have them?"

"Just what I said, we don't work on contract; they could fire us tomorrow, or we could quit tomorrow."

The next day a memo was issued calling for all of us to report to the president of QVC by appointment—we were going to be talking about contracts.

As part of his system of promotion and change, Barry Diller had named Doug Briggs, formerly vice president of marketing, to the position of president. Doug is receptive to new ideas and always maintains an open-door policy. I started at QVC with Doug; I knew him very well and liked him a lot. We're almost the same age and we often fought like cats and dogs over issues that we believed in. We liked a good row now and again, and our meetings often were punctuated by arguments like, "I think this ring will sell."

"I think you're crazy, it won't."

"I'm sure this article will go over the roof."

"No, *you'll* go over the roof."

Now, thanks to Mr. Diller, Doug Briggs, the guy with whom I'd been fighting over marketing principles, had become the president of the company. You didn't need to be Sherlock Holmes to figure out that Barry Diller had gone to the president and told him that allowing hosts to remain free agents was nuts. They wanted to lock us up in contracts, and one by one we trotted into Doug's office, where we were advised that QVC wanted to give everybody an opportunity to remain with the company and to realize lucrative financial benefits ... *if* we signed on the bottom line. During this period, there was talk about merging with the Home Shopping Network. That plan was dropped when Barry Diller decided to go after Paramount— another well-publicized undertaking. (He spent a fortune; the legal fees alone were astronomical.) While those negotiations were going on in the major leagues, I was caught up in my own negotiations in the minors. Like the other hosts, I had been presented with a contract. I didn't like it; I didn't think I was being paid what I was worth and also I was being held back from doing anything else. The contract said thou shalt not do TV commercials, thou shalt not do a talk show, thou shalt not preside over an infomercial, and leaned far more heavily on the "shalt nots" than the "shalts."

At the time of the negotiations, I received a phone call from a New York television producer asking me if I would be interested in doing a talk show. This woman had won an Emmy for a previous talk show she'd produced, had gone freelance, and had great contacts in the world of syndication. She was told that if she found the right host, she'd get all the backing needed. That's when she contacted me. The proposed "Kathy Levine Show" would originate in Philadelphia, which was not only convenient for me but removed from the New York competitive arena where there are 10,000 talk shows every hour. The idea was for me to do that program during the day and then appear on QVC at night. My interest was piqued. I went to Doug and asked if QVC would be willing to let me fly. He took my request under advisement ... which meant he'd call the big man. Barry Diller then phoned and gave me his advice.

216

Diller Meets Diva

"Listen, if you want to do a talk show, I can do it for you. I can do it best. I can get you the best writers, the best producers, the best talent. You don't have a clue what this business is like and I am this business. You're going to get eaten up and spit out. You want a talk show, I'll give you a talk show, right where you are."

I thanked him very much, hung up, and called the producer who'd been after me. I explained that QVC did not want me to go out of the company but that I perhaps would be doing something under the mantle of QVC. She turned around and said, "I could produce the show for you there. Could you get me a meeting with Mr. Diller?" I had to laugh. I wasn't setting up any meetings about talk shows because the truth was I really didn't want to do a talk show. There were so many of them, too few good ones, so why jump into a field that's already bursting at the seams?

I did want *something*, though, and decided to present my case to Barry Diller ... in person. There was so much at stake for me I wanted to be heard by the man who "held the chips." When it comes to important matters, I'm a firm believer in face-to-face. Anyone who is negotiating for her livelihood should have the right to be heard by the decision maker(s). I called Mr. Diller, we made a date, and he broke it. We made another date and he had to break that one, too. Get this, the man was negotiating a multibillion-dollar deal to buy Paramount and was in with lawyers twenty-two hours a day, but that didn't stop Kathy Levine from hocking him about her future. And the marvel is, the man was receptive! After missing each other on a few more occasions, at last we both were going to be in New York City at the same time, and he told me to call him in the morning to set up an appointment. I did, from a booth in front of Saks Fifth Avenue. "Come on over," he said. "I've only got a few minutes to spare but I'll be glad to see you."

KATHY LEVINE

This time I did not stop to buy an outfit or check my hair. I raced over to the Waldorf-Astoria, got his suite number from the front desk, and hurried to the elevator. I stood there and suddenly, out of the blue, I was overcome by stomach cramps. I'd eaten a quickie breakfast before I called Mr. Diller and I guess that in rushing to see him my breakfast turned on me. I was overcome by the spasms and instead of stepping into the elevator I raced into the ladies' room and proceeded to spend the next twenty minutes blasting my brains out at the Waldorf. I couldn't stop, and all during the siege I was thinking, Barry Diller is giving me precious minutes of his time and I'm using it up on the toilet. What happened to that brave little soldier who had learned that you don't have to be nervous when you're meeting the big boss, you don't have to be in a fancy outfit, and you don't need fancy wines and all that stuff? I'll tell you what happened—that little soldier had a monster case of diarrhea. I pulled myself together as best I could, left the ladies' lounge, and went up to the towers.

Barry opened the door and invited me in.

"Would you like something to drink?" he asked.

"Kaopectate, please," I wanted to say. "No, thanks," I answered. "I'm fine." I was next door to cholera but I wasn't about to tell him. He motioned for me to sit down and while I plopped on a chair he sat down on the sofa and put his stocking feet up on the coffee table. He reached for a pillow and, clutching it to his stomach with one hand, he began popping peanuts into his mouth with the other. I felt a sudden twinge in my stomach. I could have used a quick run to the facilities and thought of asking him if I could use his bathroom, but I brushed that idea away. I was afraid that if I got into the toilet, I might never get out again. I had visions of Barry Diller banging on the door and telling me my time was up and to get the hell out.

Diller Meets Diva

"So," I asked, "how are you holding up?" Diller had been working like a maniac to clinch the Paramount merger.

"It's tough," he said with a sigh. "This is a real struggle and it's a fifty-fifty chance that the deal will go through."

"I want you to know that we're all rooting for you," I told him.

"Thanks, I appreciate that. Now, what can I do for you?" So ended the conversation concerning the gazillion-dollar QVC/Paramount merger, and Barry Diller turned his attention to the important business of the day, Kathy Levine's future.

"I'm negotiating my contract, as you well know," I began, "and I'm not happy. The money's no good."

"I don't want to talk about money, that's not my job. I have people in your company who were hired to talk about money."

"Fine, we won't talk about money. Um, let ... let me get my notes," I stammered, and while Mr. Diller wiggled his stocking toes, I plunged into my handbag and came up with the paper. I had to come up with another topic, quick. I was prepared. I couldn't afford to let the conversation lag, and to make sure things moved I had jotted down a list of topics on a piece of paper.

"Okay," I said after glancing at the items, "money's out." I went on to tell him that I wanted to do more within the company. Although I loved selling, I also wanted to try other related venues, but I wasn't convinced a talk show was such a great vehicle. "I hate talk shows," I confessed. "I hate the idea of gabbing with someone who cut up her teenage kid, put him in the freezer, and now has written a cookbook on thirty-six ways to serve an elbow." Barry Diller smiled. "There's gotta be something else," I continued, "maybe an infomercial that QVC would get behind. I don't know. All I know is I need some latitude."

"I'm with you all the way on that," he said sincerely, adding, "you have a lot of opinions and I want you to know that your opinions are taken seriously. You do know that you're a bit intimidating, don't you? You're talent, and talent's got ego. Talent has needs, and that's what I'm trying to get across to management, the idea that talent is different. We have to make you happy because if you're not happy you'll leave." In the middle of a multimillion-dollar deal with Paramount, Barry Diller was taking time out to inform me that he understood the mind-set of talent! Our visit was short and sweet. He couldn't have been more receptive or supportive, and I walked out of the Waldorf feeling that maybe I had a chance to grow.

I went back to QVC to negotiate my contract and found Doug more determined than ever to tie me up as tight as a drum. Mr. Diller, while supportive, was busy with his own agenda. I wanted to make sure that things were kosher. I needed guidance; I needed a lawyer. I wasn't looking for just any lawyer, either. I needed one who talked entertainment turkey, someone who knew the ropes. There's just so much you can do with your own drive and common sense and then you've got to protect yourself legally, and it's important to recognize when that point has been reached.

I had to fly to Los Angeles on business, and since L.A. is an entertainment capital of the world, I got a list of attorneys to call. I phoned around, and the minute I said that I was working for Barry Diller the lawyers told me to come see them. I went to a number of firms and was disappointed each time. The lawyers weren't interested in Kathy Levine, they were looking to make contact with Barry Diller. While I was running from lawyer to lawyer, I had lunch with a friend who works in the legal department of Twentieth Century-Fox. I told her my predicament. "I've been interviewing lawyers and I'm a duck out of water. I can't find one. They don't want to handle me person-ally, they want to pass me off to an assistant. I don't want assistants. This contract is very important to me. This is my next few years and I don't want to get screwed."

"I'll get you someone," said my friend. She did, and when this lawyer called I leveled with him.

"Look, I'm a nobody. I may be a shlepper today but I may not always be a shlepper and if you handle me directly, we'll all profit down the road. I want to be handled fairly and respectfully and I don't want to feel like a lesser light."

"You have a deal," said the lawyer. And that was that. This man took my calls every time and handled me like a professional. I wouldn't have it any other way. Again, women sometimes don't assert themselves enough in situations where they have every right to be assertive. If you're paying somebody good hard cash, then that somebody better treat you in the man-ner that you should be treated, and often, that is sim-ply the way a *man* would be treated. The lawyer assessed the situation and advised me that if I wanted to go for everything then I had to be willing to risk everything.

Thanks to a good piece of advice from Joan Rivers, I was aware of the "risk." Joan had paid her dues. First she was dropped as Johnny Carson's replace-ment, and then, when she went to work for Fox, she was fired by Barry Diller. "Remember, Kathy," Joan cautioned, "everyone is dispensable. There's always someone willing to do your job, so always keep your eyes open and your mouth shut." Sure, Kathy Levine generated a lot of money, but I was expendable. QVC didn't want to lose me, but they didn't have to kowtow to me, either. Being a host was my bread and butter, not to mention my joy—this wasn't the time or place for Kathy's Last Stand.

My contract was negotiated, and although I didn't

get everything I wanted in terms of freedom, at least QVC was made aware that I wasn't simply inking my name. I wasn't a troublemaker, just a force with whom they had to contend. In a way I went through the motions as a kind of "hey, look at me" exercise, and I got my recognition. Plus, my lawyer wrote in a clause that gave me a bit of freedom—it allowed me to go on Joan Rivers's syndicated talk show, for instance, which I couldn't have done under the original terms of the contract. (It also provided for me to participate in infomercials, which QVC is now doing under the name Q-Direct.)

Meanwhile, the Paramount merger fell through and Barry Diller picked himself up and turned his sights on CBS. Another huge swell of hype accompanied the prospective takeover and then it too, fizzled. With all the takeover talk, I think the stockholders became nervous about Barry Diller's intentions. What was he doing with the company and what did it have to do with shopping? I truly believe that when he first arrived on the scene, Barry Diller was 100 percent committed. Then came the disenchantment. You can take the boy out of the glitz, but you can't take the glitz out of the boy. Barry Diller was a Hollywood executive trying to make a difference in a retail operation. That's like a race car driver selling toy cars in Kmart.

Diller moved away from his strength, and when he started maneuvering to get back into the mainstream and show Wall Street that he had some muscle, the balloon burst. We at QVC were caught up in merger fever and terrifically excited about the possibilities of being part of Paramount or CBS. It didn't happen, and if it had, it might not have meant anything better for us. We were the cash cow. As Barry Diller became more and more disenchanted, we saw him less and less. He came to the studio once or twice a week—a far cry from the early days when he was seriously thinking of moving himself into the studio.

222

Diller Meets Diva

To paraphrase, CEOs never die, they just fade away. For the many months that Diller had been hands on, we were in the big time. He instituted a lot of esthetic changes that made an overall difference in the ambience. He increased the management power and gave us permission to spend money, look better, do nicer things, and we glittered like 24 karat gold. The man had idea upon idea. He set up another cable division called Q2, which operates independently. He also was responsible for the QVC Local, a bus that's fully equipped to broadcast from anywhere in the United States and is on the road fifty weeks a year. The QVC Local made its debut in Washington, D.C., on September 29, 1994. (I was supposed to officially christen the bus by breaking a bottle of champagne over the front fender. The bottle never did break; it just kept bouncing off the fiberglass body. Another great moment in Kathy Blooper history.)

Yessir, when Barry Diller was involved, everything at QVC was exciting and fast paced. Having him there, even briefly, was a fabulous experience and personally and professionally very good for me. I'll always feel that he did something to improve my lot. On the personal side, I learned that I can go and meet with power as long as I know what I'm doing and am aware of my purpose. As for the professional side, I got lots of exposure. In essence, Barry Diller put my face out into the public eye. Yet, I know for sure that if I hadn't been a competent player, he wouldn't have pushed me. I had to keep my end up. Hey, he loved Joan Rivers, too, but when the ratings weren't great, he fired her ... and I'm no Joan Rivers.

11
To Bee or Not to Bee

❖　❖　❖

Can we talk? Can I tell you about a diminutive blond woman whose heart and mind and mouth are as big as all outdoors? "Big" is the word for Joan Rivers. I've been privileged to appear with her on QVC from the beginning, and she's been as generous and gracious to me as anyone I've ever known. Don't get me wrong, we are not bosom buddies. We don't hang out. We don't go out for lunch, we don't go out shopping together, and we don't meet each other for tea or anything like that. We travel in different circles. When I need to speak to Joan Rivers, I go through her manager like everyone else. Within the boundaries of our professional relationship, however, she is a staunch ally and one of the women I most admire in this whole wide world.

After QVC became fashionable as well as profitable for celebrities, the floodgates opened and the names came. I've worked with many of the stars, though not all of them by any means. Each host has certain areas of expertise, and we're most often paired with the person who benefits best from our strengths and with whom we have a good rapport. Electronics isn't one of my strengths, and I'm not that knowledgeable about sports, either, so it would be futile to put me with either a soft-spoken software expert or a big hunk of a football player ... wait ... I take that back—let them put me with a hunk, I'll figure out what to do. My field is jewelry and fashion, and that's how I got to be with Joan.

Joan was a pioneer, the first star to get past the stigma of being on televised shopping. We couldn't get anybody to come to us or pay attention to us until she took the plunge. Joan Rivers saw the potential before anyone else and walked right on in. She boldly went where no celebrity had gone before and didn't gave a rap about ridicule or criticism. She saw a great opportunity, snapped it up, and became the empress of television sales. Joan never put on airs about selling on the tube and, happily, her courage paid off. On a recent weekend show together, we sold $5 million worth of her jewelry. She is one of, if not *the* biggest hitter we've ever had on the show. The audience loves her and her product. Furthermore, not only does Joan do a fabulous job of selling her jewelry, she is the best person with whom to host and is definitely my all-time favorite QVC lady. I am indebted to Joan Rivers because when people tuned in to watch her, they saw me too.

Originally, Joan came to QVC to discuss making and selling duplicates of her own jewelry, much of which had been purchased for her by her late husband. He was English and had presented her with lots of gorgeous antiques. She also had a number of lovely pieces that had been left to her by her grandmother and her mother. All in all, Joan owned an extraordinarily comprehensive collection that was well worth cloning. At first the idea was simply a matter of reproducing. Later, when she got into the nitty-gritty and saw the unlimited possibilities, she began designing pins, rings, and bracelets herself. The Joan Rivers line took off like a rocket. She's a genuine crossover success story.

Joan came to QVC for the first time in October 1990. Once QVC and Joan had a deal, QVC had to choose a compatible host who'd work best with the formidable Ms. Rivers. They wanted to find someone who could hold her own against her. I can just see them sitting around trying to figure out which host had a big enough mouth to handle her. I wonder why they even wondered? In the big mouth department I stood out like a sore lip. Sure enough, I was asked if I would like to meet with Joan Rivers and explore the possibility of working together. "Of course," the producers cautioned me, "the chemistry has to be right or you can't be the one." They weren't threatening me or anything like that, rather, they were informing me that there had to be a good "marriage" of personalities. "It has to be a mutual thing, Kathy," I was told. "Joan Rivers has to like you and you have to like her. If you don't get along, we won't force you to do it." Mutual? Force *me?* I had to laugh. I got a very strong feeling that no one gave two hoots how I felt; the star had to be comfortable, and that meant Joan Rivers had the final say, not Kathy Levine.

On the appointed day of Joan's arrival, QVC was agog; we were about to have a bona fide celebrity in our midst. A lovely luncheon had been catered and set up in a small conference room. Joe Segel, the CEO, was hosting the event. Joan, accompanied by her manager, Dorothy Melvin, and her dog, Spike, had been driven down from New York in a limousine. The limo pulled up to the main entrance, and Joan got out of the car. I stood by with some of the studio muckety-mucks waiting to be introduced.

"Joan, this is one of our hosts, Kathy Levine. Kathy, this is Joan Rivers." We shook hands and two things were in the back of my mind. One: I couldn't get over how tiny she was. For those of you who've only seen Joan Rivers on stage or on the screen, you wouldn't believe how petite the woman is. Her size is not so noticeable when she's performing—then she's bigger than life. In person, she had such a fragile look I instantly felt like putting my arm around her and protecting her. She was not what I imagined. I expected a Phyllis Diller type with a shtarker persona, and here was this porcelain doll. The bawdy, loud, brassy entertainer was nowhere to be seen. I was confronted with a somewhat shy, somewhat reserved businesswoman who had come for an important meeting. Two: Knowing that the ride from New York takes a few hours, I figured she might want to "freshen up." So, instead of saying "Hello" or "Nice to meet you," I looked down at this star of stars and the first words out of my mouth were, "Do you need to use the bathroom?"

"No, I'm fine, thank you," she answered without a blink.

We went in the building and started down the hall toward the conference room. Before we reached the door, Joan Rivers complimented me on what I was wearing, a bright multicolored suit.

"Thank you," I replied, quite pleased that she would notice.

"Is your suit from QVC?" she asked.

"No," I admitted.

"Well, it's a lovely outfit."

"Glad you like it," I enthused. She looked terrific herself, but I didn't think it would be cool to compliment her right on the heels of her flattering me. Instead I offered her a nugget of information. "We've had a special lunch catered for you." That statement was about as thrilling as my first query about the ladies' room! I couldn't seem to raise my conversation to any level of competence.

"Great," she said, as though I had told her something of importance. "I'm *really* hungry."

Again I focused on her stature and thought to my-self, the woman is no bigger than a minute, a skinch over five feet; how can any one that dainty be really hungry? *I* get really hungry, probably Roseanne and Luciano Pavarotti get really hungry, but this little lady? Gimme a break. What a surprise I got when Joan chowed down like a trouper. I was thrilled to watch her eat. The luncheon consisted of lox and bagels and little pickups like strawberries and cut fruits, followed by pastries. We stood in front of the buffet table and piled the food on our plates. For some unknown reason, maybe it was my own ner-vousness, I again said to her, "Are you sure you wouldn't like to use the bathroom?"

She looked up at me with a quizzical expression. "Do you have a particular issue on that subject, Kathy?"

"No, no," I assured her.

"Don't worry about me," she replied. "I have kid-neys like a camel."

I couldn't believe it; here I was meeting a major star and with a good shot at doing a program with her, and all I could think of discussing was whether or not she should go to the toilet. Later, when friends asked what Joan Rivers was like, I said, "She has kid-neys like a camel." I didn't know what to say to the woman; I was very ill at ease, which isn't like me and certainly had nothing to do with her. I was just so nervous about the prospect of working with her. We were seated at the table when someone came over and asked if she'd like to see the studio, which is normal procedure for guests. "Studios are studios," she snapped. "What the hell do I want to see a studio for? I've been in studios all my life. I came to look at jewelry." When I heard that, *I* had to pee. Usually guests at QVC say "Oh, I'd love to see the studio." Not Joan Rivers. She was direct and forthright and scared the pants off me. I excused myself and went to

To Bee or Not to Bee

the bathroom. (I wonder if Joan Rivers told her friends that Kathy Levine had the kidneys of a gnat.)

I returned and found everyone looking at Joan's jewelry. As I mentioned, it consisted of assorted simple pieces and was not anywhere near what it is today. When the company suggested that jewelers look at the originals, Joan wasn't thrilled. She wanted to be a real part of the procedure and had her own ideas about what to do. She was big on pearls and wanted them included because her mother, her grandmother, and she herself believed in them and wore them because they were "rosy to the skin." Wearing pearls was the "feminine" thing to do. Along with her pearl pushing, she insisted that a very special item belonging to her grandmother be reproduced—a lorgnette on a long chain. Her grandmother always wore the lorgnette and used it to read programs and menus and small print. A lorgnette? In the 1990s? You bet. And so it went. Joan showed the things that were true to her and her tastes and then the time came for me to leave the meeting and go on the air. I hoped I'd made a good impression. "Nice to see you," I said to Joan. "Hope we get together someday." Hope? Pray would have been the better word. I didn't know how I'd come across although I felt that, give or take a few references to the ladies' room, maybe she liked me.

Weeks passed and nothing happened. I assumed that Joan Rivers thought Kathy Levine was a jerk, so I got to work and forgot the whole episode. (If you believe that, I still have a bridge connecting Manhattan to Brooklyn that I'd like to sell you.) A few months later, I heard that we were going to do a Joan Rivers show ... oh, and Kathy Levine was going to be the host. I'll never be able to describe my joy at being chosen. Even though I'd been wishing for it, I hadn't heard anything in so long, the possibility seemed remote, and when it actually happened, I couldn't believe my luck.

KATHY LEVINE

The day of the first show came, and once again, Joan Rivers arrived at QVC, and so did her makeup artist, her hairdresser, her manager, her dog, and some assorted persons who handled the manufacturing end of her jewelry line. Also along for the kick-off was Tommy Pileggi, her late husband Edgar's closest friend and now her best friend. (Mr. Pileggi watches over Joan like a guardian angel and stood right by her at her QVC debut.) Joan had some entourage crammed into that room, let me tell you. Meanwhile I sat alone doing my makeup, my hair, and getting ready for business as usual, only it wasn't quite as usual; it was a helluva lot bigger than usual. I was very, very nervous, because I knew that the selling of Joan Rivers's jewelry was *my* responsibility. At the time, Joan didn't know a lobster claw clasp from a hole in the ground—I did. (As some of you probably know, the former, a spring-ring mechanism, makes it easier to open and close a necklace clasp; the latter was where I wanted to crawl into at that moment.) Jewelry was my forte; it was up to me to make sure that her product moved and sold. I was doubly on edge because Joan Rivers didn't have a clue as to how our show operated. I hadn't been given any time to tell her anything because I was not permitted to hang out with her or prepare her. She was the superstar and I was the grunt. Well, at least I was a grunt who knew her subject.

The moment of truth arrived, and Joan Rivers and I walked out on the set together on September 8, 1991. I got the old rush of pleasure at seeing the camera, and in two seconds my worries went out the window. The lady was sensational; she understood instinctively what to do *and* what not to do. I went into the play by play while she provided the color commentary. As I spoke of the nuts and bolts of products like the pearls and the lorgnette, she explained why pearls were special to her and what lorgnettes were used

230

for and threw in some delightful anecdotes about her grandmother, her mother, and herself. We fell into an easy working pattern and gradually began to banter back and forth. When I said of one particular item, "This chain is long enough to double over," she looked right at me and said sincerely, "Gee, that's a great idea, I never thought of doing that." She was appreciative, and the natural flow between us built up; soon we were working together like a retail Lord and Taylor. She was cute, she was nice, and never ever cut me off in midsentence—the cardinal sin of TV sellers. To this day she is probably the only celebrity who always lets you finish what you have to say. She listens. She doesn't just wait to talk. Joan is a professional in all respects.

That first show was very well received and generated a tremendous amount of media coverage as well as a helluva lot of money. The dollars were overwhelming. I don't remember the exact amount, but, big as it was, it didn't approach what the Joan Rivers line has done since. Of course, Joan got all the kudos. The articles were written about her, and there was not even a mention of a host. Unless you knew my mother, you might have thought Joan Rivers was on the air by herself. (My mother's version went something like, "Kathy was on the air with what's-her-name.") Oh well, that's what I was being paid for, and if I had to yield the spotlight, I couldn't have picked anyone more worthy of deferring to.

QVC, delighted by the response, decided to bring Joan Rivers back in eight weeks. Joan's second appearance occurred right before Christmas, and when we finished the show, she invited me to her annual Christmas party. I was so excited. I called my current boyfriend, Steve, and told him we were going to a big celebration in the Big Apple. He was as thrilled as I when I told him our hostess's name. Naturally I went out and bought a new outfit, a darling little off-the-

KATHY LEVINE

shoulder, dark green velvet dress. (By the way, in case you're interested, 90 percent of the time I shop alone. On big occasions, the only person I'll shlep along is my mother because she's the first one to tell me if she doesn't like my choice.) I put on my green dress and wore it proudly. I didn't need my mother to tell me I looked terrific that Christmas Day. Joan's home was lovely, tastefully and elegantly decorated, and she was a gracious hostess. This was my first BIG New York party, and I've been lucky enough to be invited to Joan's Christmas gathering ever since. Although the guests are, for the most part, business associates and friends, I have seen a few celebs, like Patrick "Captain Jean-Luc" Stewart, Lainie Kazan, Tim Conway, and designers Mary McFadden and Pamela Dennis. In 1993, my new boyfriend went over the top when he spotted Phil Spector, who wrote and produced some of the best music around. My date dragged me over and, putting his arm on Phil Spector's shoulder, said, "I can't tell you how thrilled I am to see you. I had my first romantic experience in the back of a car to one of your songs. It's a privilege to meet you in person." Phil Spector is a very shy person and studiously avoids the public eye, but when he heard my date's story, he couldn't stop laughing. "My pleasure, my pleasure," he kept saying.

An eight-week cycle for celebrity appearances is a tradition at QVC. Almost all of them return on a two-month basis, particularly Joan. We work around her engagements so that when she's performing in, say, Atlantic City, we know she can come over. Her show business gigs dovetail with her selling ones. Joan comes to QVC for a three-day deal on the weekend, usually a Friday night, a Saturday afternoon, and a Sunday morning. She's on the air for approximately nine selling hours. That's lots of hard work, but she doesn't stop there—she'll do a lot in between, like commercials for future shows. We work her very hard

232

and it pays off, for her and for us. The multitudes tune in for the Joan Rivers shows whether they buy or not. I know they do because of the tremendous swell in my mail after those airings. I'm convinced if Nielsen did ratings on who watches what at those times, we'd garner one of the highest.

Joan and I continued together and soon were on a very solid basis—she began to trust me. She learned that I would not betray her, that I would not say anything that she did not want known. I would not embarrass her in any way. (Does this sound like the Girl Scouts' creed?) And I learned early on that she would not embarrass me. For a while, she started asking me about my love life while we were broadcasting. She wanted to know if I was dating or who (what) I was dating. "What did you do last weekend? Is there someone in your life? Are you happy?" She threw out these questions and it made me uncomfortable. As I said, although I share a lot of myself with my audience, I've made it a rule not to discuss my love life. Joan quizzed me relentlessly, yet I never got the feeling that she was being "newsy"; she was just curious. She's also very open about her real dating life. (I love her routines: "They take me out to dinner and they're so old," she complained, "that when the check arrives, they're dead. Anything to get out of paying the bill.") While I preferred to keep my private life off the air, Joan didn't seem to mind answering some questions. During our broadcast, I asked her if she was going out with anyone.

"A couple of people, but there's nobody really special," she answered sincerely. "It's tough dating at my age. Anyway, it's probably just too soon." Her candor disarmed me. This exchange took place not long after her husband's suicide. Joan faced that tragedy right on. In an odd way she is the most public/private, or private/public person I've known. Before she came on QVC, like the rest of the world, I'd seen her as an entertainer, an off-the-wall comedian who, it appeared, did not shy away from saying anything. I learned, and so did the audience, that Joan is not always the shocking, in-your-face persona. She comes across quite differently on QVC. She's a mother, a businesswoman, and a widow ... a very special kind of widow, too. She endured the pain and shame of her husband's suicide, did not shy away from its repercussions, and won the hearts of our viewers. They had a chance to see Joan Rivers in a much different light— courageous rather than outrageous. Women have grown to love her and are addicted to her shows, and they've provided her with inspiration.

Early on, Joan came up with a piece of jewelry, a tiny crystal bumblebee. Now, bumblebee pins were already around; Van Cleef and Arpel had been selling one for years ... for a lot of money. It took Joan to put the buzz into a reasonably priced bee, and she introduced it on our show. A viewer called and told us how much she liked the pin.

"You know, Joan," the viewer concluded, "the bumblebee is very much like you."

"Like me?" Joan queried. "How's that?"

"Well," continued the viewer, "did you know that aerodynamically speaking a bumblebee is too heavy to fly? Technically its little wings shouldn't be able to get its body off the ground. It beats the odds and flies—just like you. You don't let yourself get grounded by adversity. You keep coming back. You won't let yourself be pulled down. You beat the odds. You and the bumblebee share an ability to survive."

Joan really took the viewer's words to heart, and the bumblebee became her signature piece. She did a coin belt with a bee on it; she did birthday bees with birthstones in them. She did a mama bee and a baby bee, and every variation sold out. Women started buying the bees as a sign of hope. Some pinned them to their surgical gowns as they were wheeled into the

To Bee or Not to Bee

operating room or on their casts when they were recuperating. Others pinned them to their wedding gowns as they walked down the aisle. We got calls from viewers who told us they always wore their bees on a first blind date or on a job interview. Women wore those little buzzers up, down, and sideways. The upshot was that Joan worked the little critter into her logo and became known as the Bee Lady. We are bee-set by viewer interest and enthusiasm over the bumblebee and have come to the point where we laugh and tell the viewers if we see one more bee we're going to "bee" sick.

I became utterly comfortable being on the air with Joan. We'd laugh and have a great time. Although we tried very hard not to cross that line of good taste, occasionally we did. Once we got into a riff about how Philadelphia was going to have a gay football team and we were going to sell them pink jerseys, etc. etc. It was silly, but we just went with it. The gay community was not amused and let us know their dissatisfaction. I think that while Joan was a bit miffed at their reaction, she recognized that they had a point and maybe it wasn't fair to take shots at them on the air, even if it was done without rancor. It did seem ironic that they chose to take affront—Joan has been an incredible supporter of gay rights and did a lot for the AIDS cause from the start. Long before the red ribbon became de rigueur, she was in there fighting.

One thing about Joan Rivers, she's an equal opportunity offender. I can't think of anything or anyone she's missed, from the Queen of England to Elizabeth Taylor. She hits everyone. She's a lady with opinions and is not afraid to express them. Boy, you should hear her go after people who start complaining about America. "If you don't like this country, get the hell out!" she told a ranting viewer on one broadcast. I know from working with her that she does not intentionally want to hurt. But, hey, humor is dangerous;

you take a chance and sometimes you miss. You have
to miss in order to connect. For the most part, viewers
love her bluntness. They'll call and shmooz, and she
can say almost anything without raising hackles. One
time a viewer phoned in when we were selling a gold
bracelet. "I love that piece," cooed the listener, "but
I couldn't buy it for myself. I'm going to wait for my
boyfriend to get it for me."

Joan countered faster than you could say "fourteen
karat." "Listen, dear, if I waited for a date to buy me
a piece of jewelry, I'd be a hundred and six and my
teeth would be in a cup. You want something, get it
for yourself!"

Joan's philosophy is similar to my own. I'm always
telling the viewer, "Do something nice for *yourself*,
it's a long day."

Hosting with Joan is a pleasure, but you've got to
be on your toes, because you never know what she's
going to say. I think she's the brightest woman I've
ever worked with, and believe me I've worked with
plenty of smart ladies. It's like playing tennis with a
professional; whatever garbage you lob over the net,
she can whack it back. Joan's brilliant and knows history, literature, and lots of other things, all of which
makes her the ideal partner. But when the devil gets
her tongue, look out, she'll say most anything, and
there's nothing I can do because it's 100 percent live.
In the last year, I can recall two incidents where I
broke up, one temporarily, the other almost permanently.

Joan has a couple of Yorkshire terriers, and one of
them, Spike, had just had a prostate operation. Joan
brought her pups on the show, and that little son of
a gun Spike started nipping my ankles.

"Hey, cut that out!" I cried, pushing him away.
"That's a nasty dog," I commented to Joan.

"If you had a prostate operation, you'd be nasty,
too," she shot back. I totally lost it.

To Bee or Not to Bee

Another time, during a recent airing, Joan really got me. I was showing a ring and doing my spiel. The camera was in close on my hand, and then pulled away to a full shot of me and Joan. I said something to the effect that the ring would go anywhere and be admired even at a formal dinner party. I paused and Joan all of sudden said, "Have you ever been at a formal dinner party when somebody farts?" I couldn't believe what I had heard. I could see the mail pouring in from the hostile members of the audience who always are looking for something to snipe at. I knew they'd blame me for what was said because I was the host. I looked over at Joan as she sat there and continued to talk about passing wind. "I'm trying to sell a ring," I interjected. That phrase turned out to be the last coherent thing I said. I started laughing and buried my head in my arms. Joan was on a roll, and all I could do was let her rip, so to speak. I doubled over in my chair. My hair was damp, the glue on my eyelashes loosened, and they were hanging off my lids. I couldn't draw a breath as Joan Rivers was doing a monologue on the subject of farting at dinner parties. The producer was screaming at me but I laughed so hard, my earpiece fell out. I went into a trance and only remember thinking, "Oh Lord, get me out of here." I never got back control of that show.

Over the years, as our partnership became more and more popular, it dawned on me that there was a glaring discrepancy in the way we looked. When people turned us on, it was immediately apparent that one woman was a star and the other was not. Joan looked so damn good and I looked so frumpy, it bothered me. Now, I didn't think of myself as another Joan Rivers; I couldn't pretend to be in her league—the clothes, the shoes, the hair, the makeup, the style, the mind were beyond me. I didn't want to compete with her and even if I had wanted to, I simply didn't have the means. I did think, however, I deserved a shot at

looking presentable, and I started with the greatest
cross I have to bear—my hair. At my insistence, the
company agreed to pay for me to get it done, at least
for that show. This was a minor triumph.

I learned about dressing well from Joan Rivers. She
doesn't wear prints or patterns, she's solid and neutral;
that way she can repeat an outfit, accessorize it differently, and nobody knows she's in the same clothes. It
didn't take me long to catch on. All my clothes are
solids now. I learned, too, that it's better to buy one
good outfit than three junky ones. My budget is limited; still, I buy a much better quality of clothing, especially if it's something I know I'm going to be wearing
a lot, like a suit.

Joan continues to be a role model as far as fashion
goes—she's usually 100 percent coordinated, but even
she has an occasional "breakdown." We appeared together recently on a jewelry show and Joan was for-
mally dressed in an exquisite Pamela Dennis long
black skirt and black beaded jacket. As the program
proceeded I looked down and saw that between the
black skirt and the matching black shoes, Joan Rivers,
fashion maven, was wearing *blue* stockings. During the
first break, I leaned over and whispered, "Joan, you
must have grabbed the wrong panty hose, they're
blue." Joan laughed, pulled one foot out of her shoe,
and there was her big toe sticking through a hole.
"Yeh, they're blue all right, and I didn't grab the
wrong ones . . . they were the only clean pair left in
my drawer." See, even Joan Rivers can run out of
panty hose.

When Joan hit the $10,000,000 mark in sales, QVC
threw her a party. (Now they do it for all the celebrities who reach those heights. Joan was the first,
though, and it took the others a long time to catch
up. Richard Simmons, Susan Lucci, Tova Borgnine,
Kenneth Jay Lane, and Nolan Miller have all done it
since, but no one reached that level with Joan's

speed.) To celebrate her achievement, Joe Segel hosted a party and during the festivities stood up to make a speech. First, he acknowledged my contribution, which I was hoping he'd do—it seemed only fair. I stood up and got a big round of applause. Then Joan was recognized and presented with a magnificent bracelet encrusted with tourmalines and diamonds, and I mean d-i-a-m-o-n-d-s. Of course, being the consummate businesswoman, Joan had the bracelet copied and sold it on QVC. Joan is like that—give her something or show her something and boom, she has it copied. After the party, Joan came over, gave me a hug, and said, "You should have gotten a bracelet, too." I smiled.

When Joan hit $25,000,000 in sales, they threw her another party. Again, my contribution was recognized and I stood up for another round of applause, sat down, and watched as Joan was presented with an antique platinum, diamond, and sapphire bracelet. She came over, gave me a hug, and said, "That was wrong, you should have gotten a bracelet, too."

"Joan," I answered, "it's my job to sell your product, and my pleasure, as well. You've given me a lot more than you know; I have recognition now—I'm known because I'm the host who works with Joan Rivers. Don't worry about the bracelet, I'm doing my job and everything's fine." That's what I said. Although I really did mean what I said about her, the truth was, in my heart of hearts I was thinking it would have been nice to have a platinum and diamond and sapphire bracelet!

Here's another thing I learned from Joan Rivers. Joan's Jewish and makes no bones about it. She's very relaxed about sprinkling Yiddishisms in her speech. Working on a network like QVC had made me a bit more guarded about saying things that the majority of our audience might not understand. I used certain crossover expressions on occasion, words that had pushed their way into the language and were known by most everyone. I often referred to my "dates" as shleps, and I believe that America understands the word *shlep*. I think people also understand *schlemeil*, so when I say that someone is a schlemeil or that you're dressing poorly so you feel like a schlemeil, I believe viewers get the gist of it. In the beginning, I was pretty careful, though, because I didn't want to say anything that my audience didn't get. Then, along came Joan, whose Jewishness is writ in neon and whose speech is filled with Yiddishisms. Hearing her loosened my tongue. I began to use expressions that were not universally understood but when I used them, I also defined them so no one listening in would be left out. I ran into a bit of trouble one time by calling some article a piece of drek. I was using the term to mean "garbage," which is one of its uses. I got calls from Jewish viewers who were offended by my using that word because they knew the literal meaning, "sh—." I thought they were being too fussy. My mother called and told me they were absolutely right. "Even though your viewers don't know exactly what you're saying, that doesn't give you the right to say it." Mother knows best, and I don't use the word anymore. Other hosts who aren't Jewish use Yiddish expressions and sometimes get into "gray" areas of translation. Thinking that the word meant something like "dope" or "jerk," Mary Beth Roe once announced on the air, "What do I know? I'm just a schmuck from Minnesota." After the broadcast she asked me if *schmuck* was a bad word.

"It all depends on who you're calling and what you're calling," I answered.

"Well, how about if I called myself a schmuck on the air?"

"Hmmm," I replied, "it's not real good, Mary Beth, but you'll get by, don't worry, it's okay." (Just so you

240

don't have to go running to the glossary of terms right now, the *literal* meaning of schmuck is "penis"!)

There is another side to this issue, a darker one. Some people out there are bigots and on occasion they'll send disgusting mail. I admit I was a little nervous and shied away from any mention of religion because I didn't want to provide ammunition for any anti-Semitic putz to start sending letters. I kept quiet as Joan spoke openly of her Jewishness. When she sold her first Maltese cross, she made very clear what it was about. "I'm a Jew," said Joan, "and I designed this as an item of jewelry. It's not an insult to have designed it or to wear it." Joan helped me to relax about the religious angle; she kind of gave me permission to be Jewish on the air. So in case any of you viewers thought I was a Buddhist, now you know.

A final note about Ms. Rivers. When Barry Diller came to QVC, everybody wondered what would happen. In case you don't remember, Barry Diller was the man who hired Joan for her Fox Network talk show and then fired her. (Joan also believed he was partially responsible for some of the problems that led to her husband's suicide and has been very up front about that in her own book.) The question was, would she want to stay on and work for him and/or would he keep her on? At the time of Diller's ascension, Joan was in London, where she appears twice a year. Apparently, Diller called her there and told her in effect that business was business, kind of, "You're making lots of money for this company, stay where you are and I won't bother you." Joan was happy with the arrangement and remained. Joan and Barry did not kiss and make up for a long time, and he always had the courtesy to be out of the building when she was there; his good friend Diane von Furstenberg wasn't around either. Ultimately, things resolved and Barry Diller and Joan Rivers were fine. He'd come by, say a quick hello, and that was that. Money sure does talk.

I still get very little time with Joan prior to doing a show, and our preparation, if you can call it that, is pretty much a last-minute visit to her dressing room where I say, "Hi, how are you? What do you want to talk about?" She'll say something like "Oh, let's talk about Melissa's new show" (her daughter was going on television and Joan was as excited as any mother would be) "or, we can talk about my trip to London, or Spike and Veronica." Veronica is Joan's new Yorkshire and cute, cute, cute. Joan and I prattle on and on, and she's always good and always up.

She's generous, too, and often gives items away to a deserving viewer. "Joan, I'm going in for surgery and I'm going to pin your bee on my gown," one caller said. "Oh," cried Joan, "let me send you these earrings, you can wear them, too!" And out those earrings are shipped. She's learned the jewelry business and knows exactly what she's doing. She can talk about a lobster claw clasp with the best of them. All in all, she is so very entertaining that the time goes quickly and profitably.

She continues to be generous with me and invited me to appear as a guest on her original daytime talk show and later on the "Can We Shop" talk show. Sadly, that concept didn't fly. It didn't stop Joan. She went on to write and star in a play about Lenny Bruce's mother, which garnered her lots of critical praise and a Tony nomination. Let's face it, the lady has a bit of the invincible in her; when she reaches $100 million in sales, I think QVC should give her the Hope Diamond . . . oh, and maybe this time they could throw in a little bauble for me, too.

12
Who's Afraid of the Big B.H.D.?

❖ ❖ ❖

Linda Ellerbee had them in the seventies. Jane Pauley went under attack for them in the eighties, and even perky Katie Couric takes her knocks about them. I'm talking about Bad Hair Days and with great pride and no choice, I carry them into the nineties.

For those of you who know and love me (and hate my hair), this book wouldn't be complete without a brief ode to my loveless locks. I was born under the sign B.H.D.—from the moment they broke through my scalp my stringy strands pointed toward all the planets and throughout my childhood they were never in agreement as far as direction. Every school picture of me shows a cute face, nice smile, sweet demeanor, and weird hair. Coiffure-wise, my adult life has been more of the same—B.H.D. followed by B.H.D. Nothing sets the tone for a woman—not her clothes, not her makeup, not her jewelry, not even her weight—as much as a Bad Hair Day. I have coaxed, colored, curled, cut, filled in, gelled, glued, ironed, lifted, moussed, permed, pieced, pulled, sprayed, straightened, and teased my hair, yet every day remains a

243

crap shoot. And, to add insult to injury, each evening I have to step into the living room of millions, with no hairdresser in sight. I torture my locks into position and go on camera dreading the inevitable and, when I glance into a nearby monitor, the inescapable is there—a hole, a flat spot, a curl gone mad, or a limp tress—and my concentration is broken.

Viewers are always eager to help. "Kathy, what did you do to your hair?" says Mary, a call-in. Now, that's a loaded question. Do I answer, "Oh, I worked hard on it today and it's cooperative for a change" only to have Mary harpoon me with ... "You don't understand, Kathy, I think it looks terrible. I liked the way you wore it on Christmas Eve." Christmas Eve! Today's June 9th ... does that mean I've looked like a dog for six months?

Experience has taught me to be humble in discussing my crowning unglory. Let's face it, my hair and I are like a bad marriage—we don't speak, we don't argue, we just stick around to keep the family unit alive. We're codependent. Look at it this way, five days a week, fifty weeks a year makes a whopping total of 2,000 Bad Hair Days that I've presented for your viewing pleasure. Believe me, I'm grateful to those of you who have endured my B.H. presence for the past eight years. I once saw Cindy Crawford in person and couldn't get over her. She appeared to be about five feet seven of gorgeousness topped with an additional three feet of an incredibly thick, shining mane. In my next life I'm coming back as Cindy Crawford's hair. Unfortunately, while finishing out this life, I have to bear the burden of my lean, limp locks and endure all the jokes. In the words of the wise and witty Ms. Ellerbee, whom I admire and respect—"and so it goes."

13
The Stars Are Out Tonight

❖ ❖ ❖

Ever since celebrities began coming to QVC to sell their products, I have been asked the same question over and over—"What's he or she really like?" I ask the identical question whenever a friend of mine meets a well-known personality. Everyone is curious about the famous—even the famous themselves. Many celebrities ask me about the celebrities I work with. I've gotten a big kick out of meeting and working with the celebrated, and I think you'll get a kick out of hearing about my experiences. So here, for your enlightened entertainment, is a Kathy's Eye View of the Stars.

I'll begin with one of the first celebrities with whom I appeared, Carol Channing. Live TV is not easy for Carol; she goes by the script, but she's a trouper and gives 100 percent 100 percent of the time. As flamboyant and daffy as she is, she is, at the same time, a generous, warm, and kind woman, and a courageous one as well. Carol appears to suffer from arthritis and does not believe in taking medication. On more than one occasion she's gone on television in great pain. I noticed that many times she had to lie down before her appearance, and each time this happened, she got up, put on her hair, put on her lashes, put on her smile, and went out and knocked them dead.

On QVC she sold a line of jewelry called the Broadway Collection, which was derived from actual jewelry worn by Broadway stars. My favorite item was a copy of a ring worn by Barbra Streisand. Carol and Barbra had vied for the film rights to *Hello, Dolly*. Although Channing had been the Broadway musical's original heroine, Streisand won the screen rights. Later the two women met each other at a Christmas party and, putting all differences aside, shook hands. Carol admired Barbra's ring and sure enough, a copy of it became part of the Broadway Collection. That's show biz.

Blond skinhead Susan Powter is very show biz. She flashed onto the screen, and her "Stop the Insanity" infomercial took off like gangbusters. Ms. Powter's aggressive approach pushed her product over the top and after a tremendous run, she's moved on to the next level ... a talk show. Meanwhile, she's established herself as a known personality, which doesn't hurt when you're attempting to build an audience. She's also an attractive woman—believe me, if you're sporting a crew cut and look that good, you've got something basic. Whatever else, Susan Powter doesn't have to worry about Bad Hair Days. She is, by the way, much littler than you'd expect ... probably a size 4.

Susan Lucci's another big-name "little" woman. Ms. Lucci's tiny—not an ounce of fat—absolutely beautiful and always in complete control and very self-contained. She sells her beauty care products efficiently and intelligently and guards her privacy like a pit bull. I don't know anything more about her than I did when I met her three years ago. She talks product, period. I once asked her if she had a dog. She looked at me as

though I'd asked about her sex life but quickly recovered and replied that she did have one, a Bijon named
Oscar. "And," she added, "I use my Lucci shampoo
on him." From then on I referred to her dog as the
"Lucci poochie." I finished doing a show with Susan
and noticed her ring. It's hard *not* to notice a search-
light-size diamond that you could die for, especially
when it's around a size 3 finger.

"That is one hunker of a ring," I said admiringly.

"Ha, ha, ha," laughed Ms. Lucci.

I couldn't stop looking at that ring. It was the biggest thing I've ever seen in my whole life. There's
something about being in the presence of a huge diamond that's totally exhilarating ... at least for me. Her
reticence aside, I admire Susan Lucci's professional-
ism. She may have lost out on the Emmy for fourteen
years, but she's been winning QVC audiences since
the day she arrived.

Generally speaking, actors selling product can be
quite effective; after all, they're trained to talk. However, acting and selling are different, and just as I
would not skip out onto a stage and expect to stun
the audience with my version of Lady Macbeth, I
would caution the best actor to take direction from a
professional seller like me. It's very important for the
host to get a sense of who the seller is, and the seller
has to realize that a) the host isn't stupid, and b) the
host runs the show. Whoever appears with me is a
guest on my program and not the reverse. I run the
show. I ask the questions and I handle everything. I
will never let a guest down. I always tell them before
we go on, "Don't worry, you're in good hands. No
one has ever died in my arms." I also give my sellers,
no matter who they are, one piece of advice every
time. "Please," I request, "no matter how tempted
you are to ask how we're doing, do not whisper to
me. Your microphone is always on. And do not get
off the air and say, 'Oh, thank God that's over,' be-

cause your microphone is *still* on." So far none of my
sellers have embarrassed me, but there have been any
number of glorious moments at QVC when a real pro
didn't make the adjustment, and one of those incidents
concerned a classically trained actress.

Joan Collins attended London's Royal Academy of
Dramatic Art. The lady had been a movie star and
then moved over to television where she prospered on
"Dynasty." "Dynasty" ended and Ms. Collins went
into other pastures and at one point was hired as a
kind of "talking head" to represent a line of jewelry.
That's how she wound up on QVC. (Being hired by
a company as a spokesperson is a different kettle of
fish from being a product originator like Joan Rivers.
When the product is *yours* from the beginning, you
feel very strongly about how it's made and how it's
represented, as opposed to representing a product
with which you have little or no connection.) Jeff
Hewson worked with Joan Collins, and boy, did he
have his hands full.

The first time she came to the studio Ms. Collins
had the misfortune of arriving on the day that a very
favored mayor of Philadelphia was being laid to rest;
all the press was at Frank Rizzo's funeral. Ms. Collins
walked in, head bowed and eyes covered with huge
sunglasses. Shaking her head and waving her arms in
front of her, she said, "No press. No press," as she
marched forward. After a few moments, she looked
around and switched her tune to "Where's the press?"
Obviously she was looking for it, and even after we
apologized and explained the special circumstances to
her, she remained rather frosty.

Once she got on the set, matters became even more
strained. She sat there as people buzzed around doing
what had to be done. Workers were delivering products, setting them up, and confirming what item was
next. Item numbers were being projected and various
shots were being considered. This is an extremely

important part of our procedure, because there's nothing worse than having a host talk about one product while the TV screen is showing another. The person delivering the product to the host has to double-check and make sure he's giving the right product, and before that person can hand the product over, he has to get approval through an item number. So, he'll stand off-camera about two feet away from the host and say, "Checking item number J-1234, red ruby necklace." Once he gets the okay, he'll put the product down on the table or hand it over. Put it this way—you can't hand rubies to someone who's selling sapphires. What the viewer sees on the screen is a serene picture of the host and seller and the models and the product, but just beyond the camera's frame is a hubbub of activity.

In the midst of this usual ruckus, exasperated by the commotion going on around her, Joan Collins cried out, "It's too noisy. Everybody clear the set!" In her mind, this was a rehearsal. Movie sets may be still when cameras roll, this was a *selling* set, and her comment was heard not only by the staff and crew but by the entire listening audience. She was on the air and continued to act as though this were the preparation for the real thing. Poor Jeff kept trying to steer her in the right direction as she continued to interject remarks like, "Can we do this again? This isn't working. There's too much noise!" Jeff would come back with, "Yes, we're right here LIVE! on QVC" or "We're so happy to have Joan Collins with us, LIVE AT THIS VERY MOMENT." His direct hints went right by her, and she kept asking for retakes. Near the end of the first segment, she leaned over to Jeff and out of the corner of her mouth quite audibly asked, "How're we doin'? Makin' any money?" *Nobody,* but nobody, talks about making money on the air. Jeff threw up his hands and said, "We're doing fine, LIVE!" During the break, Ms. Collins was informed that she had been on the air. She's a real pro, so when the show continued she got into the spirit and chattered away. She and Jeffery were discussing watches. "A lady," Ms. Collins pointedly stated into the camera, "never has a watch on after six." I'd never heard that before and later repeated the story to Joan Rivers. Joan laughed. "Some ladies don't wear one after six because it's tough to read a watch when your legs are up in the air."

Over the years I've developed a sense of who's going to be good to work with and who's going to be difficult. Some people think that selling is beneath them and that's it. Most people love it. They get a kick out of the energy that is part of the QVC ambience. They love being live on TV and they love the sales. Nolan Miller, the man who designed the fabulous wardrobe for "Dynasty," is a frequent QVC'er and a real gentleman—handsome, tall, and soft-spoken. He works with Mary Beth most of the time, but I've had occasion to do shows with him and have had a ball. Nolan's designed for the great ones like Barbara Stanwyck, Lana Turner, Barbra Streisand, Elizabeth Taylor, and on and on. One time he called me from Aaron Spelling's house. Candy Spelling, Aaron's wife, was a client of Nolan's, and Nolan thought she'd be good on TV. Eventually she did sell a line of designer dolls. Nolan told me that when she came to QVC she was booked for the weekend into a bed-and-breakfast that had been converted from a lovely little 1760 Pennsylvania farmhouse. Mrs. Spelling arrived along with a few pieces of jewelry—like 50 zillion dollars worth of stuff. She asked the owner of the bed-and-breakfast to please put them in the vault. Vault? The man looked at her like she was nuts. Vault? in a little PA hideaway circa 1760? (I don't know what happened to the jewelry—maybe she stuffed it under the mattress.)

Bob Mackie is a couture celebrity who's funny and fine and hasn't got one shred of celebrity attitude. He's a really kind person, which I found out when we met. At the time my weight was high as an elephant, never mind his eye. Mackie brought dresses for modeling that were all size 6. I was busting out of my 12s and 14s. That day, I wore a straight black chemise dress with a pleated bottom. Before the broadcast I went to talk to Bob about his presentation. Bob Mackie doesn't leave anything to chance. He draws a precise sketch of how he wants the models dressed, which includes every aspect of the total appearance. The drawings are a wonderful aid because the models know exactly what he's after. Those sketches are perfect little works of art and after the show, he autographs them and everybody tries to get one. They're real collectibles. Anyway, at our first meeting, I was the size of Rhode Island in my black chemise dress. Bob Mackie and I went over the sketches together. We finished and I walked away toward the set. "Nice legs," Bob Mackie called after me. I can't tell you how good that made me feel. He could just as easily have said, "Big ass," but he's not that kind of a guy.

Another famous American designer, Bill Blass, is great to work with, too. He's got style and taste and speaks very articulately. I have a feeling he must have been raised in some fancy Massachusetts-type place. He said he liked working with me, although he liked me better when I had blond hair and made no bones about telling me. (Re: the blond hair. Check page 182 of this book, Mr. Blass, and forget it!) Bill Blass is another one who always has something to say—there are no deadly awful pauses that have to be filled in; conversation flows and sales are brisk. Sometimes, for one reason or another, sales may not be so brisk . . . take the case of Loni Anderson and her collection.

Several years ago, Loni came on to introduce her Memories Collection of jewelry—duplicates of an original group of baubles that had been given to her by Burt Reynolds. The collection was very pretty, and each item had a charming love story connected to it. Loni herself was charming and delightful as she related her tales of love and jewelry. Then, lo and behold, the Anderson-Reynolds marriage blew up, and QVC was left with the jewelry. What were we supposed to call it—the Broken Memories Collection? We took somewhat of a beating on that line, and it's just one of those sad stories. Thank heavens, more good stories are around than bad.

Victoria Principal has to be among QVC's biggest success stories. She had one of the longest-running, most prosperous infomercials in the history of that genre, was consistently one of the top five moneymakers, and is a dedicated, focused woman who's great on camera. I'd guess that she's in her mid-to-late forties, but she looks about thirty. Victoria had a skin problem in her youth which was remedied. Later, she consulted with Aida Thibiant, a skin specialist, and with Thibiant's help she devised the Victoria Principal Skin Care program. Victoria's a walking testimonial to her own product, which is about the best selling point imaginable.

Sometimes our celebrities aren't performers, and we add a little pizzazz to their presentations. Kenneth Jay Lane is a big name in costume jewelry—he's the man who made it okay for the rich and famous to wear fakes and got his start by duplicating Jackie O's diamonds. He's a very witty, wry gentleman, and actually, I thought his wit might be a little *too* dry for our audience. They love him, though, and we've brought him down to earth a bit by jazzing up his displays. We built a cardboard "limousine" in which he makes his entrances. Viewers get a kick out of watching him spoof the high life. The limo comes on and he waves out of the window to the audience. On one show when he stepped out, the limousine door fell off and he tripped over it. All that day we kept showing the same video clip of Kenneth falling out the door. We got big laughs out of it, and no one laughed harder than Mr. Lane himself.

Speaking of distinguished gentleman, Charlton Heston has been on QVC selling videotapes—elegant, illustrated

stories of a religious nature. He went to Israel to research Moses and the creation of the Torah and was
scheduled to appear with me for his first outing. I called
him at his hotel. "Hi, Mr. Heston, this is Kathy Levine.
I'll be your host this evening, and I wondered if there
was anything you want me to ask you?" The voice that
came back at me was the voice of Moses, Ben Hur,
and probably God himself if he decided to speak to us
directly—it's so rich and resonant, I got chills listening
to him. He thanked me for calling and asked me what
I thought would be appropriate for me to ask him.

"Well, I was wondering what compelled you to do
these tapes?" I offered.

"*Im*-pelled," corrected Mr. Heston. He wasn't the
least bit critical when we went on the air, though. As
a matter of fact, he was delightful.

"Do folks tremble when they meet you?" I inquired.

"Not at all," he answered, adding slyly, "of course
sometimes the waters part for me, and that im-
presses them."

I've confessed that sports aren't my strong suit;
however, I know the great ones when I see them. One
day I walked off the set and bumped into an upcoming celebrity.

"What are you selling tonight?" he inquired.

"I'm selling rubies," I answered. "Buy one, sir, and
help a poor working girl save her job." Hank Aaron
laughed and went on for his segment. That's what you
call a "brush" with greatness. When you think of baseball superstars, Hank Aaron's right up there. So, too,
is Mickey Mantle.

Mantle came to QVC and it was evident that he
had a problem. Put it this way, he did an effective job
of selling, but you could see how eager he was to get
out of the studio and into a bar. He was in the throes
of alcoholism, and you could smell the liquor on him.
Then he went to the Betty Ford Center, turned things
around, and came back to us a changed man. Dan

Wheeler worked with him and said it was like night and day. Previously, it had been difficult to deal with Mantle because he was bogged down in alcohol—now he was on top of everything. We were very, very happy to see him turn his life around. The man did a lot for baseball and now he had done something for himself as well. Guys like Mantle are an inspiration for us at QVC just as much as for you out there. There's nothing better than seeing someone turn his life around for the better. That's a real home run!

I don't know sports, but I sure know food! If you're into eating big time there's nothing like watching Chef K Paul at work. Paul Prudhomme is a nice guy, very respectful and very quiet and very focused. He's the man who put Cajun cooking on the map and is a popular repeat guest on QVC because after his shows, the entire staff eats well for days.

Tova Borgnine's another self-made success story. She's married to Ernest Borgnine, a delightful and charming man, and she's been selling her fragrance and skin-care products (which come from cactus plants) in magazines for years. On the last page you'd find a picture of her and the promise that you could learn her secrets. One look at how she looks is an incentive to discover how she does it. Tova's dedicated to her craft and cares about the packaging as well as the content. I could never understand when I read or heard about women who wear only one fragrance all their lives. I didn't understand until I began wearing Tova. It's the only scent I wear well and I continue to receive compliments year after year. (I don't have to say this, I mean it.) Tova's a really elegant lady; when she walks into a room, everyone knows that "somebody" has arrived. She dresses divinely. I asked her if she had ever owned a pair of jeans. "Once," she answered, "I had to buy a pair to go horseback riding." Tova invited me to give her a call if I ever went to California and, naturally, I did just that (remember, don't invite me unless you mean it or you'll get the shock of your life when I show). She picked me up in a Rolls Royce, and we drove to a fabulous restaurant for Sunday brunch. I'm always delighted to participate in the lifestyle of the rich and famous if only briefly. Tova is always fun to be with.

The rich and famous always have been into exercise, and now exercise and body building have taken over the airwaves. You *know* there's something in it when a guy like Regis Philbin, not exactly a Schwarzenegger, makes a workout tape. Regis had a good reason; he had to exercise for his health's sake and was so successful he decided to put his program on tape. We had a good time together on the "Regis and Kathy Levine" show—just kidding, Kathie Lee. By the way, Mrs. Gifford also appeared on QVC with *her* personal exercise program and did extremely well.

When you're dealing with people in show business, how they do on QVC has a lot to do with the format in which they work. Performers like Regis and Kathie Lee are "live" and can handle just about anything; others are used to taping and are like fish out of water when they go on QVC. In these cases, a host really has to be on his or her mettle and guide the celebrity along.

Some guests are welcomed if for no other reason than they are just a pleasure to look at. George Hamilton falls into that category. He is *the* tannest man in the universe—at the studio, we refer to him as George Hamil-tan. Years ago, Johnny Carson did a monologue and said something to the effect that an atom bomb had fallen on Los Angeles and George Hamilton was spotted heading toward the blast's center with his reflector. When the sun got a bad name, George created a line of self-tanning products. On QVC he always tells the host to "touch my skin; it's very soft because of my product." The host (female) leans over to touch his face and gets a "power surge." George is handsome, handsome! And a gentleman, to boot.

KATHY LEVINE

QVC had another breakthrough in quality products when Mary McFadden, world-class designer, came to us with an accessory line. She's incredible and, in her own beautiful way, the most bizarre woman I've ever seen. She wears white, white makeup and her face is framed by short black, black hair. She dresses magnificently in long togas and tunics of the most exquisite colors and cuts. All told, you would not be likely to run into a Mary McFadden in your local supermarket. She's remarkably innovative and gets her inspirations from all over the world. She made marii pleating world famous. Marii is also known as knife pleating and is made with a hot knife that puts a permanent crimp in the fabric and never comes out. It's used in every possible kind of nightgown, skirt, and palazzo pant. Mary McFadden found it, loved it, incorporated it into her work, and became famous for it. Before Mary went on QVC, I had the pleasure of visiting her showroom. (Not just "pleasure" really, I went there to look over the merchandise and work on the presentation.) The rooms themselves are works of art and decorated so splendidly—it's like being in a museum rather than a clothing emporium. Some special gowns are hung on the walls in acrylic frames. One of these frames contained a striking beaded dress. It was so beautiful I couldn't help asking if she wore ever it. "Yes," answered Ms. McFadden, "I take it out for the Academy Awards and then I reframe it."

Mary McFadden may be off the wall but she's also laid back, if that's the expression, and I'm the exact opposite; rapid fire is my middle name. It took me a while to learn how to adjust my sights to hers. I had lunch at her showroom one day and it was scrumptious, shrimp curry and caramel apples for dessert and a delicious Madeira wine. Where was Madeira, I wondered? I asked my hostess. She requested one of her secretaries to look it up. Meanwhile, we continued to eat. The food was served on the most attractive dishes

256

and again I asked a question. "Where did you get these dishes? They're so beautiful." Mary continued to eat and didn't look up. I waited and waited and when there was no answer, I started talking about something else. After a few minutes of conversation, I got onto the subject of the upcoming QVC show.

"Tell me about your line, Mary. Are you going to do gold braid?"

"Bendel's," she said.

"What's a bendels?" I asked.

"Bendel's, the dishes—I got them in Bendel's."

Do you think I was surprised when I saw Mary a few days later and she greeted me with "It's a Portuguese island." I knew immediately that she was talking about Madeira. You'll get your answer from Mary McFadden, it's just a question of time. She's a bit hard to follow, which is fine because I can make the connections pretty quickly. When she joined me on QVC, I gave her the time to back up and go forward and back up again. She was charming and full of stories about her travels to India and Nepal, and viewers were enthralled with her tales. She "romances" her products, and people are fascinated—they're not only buying scarves and belts, they're buying "myths." I really like Mary McFadden, she's talented, good company, and a lot of fun.

Not only have bona fide celebrities appeared on QVC, we've actually *created* celebrities, and one of the earliest was Susan Graver. This lady is a legend in apparel. She was the *first* manufacturer of very affordable, washable, polyester clothing offered on QVC. She clicked with middle America and her name became as recognizable to our viewers as Donna Karan's is to the high-fashion-minded public. Susan Graver is an institution unto herself and, at this writing, is *the* most popular label on QVC.

Joy Mangano, an active mother of five, is another example. She brought her Roly-Kit™ and then her Miracle Mop™ to QVC and both items hit big. Joy has a team of dedicated women partners and a loyal following of fans.

Harvey and Ilene Tauman wanted to make the best skin-care collection possible and, using a patented polymer, they realized that dream with their Hydron cream. Most of the hosts use it and love it. Viewers notice our "glow," and we're walking testimonials to Hydron. Harvey himself has become a favorite on QVC and is fun to work with.

Noncelebrity celebrities may not make front-page news, but they're the real success stories, and we at QVC are proud of our participation in boosting the entrepreneurial spirit of the American dream.

So far everyone I've discussed in this chapter has been someone I've worked with or met. However, I simply cannot resist mentioning one star even though we've never actually been introduced. I sold her products, and I'd happily do it again and again, because I'm crazy about her and my adoration dates way back. I've had a thing for her since I was a teenager. Remember, I was the gawky, funny girl with a big nose, a big mouth, and long fingernails, and the minute I saw Barbra Streisand, a gawky, funny girl with a big nose, a big mouth, and long fingernails, she became my idol. I still refer to my early teens as my Streisand years, and in those days I studiously cultivated her "look"—big wings of black eyeliner, blue eye shadow from lid right up to the eyebrow, hair parted on the side, cut long on one side and short on the other ... and fingernails that never stopped. When Barbra Streisand appeared in *Funny Girl*, I went nuts. I looked like her; I had her nose, I had her nails and did everything to emulate her. Truly, the resemblance was amazing. Over and over again, people would come up to me on the street and say, "You look just like Barbra Streisand." Well, I sure wanted to look like her—I thought she was gorgeous. I followed her career closer than her manager and always maintained a special feeling for Streisand and when our paths finally (almost) crossed, happy days were definitely here for Kathy Levine.

In the summer of 1994, Barbra Streisand went out on her first concert tour in twenty-seven years. She had stopped making personal appearances for a quarter of a century because of an incident at her last public performance. While on stage in Central Park she went blank and forgot a line. That teeny-weeny slip frightened her—Ms. Streisand is a perfectionist (aside from her extraordinary, abundant gifts, *that's* the big difference between us)—and was so spooked, she could not appear in public. She came out of hiding as part of her therapy and arranged to do a final concert tour, which would include London, California, New York, and Washington, D.C. As you probably know, the tour became an international happening. Tickets were high priced and hard to come by.

Barbra Streisand records on the Columbia label, which is owned by the Sony Corporation. Sony also has a division that sells concert tour paraphernalia. (When The Rolling Stones, Pink Floyd, or outfits like that go out on tour, merchandise is always available, things like T-shirts, sweatshirts, key chains, night shirts, paperweights, and photographs.) No one generates as much money as Barbra's fans and when she went on this tour, a series of Barbra boutiques were set up at each concert, and her collectibles raked in the money. QVC was contacted and asked if we would be interested in selling the merchandise on the air. Sony offered to send tickets for the Madison Square Garden concert and suggested that some of the hosts attend to get a "feel" for things. I was called and asked if I would like to go. I thought it was joke. Would I like to go to a Streisand concert . . . for free? Were they kidding? I would have hocked my jewelry to *buy* a ticket. Another host, David Venable, was also asked. We were to go to the concert, meet the

Sony people, the boutique people, and various assistants to discuss how best to sell product. I naturally entertained the hope that one of the people we'd be discussing things with would be the one and only star herself. There was one little hitch—before I actually got to go to the concert, I had to speak to Barbra's manager, Marty Ehrlichman, and convince him that I had a genuine appreciation of his client and that I was the right person for the job.

"Hi, Mr. Ehrlichman," I said over the phone, "my name is Kathy Levine and I understand that you wanted to speak with me. I'm from QVC."

"Yeah," came a voice over the phone that in politest terms one would have to call gruff. "I'm after the right person. I want someone who lives and breathes and dies for Barbra ... like Richard Simmons. What makes you think you're a candidate?"

Much as I loved Barbra, I knew I wasn't in Richard Simmons's adoration league—he is her number one fan. The man has a shrine to her in his home.

"Well, first of all," I replied, plunging into my qualifications, "I've been told I look just like her. When she came out with *Funny Girl* I was stopped for two years running and asked if I was Barbra. My eyes are somewhat like hers and I wore my makeup like hers. I had my hair cut like hers and my nose *used* to be like hers. Most of all, though, I think she is the greatest entertainer, ever—the supreme talent."

"Hmmm," mused Marty, "I'll get back to you."

Turns out I passed the test, and so did David Venable. We received two tickets to Barbra and were given limited backstage passes. The performance was a dream—everything I'd ever imagined a Streisand show would be like ... and more. I sat there with tears rolling down my cheeks throughout the entire evening. Afterward, David and I met with the Sony people and the boutique people and the assistants but alas, not with Barbra.

260

The Stars Are Out Tonight

David and I returned to West Chester to prepare for the Streisand Collectibles. QVC decided to build up the sale by showing different video bits, and the professional voice-over man was called in. As taped scenes of Barbra rehearsing were shown, he read the copy: "QVC was there when Barbra Streisand stepped on to the stage after twenty-seven years," and so on. He had a wonderful voice; however, when Barbra Streisand heard the spot, she went into orbit. The professional spoke beautifully, but he kept pronouncing Barbra's last name as "StrieZand," and the lady is very particular about such things. She called Marty and said she wasn't going to do anything with us because we didn't know how to pronounce her name. The spot was pulled immediately, and I think the announcer was put in front of a firing squad. Marty called our boss and laid down the law. "Listen," he growled, "I want the show hosts working on this project to call me. They're going to have to audition. I want to hear the name Streisand pronounced like the 'sand' in sandbox, not Zand like in Zanzibar." The next thing I knew, I was on the phone with Marty and reciting "Streisssand" over and over again. Then it got to me. I was forty-two years old, a television personality for eight years, and I'm standing there going "Streisssand, Streisssand" like a nitwit.

"Marty, this is silly. I'm a big girl now. I shouldn't have to do this. I know how to pronounce her name."

"Okay, okay," barked Marty, "okay, you know how to pronounce the name. BUT . . . let me tell you something right now. I don't want to hear any more about how you resemble her. You don't look like her and you never looked like her!" Amen. I wasn't going to argue with the man.

The night of the Barbra Collectibles on QVC, the Sony people arrived and sat in the green room while David Venable and I went on the air. This was a big opening night for the collection and a real test. As

261

terrific as the merchandise was, it was also pricey, and
selling it would be an iffy situation, not a shoo-in by
any means. David and I worked our tails off that first
night and we did real well. Afterward we joined the
Sony people and they were applauding and shaking
our hands. As we stood around making nice in the
green room the phone rang. Marty Ehrlichman was at
the other end and someone handed me the receiver.

"Are you happy, Marty?" I cried into the mouth-
piece.

"I dunno," came the reply, "should I be happy?"

"I think, Marty, you should get down on your knees
and thank David and me."

"How come?"

"Because, Marty, we sold an incredible amount of
merchandise and the viewers never saw the concert.
You busted my chops with the pronunciation of her
name. You told me I don't look like her and I don't
know her. You gave me stuff that costs lots of money
to try and sell, Marty, and on top of that, now you
want me to tell you whether or not it's good?" (I was
on a roll.) "Don't you ever give it up? Don't you ever
say congratulations, nice job?"

All I wanted was a simple thank you, and he just
didn't get it. I gave the phone back to one of the
assistants. Even though management wanted me to
stick around for the other shows, I take my time off
very seriously, and Streisand or no Streisand, I left the
next day on a scheduled trip to the Berkshires with a
friend. David Venable would finish off the rest of the
Barbra shows. Naturally, when I got to Massachusetts,
I wanted to find out how things were going. I turned
on the TV just in time to hear a viewer call in and
say, "Hi, David. I was watching you and Kathy last
night. She looks just like Barbra Streisand. They could
be sisters." I sure hoped Marty Ehrlichman was watching! A few weeks later I received an autographed picture of Barbra in the mail. I really appreciated the

gesture. Whether Streisand actually sent it, I don't know. Who cares, the picture's mine. So that's the story about my near brush with greatness, and although I never met Barbra Streisand, the experience was thrilling. She is the epitome of excellence, and that's a burden that only a Barbra Streisand can handle. God bless her, she really is gorgeous.

Richard Simmons is Barbra Streisand's number one fan. He's devoted to her. *His* fans are as crazy about *him* as he is about her! I love Richard and I've saved this very special gentleman for the ultimate place in my passing parade of prominent persons. Richard has made such a difference in the lives of so many people that I am convinced there's a special place in heaven for him.

Briefly, Richard was a fatty and suffered all the indignities heaped on overweight people. He got his act together, slimmed down, and then made weight loss his cause. He made infomercials—mini-dramas in which Richard would get into his car and go and visit a man or woman who had lost weight using Richard's Deal-a-Meal plan, and they were watched by millions. Deal-a-Meal was a brilliantly conceived method of getting people to control their eating. You had a deck of cards and each day you dealt yourself a certain number of cards in the major food categories. Every time you ate something from a category, you gave up a card. If you ate a strawberry or an apple, you gave up a fruit card, if you had milk or ice cream or cottage cheese, you gave up a dairy card, and so on, and, if you went through all your cards by four in the afternoon, you were finished eating for the day. On the other hand, if at the end of the day you had cards left, a couple of fruits, say, and a bread, then you could sit down at midnight and "binge" on an apple or a pear and rye toast. Meals were defined and you didn't have to use any guesswork; you did or did not use all your cards. (The plan is pretty clear-cut, yet

263

people used to call up and ask if they could buy *additional* cards. No doubt about it, hope springs eternal in the human stomach.) Richard became famous and rich from those infomercials. He took a lot of razzing because he always seemed to be in tears along with the people with whom he was speaking. The truth is, they touched his heart. He really was (is) the champion of the overweight, the first one to come out and be openly sad for people who couldn't go to restaurants or movie theaters or in airplanes or who weren't able to sit in chairs. He was sympathetic and empathetic and would seek out clients. He'd go to shopping malls and hold exercise-a-thons. He augmented the Deal-a-Meal with his "Sweatin' to the Oldies" videos and brought people together to lead them through the steps. Everyone had a ball. With Richard urging you on, it wasn't like work, it was play. There were at least four videos in the series, and they were wildly successful. Richard really works a crowd; he talks, signs autographs, and listens to all the sad stories. Because he's so "out there" he has his detractors, and guys like Howard Stern love to rip him up. Lots of people do imitations of Richard Simmons but the truth of the matter is a) he has made terrific inroads for people with weight problems to lose weight in a simple, healthy manner and b) he has made a lot of money.

I can tell you something else you might not know about Richard—he has a fabulous singing voice and is a terrific dancer. For my money he could have had a Broadway career, he's that talented. But he shied away from doing anything other than working with the weight afflicted. I once asked him why he wasn't a public presence. Why had he only catered to people with weight problems? Why didn't he broaden his horizons and do fund-raisers and public speaking? He told me he was too shy and only comfortable doing what he did. He's an extraordinarily generous man, too. He's given away thousands of Deal-a-Meals to people who need them but can't afford them. On the quiet, he's also given time and money to terminally ill AIDS patients. He simply is not interested in accolades and does what he does because he wants to. I probably shouldn't be going on about this; still, I can't get over how unselfishly Richard Simmons gives of himself. Richard's always giving to the QVC hosts, too. We're not supposed to take gifts and we try to obey the rule. Ha. Try keeping Richard from giving presents, you'd have better luck emptying the Pacific Ocean. When he's coming on the show, he'll call and say, "I'll be there Friday, what do you need?"

"Thank you," I'll answer, "but you know damn well I'm not allowed to take anything."

"I'm coming in, what do you need?" he repeats. Just to get him off my back I'll pick some silly little thing to say like, "Well, I do need a new lipstick." Richard will arrive at the studio with an assortment of lipsticks in all different shades. Or, I might say, "Gee, I just ripped my panty hose," and Richard will appear with dozens of pairs of stockings. He used to bring gifts from places like Chanel and Hermès until he got called on the carpet by the president of the company. The hosts were ordered to give back any gifts we'd received from him and Richard was informed that if he continued to give us presents, it could cost us our jobs. You'd think he'd give up—not Richard Simmons. He told the president that the hosts worked so hard we deserved something. He found out our home addresses and sent ties to the men and scarves to the women. The man is not generous, he's maniacally generous.

Richard is brilliant on the air. He's so good because he knows his stuff better than anybody; in fact, he usually doesn't need a host and handles everything by himself. Richard's hourlong segment of motivational speaking was listed in the schedule as "Project Me."

KATHY LEVINE

(Until I watched the show, I thought the name was pronounced "Pro-*ject* Me," and had visions of people hurtling through the air.) "Project Me" provided the opportunity for people to call in and purge their souls. Some of the stories were unbearably heartbreaking, but nothing fazed Richard. No matter what grievances were voiced—"I weigh 400 pounds; my family hates me; people make fun of me"—Richard had words of encouragement. "Today's the first day of the rest of your life," he'd say and then would talk to the person about planning the next day, and the next. In the best scenarios, Richard would get a call and someone would say, "I spoke to you last year and you saved my life. I lost 182 pounds because of you." "No," Richard would answer back, "it's because of *you*," and then they'd cry ... everyone would cry. Each time Richard comes on we all cry. He should do a tape of "Cryin' with the Oldies." The "Project Me" programs are heart wrenching and absolutely addictive even for those without a weight problem—surely someone falls into that category!

Never one to remain satisfied with the status quo, Richard keeps adding different strategies to help his followers. One of his masterplans was the "Cruise to Lose," which he did through the Carnival Cruise Lines. Vacations are tough to deal with when you're trying to control your weight and cruises can be the worst. By setting up a floating "spa," Richard made it possible for people to enjoy a holiday and not pay the weight gain consequences. Richard invited QVC show hosts to make scattered appearances throughout the cruise. I flew to Jamaica and picked up the boat there. (I don't mean boat, I mean "ship"; I'd never been on a cruise before and had no idea that you don't ever say boat.) Richard had scheduled activities for every minute of the day. His group of around 200 people sat at special tables where they were offered a selection of meals that featured beef, chicken, or fish, cooked in the most healthful manner while the rest of the passengers stood in salad bar lines dumping the macaroni and potato salads on their plates. Meetings were held in the nightclub and so were the exercise classes.

Richard arose at 7 A.M. and everyone had to join him for a walk around the deck, including the QVC host of the moment. I would have passed on that one, but Richard wouldn't let me. I'm a night person, to begin with; and besides, getting up that early would not allow me to put on a face. The first evening I told my fellow cruise-to-losers not to be surprised at what they saw the next day. "The face you see on television won't be the one you see tomorrow morning. I'm coming out as I am, no makeup." At 7 A.M. I crawled out of bed, brushed my teeth, and joined the gang on deck. I learned a lesson. The ladies had their cameras at the ready and were snapping away. I saw some of those pictures of me with "no" face, and I looked like a dog. My mother was right (again)—when you're in the public eye, you don't want to be captured for eternity with your face off, and I made a vow that I never again would appear sans makeup for a public appearance. (If anyone reading this was on that cruise and has one of those snapshots of me, please, please destroy it!)

I walked the decks, I did the exercises, and I sat in on the meetings. At the formal gatherings, a bowl was passed around, and if you wanted to share your story, you wrote your name on a slip of paper and put it in the bowl. Richard drew the names. There was time for about three people to talk at each session, and Richard wanted to give as many people as possible the chance to talk. The single biggest issue was self-esteem. As kids, these people had been attacked for their weight and from early on learned not to expect anything nice for their lives. Hearing their stories, I was overwhelmed by feelings of sadness. Sure, I battled my own bulge but on a far smaller scale than my fellow passengers. I felt like an outsider looking in. I was sad that their weight was the focal point of their lives. Jobs, love, school—everything was affected by the weight issue. I became acutely aware of their pain, but I also became aware that if the issue always is that you are going to be fat, then for God's sake, be fat.

I repeat, when I present large-size clothing on QVC, I don't say, "Buy this and you'll look thinner." Hey, how much "thinner" can an article of clothing make you look? I wouldn't insult anyone by offering her the possibility of looking like a size 20 instead of a size 22. It's better to buy something you like and then go out and have a good time. Richard helped me to fix my focus. Health is the object, and if you can be reasonably sound of mind even if it's in a large body, well, that's great. Richard was everywhere on the Cruise to Lose, walking around and shaking hands, calling out names (I swear he knew everyone by name), and giving quick words of encouragement. Richard has more energy than twenty Olympic gymnasts. He's something to watch, and people love him because they sense his sincerity. He'd go through the bar and into the dining room greeting everyone along his route and then return to his cabin leaving a lot of happy cruisers in his wake.

Richard's such a role model that there's no room for him to stray. One day I was in his cabin and I saw him take a candy bar and begin to eat it. I reacted as though he were ingesting poison.

"What are you doing?" I cried. "I've never seen you eat a candy bar!"

"That's because I can't eat them in public. I'm supposed to be perfect. I'm supposed to be watching my diet all the time."

"That's insane," I replied. "Your weight is under

control, you work out, you eat sensibly, you can have a candy bar."

"No," Richard said, "people expect me to set an example, and I don't want to disappoint them. If I eat sweets, I do it in private."

I was very impressed with his dedication. He maintains a public image for his fans. He hasn't been a fat person for many, many years yet he's never forgotten what it felt like to be overweight. He is so sensitive to other people's pain, it's a wonder he can get through the day. He's so very upbeat, though, he truly believes that everyone can be helped, and when people listen to him, they believe it, too. The guy is simply a great human being and I really admire him.

P.S. Richard Simmons's favorite candy bar is Kit-Kat.

14

Life Is Short, Death Is Long . . . Eat Dessert First!

❖ ❖ ❖

At the start of my broadcasting career, viewers made all sorts of speculations about me. Was I married or single or divorced or what? We're all in the same boat when we're in our thirties and unattached—you either make your own life and adjust to it and be okay with the fact that you're going to be single, or you powder, primp, and do your best to wrestle up a man. Viewers watched carefully to see how I reacted to my situation and how I handled myself. I seemed to be doing fine, and I was. Remember what I told you at the beginning of this book—have fun, be good to yourself, don't hurt anyone, and make a difference? I really try to follow my own advice, and so far, I *think* it's working. I'm having fun, I'm good to myself and to my loved ones, I don't hurt anyone, and I may even be making a difference. (Recently I've done some fund-raising, and volunteer work with kids—I don't know who had more fun, the kids or me.) One of the "differences"

Life Is Short, Death Is Long . . .

I've tried to make has to do with giving women a kind of mandate to do things for themselves—to work, thrive, learn, grow, think, assert, *and* to buy something nice for themselves even if they aren't wearing it for a "him." I've tried to make it okay for women to shop, spend, and put themselves in first place. In these instances, I do what I say and invite viewers to follow along. I *am* always self-centered and I'm all right with that. I am number one, and though I'm real good to number two, I take good care of me first.

I make my choices and I don't have to make excuses to anybody for choosing to do whatever I do on any given day, *provided* I don't upset or hurt anyone else. If it's my day off and I decide I want to stay in bed all day, that's my choice and I don't beat myself up about it afterward. (Unfortunately, I haven't made that choice in years. I'm too damn busy.) Viewers who are hard on themselves look to me for inspiration. Listen, I can't give you a blanket authorization to stop beating on yourself; all I know is, you're going to feel great when you do!

I want viewers to feel good about themselves and I try to answer all the questions that people write to me . . . to the best of my ability. Because there's so much mail, we use a form response. I always try to add my own P.S., though, and attempt to answer *direct* questions directly. I receive all sorts of requests, which boil down to people asking for a vote of confidence. Very often all anyone needs is a good strong pat on the back, and I'm there to provide it.

I guess I'll never get over how lucky I am. Who gets a chance to go on national television for three hours a day and have a party . . . and get paid for it? I have my own little Broadway show. Sure, I'd like my viewers to shop, but truthfully I think it's fine if they watch and have a good time. My original fears that I was too upscale and too snotty were wrong. I'm not upscale and I'm not snotty and I don't talk down

KATHY LEVINE

to viewers and I don't talk up to them. I believe that when I "meet" a viewer we may come from different backgrounds, educational experiences, travels, and tastes, yet the viewer immediately senses a kindred spirit. Maybe it's the shopping itself, but there's no upper or lower class here. We're all girlfriends and like girlfriends we have our spats. The letters tell me when my pals are put off, and though I don't spend time with nasty letters, I do pay attention to any constructive criticism. Bottom line, I guess I'm always going to be someone's meat and someone else's poison, but that's okay. As long as I reach some of the people some of the time, I feel good. I'm content with my life and, as I've been pointing out, one good reason is I've learned from my mistakes.

Many years ago when I was floundering from job to job until at last I realized that I had to look for work that called on my strengths, not my weaknesses, I made up my mind that I would not take a job just because it was a job, I would only work at something I liked. I knew I would never again be a doormat, personally or professionally. When QVC came along, I really didn't know what it was going to be; I only knew it played into my good points rather than the weak ones. I knew I would love being with people and sharing information, and I knew I had real knowledge of jewelry and shopping and trying to keep myself in good physical condition. The things I liked to do for myself were the things that I now could share with others.

QVC and I were an instant marriage. I knew the second I was on that not only did I love television, I loved what I could do for people . . . all the things I've mentioned, from doing something nice for yourself to looking good regardless of your size and putting *your* desires ahead of the pack. So many women tell me that they will not treat themselves because they have to "do" for their children or "do" for their husbands.

272

Life Is Short, Death Is Long . . .

I listen for clues as to whether these people will be depriving themselves or their families of the basic necessities, and if I determine that buying a ring isn't going to put them into the poorhouse, then you bet Kathy urges them to make the purchase. Later I'll get calls saying, "I bought that ring because you told me to, and every time I see it on my finger, it makes me feel great because I did something nice for me."

At this point in my life, I'm really feeling at the top of my form; I have strong family ties and *great* friends, really good girlfriends and lots of male friends. Most of my girlfriends are single, and they're not stereotypical "single" women, either. Like me, they're upbeat and content with their lives. I actively seek the company of strong, competent achievers. The philosophy is, we don't need someone else's opinions to make us feel worthy. I've been in *that* place—there was a time when I let other people influence my decisions about my looks, my jobs, and my relationships. No more! I'm not saying I'm insensitive to others; I'm very sensitive, but now I pick and choose the people I pay attention to. (One bad fan letter may upset my day; it won't, however, make me change my hair color.) I feel sorry for women who are upset because they're convinced that they'll be unattached for the rest of their lives. My answer to them is, get a life ladies, Prince Charming may not be the answer. I'm not desperately searching for a somebody anymore. I'm at peace being alone—not lonely, and there's a difference. I enjoy my neat, little home, I enjoy making my own decisions to do what I want. It doesn't mean I'm selfish or that I don't share with other people; I'm a dedicated daughter, sister, and friend—I just know what I want. And it took me all this time to figure it out, too.

Here's the real poop. Being a single woman is *not* a curse, it's not a sentence, it's a choice. A woman can find a man if she wants to pay the price. Trust me, there's someone out there. The question is, is it worth it to you? I made my choice. I do believe that although you don't necessarily need a "man," you do need a purpose, one that you determine for yourself. I come from a very strong work ethic on all sides, parents and grandparents. I couldn't imagine getting up and not having anything planned except to shop. It would be very boring for me. I like to work, yet until I reached forty, I really thought that there would be a *somebody*. Of course, I *had* a somebody way back when, and I've been in long-term relationships since my divorce; still, I kind of figured that maybe one day, old Kathy would get married, settle down, have kids, the whole shmear. Then, when I finally realized that not everybody is superwoman, not everybody can do the nine to five and come home and do another eight-hour shift of nurturing, caretaking, and listening to the other person's day, I gave up on it.

For most of my life while I went through the painful process of seeking a purpose, I was fortunate to have someone who always was there for me—my mother, the most influential woman in my life. She never said "never" to me; it was always "Try it, do it, buy it. Try everything!"

My mom knew from day one I was going to be a "late bloomer." She was sure that I would find my niche, my personal look, and my personal power. She also knew it would take time. It has, and one of the things that sustained me through those years was her love and support. She is thrilled at my success and remains my most honest critic, my cheerleader, and my best friend. Lucky for me, my mom was able to combine a career and motherhood. I mean, where would I be if she hadn't! When you don't have children to take care of, though, I think life is about having a good job, good friends, a good dog, a special someone, and a nice, comfortable bed. If there's one thing I'd like to share with my viewers, it's this: Don't simply live out your days. Seize them and experience life to the fullest. I've practiced what I'm preaching and I feel centered, focused, and directed. My cup isn't empty nor is it half full—it's bubbling over every day with endless possibilities.

I love coming home at night after a day's work, taking Chelsea out for a quiet walk, and then getting into my cozy bed with a hot chocolate and a couple of graham crackers and a good book or a bad magazine. I like it because my life is very full, very rich, and every night when my doggy crawls onto the covers, spreads herself out, and looks up at me, I look down at her and say with total sincerity, "Life is good, Chelsea, life is good." I smile, then I laugh. I've cried before and, trust me, it's better to laugh.

Vaddaya Mean?
Kathy's Glossary of Yiddish Words

(To assist those who aren't conversant in the language)

Bar mitzvah	coming-of-age ceremony for boys
Bupkis	nothing
Chutzpa	nerve
Drek	garbage; literally, sh-t
Farpitzed	dressed up
Ferkakta	mixed up
Goy	Gentile
Hock	nag
Kvetch	complain
Lox	smoked salmon
Maven	authority
Mishugena	crazy
Mumzer	bastard
Nebbish	nerd
Nudnick	pest

Glossary

Oy	oh oh, often followed by "vay is mir," meaning, Oh, woe is me!
Plutz	drop
Putz	*a jerk; literally, penis
Schlemiel	*a jerk
Schmear	spread it on
Schmooz	chat
Schmuck	*a jerk; literally, penis
Schnor	beg
Schnozz	nose
Shlep	drag (verb) or low-life (noun)
Shtarker	strong (person)
Shtick	routine
Shtup	stuff
Spiel	routine, explanation
Tchochke	bric-a-brac, nik-nak
Tookus (tush)	rear end
Zaftig	plump

(*There are lots more words for a "jerk," I just didn't use them.)

278

Afterword

❖ ❖ ❖

Many people have asked me how I managed to get a book published. The story is much like the apocryphal story of Lana Turner at Schwabs Drugstore—right time, right place.

I had no thoughts whatsoever of doing a book. But in December of 1993, I received a letter from Amy Einhorn, an editor at Pocket Books, telling me she'd been watching me on QVC (thanks to her mother's urging) and asking whether I had ever considered writing my autobiography. Judging by what she saw on TV, Amy thought that I would be able to write a funny, entertaining, and inspiring story. My reaction: What story? I could talk about my job, my dog, my friends, my lack of dates—but a story?

Amy felt that loyal viewers like her mother would love to know more about the personal details of my life, as well as the ins and outs of QVC. She thought I could be a good role model, inspiring other women to recognize their potential and make positive choices

Afterword

for themselves. Me, a role model! I work, I eat, I walk
the dog, I sleep—some role model!

I assumed this letter was the work of a friend who
was just goofing on me, so I ignored it. I also ignored
the additional letters that followed from Amy. Finally,
a message from her on my voice mail prompted me
to call and get to the source of this joke.

But the joke was on me. It turns out she was legit.
And not only that, but Pocket Books was an impres-
sive force in the publishing world—they've had more
New York Times bestsellers for the past consecutive
eight years than any other publisher! They've pub-
lished everyone from Kathie Lee Gifford to Rush
Limbaugh to Judith McNaught and Mary Higgins
Clark. Talk about impressive.

A meeting took place, and, long story short, Pocket
Books and Kathy Levine agreed to do business. Inter-
estingly enough, within six months two other major
publishing houses sought me out. I was both flattered
and floored—as I say at the beginning of this book,
who would've thought?

I am not a writer. I have the gift of gab and can
tell one hell of a funny story, but putting pen to paper
leaves me cold. I needed a co-author, someone who
could capture my humor and my voice without putting
too much of him/herself into the script. So how do
you find a co-author?

Amy furnished me with as many names as would
be needed until I could locate my dream writer.
I scheduled each of them for a personal interview.

I met with a few writers before I found the one I
clicked with—Jane Scovell. The day I met Jane, I
had scheduled an interview with another writer an
hour before. I came into New York City to meet
with the writers because almost all of them (and
almost all of the major publishing houses) are
based there.

Afterword

For these two interviews, I chose the Waldorf Astoria's Peacock Alley—for tea at 2:00 P.M. and at 3:00 P.M. I brought along my friend Frank. He has a very good gut instinct for talent and personality types. Since he knows me well, I thought he could help me choose wisely.

We ordered tea and waited for our first appointment to show. As luck would have it, the weather was terrible, and he was late (he could not get a cab, he later explained). Jane, on the other hand, was anxious to get this half-assed interview over. You see, Jane was a seasoned pro. She had co-authored Elizabeth Taylor's 1986 autobiography, as well as Kitty Dukakis's, Marilyn Horne's (the opera singer), and Cheryl Landon's (the daughter of actor Michael Landon). She did not need to do a book on some cable-shopping maven. This was a courtesy call to the publisher, and she came extra early, fully prepared to blow this turkey off ASAP. She came sloshing in from the rain in an oversized trench coat, shlepping two huge shopping bags. I was surprised that security at the Waldorf didn't throw her out.

Of course both of them arrived at the exact same time. I went off with the male author—after all, he did have the first appointment (and he was incredibly cute, which didn't hurt)—while Frank joined the bag lady.

The male author had a string of successful books. But typical Kathy, all I kept thinking about was how much fun it would be to tell my life story to this amazing-looking man. He was funny, charming, candid, and I thought perfect. I began to think that this author business was going to be quite fun.

But across the way sat Jane and Frank, best buddies by this time. Jane told Frank, "Look at her. She's leaning forward into him, she's mesmerized, she's gone." The object of my attention left, and Jane came

281

over for her interview and proceeded to eat everything short of the tablecloth. And oh boy, did she start to complain when she realized there were no more smoked salmon tea sandwiches! I looked at this loony woman and immediately loved her.

I asked her how she worked as a co-author.

"I live with you, I follow you, I meet your friends, your family, your coworkers," she answered. "I become you, I learn your thoughts and I become your voice. You will be so sick of me when this is over, you'll never want to see me again." Jane was thorough, and I liked that.

I then asked, "What if I say something to you one day and then change my mind about putting it in the book the next day?" She said, "Honey, it's your story. We don't exploit you, embarrass you, or hurt you." She was a little bit mom, grandmom, sister, friend, and teacher in one. We agreed to speak again soon, and Jane departed—I kid you not—with six lox sandwiches stuffed into her shopping bags. A real class act. I hired her instantly.

True to her word, starting in May of 1994, Jane shadowed me for three months. I talked into her little tape recorder anywhere and everywhere. We rode the Amtrak trains together, we ate our way up and down New York City, we shopped, we partied, we met each other's families, we toured QVC, and we vacationed for five days at Canyon Ranch in Massachusetts. We worked everywhere. I talked and talked and talked, and she taped and transcribed and organized and wrote and rewrote.

One year later, here we are, the Bag Lady and the Shopping Maven. We laughed, we cried, and we made a book. I have never had so much fun, and I never could have written this book without Jane. She is a kind spirit, and a forever friend. Everyone should have a Jane in their life.

So that's how this book came about. I hope you

enjoyed it and had as much fun reading it as I did writing it. Now let's hope some really fabulous things happen to me in the near future (isn't Richard Gere single?) so I can write an interesting sequel!

Love,

Kathy

One Year Later

So who knew this little girl from Allentown, PA, really had a book in her?

I still can't believe I did it! I remember thinking when the project began, "Do I have anything to say?" (Yes, to all of you in North Dakota, I now know that Bismark belongs to you—I accidentally placed it in the wrong state. My geography teacher always said I didn't know north from south.)

"Well, here I am, one year later, amazed, delighted, thrilled, you name it, at the wonderful way my literary endeavor was embraced by readers. Furthermore, I'm proud as can be that my book accomplished exactly what I hoped it would. "Have fun. Be good to yourself. Don't hurt anyone. And—make a difference," I wrote up front, and you know what? From all the letters I've received, lots and lots of readers took my advice to heart. Plus, and maybe this is my happiest achievement, it turns out that many of you were helped in some way by what I had to say. In a sense, I followed my own advice—I made a difference.

Believe it or not, one of my hurdles when writing this book was to get out there and hustle my own product! On QVC the biggest bugaboo, for even the biggest names, is the fear that nobody will be interested in what they have to sell. As a host on QVC, I had it real easy to calm down a nervous guest. I do it all the time, and my experience with John Denver provides a perfect example. He came to us to sell his albums. Before we went on air, John turned to me and said, "What if nobody buys?"

"Trust me," I told him, "you'll be fine."

Meanwhile, I'm thinking to myself, This is silly, what's this guy talking about? He sells millions of records and he's worried about people buying? It's crazy. Needless to say, John Denver did just fine—great, in fact. And that's only one example. I could go on and on about mega-celebrities who just couldn't believe that the public was out there waiting to buy their products.

Okay. With all my knowledge, with all my experience, when *my* book was ready, suddenly I was in the hot seat. I was no longer simply the selling host for someone else's product, *I* had something to sell. Me, Kathy Levine, the one they all say could sell refrigerators to Eskimos and snowblowers to Hawaiians. Me, the one who received two NIMA (National Infomercial Marketing Association) Awards for best show host in the country, two years in a row. Me, the huckster who can huck anything. That "Me" went on the air one fall evening to sell *It's Better to Laugh* . . . and you know what? I was positively terrified! All I could think was, What if nobody buys my book? What if I put this sucker out there and nobody wants it? Never mind that I'd proved I can talk about product and can ring all the bells and blow all the whistles and wax poetic and glow over almost anything. This was different. I was holding "my life" in my hands, and all of a sudden I had an attack of humble pie. I didn't want to talk about how I felt that this was a great book and a wonderful story. I just thought, Oh my gosh, I have cut myself open, I have bared all my guts, and ... what if they *don't* like me? The ego is a very fragile thing, and *my* little old ego was on the line. Believe me, I was very, very sensitive about how the public would react to my story. Would people actually call and *buy?* What would the numbers be like? I don't think any Broadway actor ever had more butterflies in her stomach than I did that first selling night. (Butterflies? I had locusts zooming around my insides.)

It's Better to Laugh ... went out on a Joan Rivers evening ... and what better time for me to make my own selling debut than with her. Joan was getting on her makeup when I ran into her dressing room.

"Give me something for luck!" I cried.

"Sure," said Joan, and she looked around for an appropriate token. Now, Joan had no idea what I was talking about. She didn't know I was going on air to sell my book; she just thought I was asking for some stupid thing to take on with me for whatever cocka-mamy reason. Joan usually puts a safety pin on her bathrobe in case she needs to pull something together at the last minute, and for want of a more suitable keepsake, she pulled the pin off and handed it to me. I grabbed it, pinned it to the inside of my jacket, and ran off to the set.

I went on air with Jane Rudolph Treacy and, with the locusts doing squadron formations in my belly, began my spiel. Meanwhile, back in her dressing room, Joan was watching on the monitor, and she immediately realized what was happening. She felt real bad about giving me a ferkahtka safety pin for luck instead of something meaningful (like a platinum-and-diamond bracelet— that's gotta be pretty lucky, not to mention meaningful!) and, typical Joan, she decided to take action. I was sitting talking to Jane when out of the corner of my eye I spotted Joan walk onto the set. Wearing her bathrobe and with half her makeup on, she strolled in front of Jane and me holding *It's Better to Laugh* . . . in her hands. Her head was buried in the book, and ignoring us, she pretended to read.

"Wow," Joan said, looking up at the camera. "Paul Newman! She did everybody. Boy is this book steamy!"

Not for the first time, and probably not for the last, I owe Joan Rivers a big thank you. Her antics really broke the ice, and Jane and I went on to sell up a storm.

Joan got out there and supported me right from the beginning. Later, when my book was well on its way, people would call in, talk to Joan, and then say, "Oh, by the way, Kathy, I loved your book." I wasn't sure how Joan would take it. After all, those shows weren't about my book, they were about her jewelry—and the last thing I as a host want to do is to take the spotlight off the product. But Joan, so gracious and kind, didn't lose a beat and kept saying, "Buy the book, buy the book." Bless you, Joan. Time after time you prove that you're one helluva lady in the heart as well as the head department.

Jane Rudolph Treacy was terrific that night, discussing *It's Better to Laugh* . . . with such enthusiasm that I was ready to go out and buy it myself. Actually, all my colleagues came through for me—just as you'd expect they would. Mary Beth was, of course, very helpful in recalling key facts I'd forgotten as well as in selling my book on the air. In fact, I tried to give a copy to all my fellow hosts. But that darling David Venable ran out and *bought* my book before I got to him. It was such a generous thing to do, and I told him he was a sweetheart. "Listen, Kathy," said David, "friends support friends. You wrote this book for a reason, and I went out and bought it for a reason." (Oh, David, may your magnanimous philosophy govern the sales of any future books I might publish! While you probably think I got unlimited copies of my book, in fact authors get a set amount—in my case enough for my family members—so while people were expecting free copies from my imaginary unlimited warehouse, I was running to the bookstore like everyone else.) My colleagues were wonderful, and my number one fan was Bob Bowersox. Bob had put out his own smashingly successful book a few months before mine, and he knew the ropes and really stood behind me.

After the book went out, I sat on pins and needles waiting for viewer response. I don't think I could have handled it if the first reports had been negative. If I had received letters saying, "Your book stinks, it's boring, and I'm sending it back," I would have been devastated. Surprise—it didn't happen. The comments started coming in and, I swear, I felt like Sally Fields at the Academy Awards. I wanted to get out there and cry, "You like me!" Honestly, viewers were so supportive and the letters kept coming . . . a thousand a week! And of the thousands I received, unless someone was censoring my mail, only three were negative. Of course I always like to accentuate the positive, but I'm going to address those three first and then get to the majority.

The writer of my favorite among the disapproving trio said, "It might be better to laugh, but sometimes it's just better not to know." This person didn't want to hear my story and felt that all I had bared was my sex life. I think she missed the point. I shared my experiences in hopes that I would strike a responsive chord in the reader and that women could learn from my mistakes ... as I had.

Okay, that was one downer. The other two felt that I had treated Jeff unfairly and that, as a friend, I should not have taken sides. Look, everyone is entitled to his or her opinion. I'm only sorry even three people got hung up on what I considered little issues and didn't get the big picture. I used myself as an example simply to show that if I could do it, *anyone* can make his or her way in the world. To paraphrase Abe Lincoln, you can please some of the people all of the time but you can't please all of the people all of the time.

To get to the positive side, the rest of the mail was absolutely enthusiastic and the letters are still coming. I get E-mail at QVC, and all the way down the screen it reads, "Your book ... Your book ... Your book. I loved your book. I laughed, I cried. I saw so much of myself in you." I was dizzy from praise. I just loved the mail and, truly, not simply because everyone was patting me on the back. What really pleased me was that people got something out of my story, and I just have to comment on a few of those letters.

One woman who was going through chemotherapy wrote that if she read a chapter before her treatments, she was better able to handle it—that letter alone made me glad I wrote the book.

Deeply moved by my father's plight, many readers were very interested in how my family handled his illness. One woman wrote to say that for quite some time she had noticed that her mother was acting oddly, but chose to ignore the strange behavior, hoping it would go away. When she finished the chapter dealing with my father's decline, she realized that she could not disregard her mother's obvious symptoms. She began to consult with doctors and to make inquiries about nursing homes. Within a matter of months her

mother succumbed to Alzheimer's and had to be insti-
tutionalized. But because of the preparation, everything was accomplished with a minimum of stress. And
trust me, even if it's only one tiny degree less stressful,
that's a lot!

Then came the letters from high school kids who
identified with the Barbra Streisand wanna-be from
Allentown. These kids wrote that they were overweight and/or scared about making grades and/or getting into college. They felt hopelessly unable to make
decisions about what to do with their lives. "Thanks
to your story, I feel it's okay if I don't know exactly
what I'm going to do and that sometimes floundering
around is how you find your way," wrote one kid. Yet
again, I was struck by the power of the pen.

Granted, most of the responses were from women;
however, the men were right there, too. One of my
favorite male replies came from a guy who had owned
a pet store for ten years. His business did pretty well,
well enough for him never to consider doing anything
else. One day a woman walked in holding a dead
guppy in a plastic bag full of water, slammed it on the
counter, and said, "My kid's guppy is dead, and it's
your fault. And what are you going to do about it?"
This was *the* moment for the owner. "I knew then that
I had to change careers," he wrote, "but after ten
years I didn't think I could do it. That evening, I happened to pick up my wife's copy of your book, read
it, and decided that if you could do something, I could
do something. Thanks to you, I'm going to change
careers and I'm going to be fine." I don't know
whether he should have thanked me or the guppy, but
either way, I was delighted to play a part in inspiring him.

Many of you were touched by the breakup of my
marriage to a really "terrific guy," and not a few were
directly influenced. "Something wasn't there in my
marriage," wrote one man, "and I agonized for two

years. Ultimately I knew it wasn't working, and I left. I was able to make a clean and gentle break, as gentle as possible in such circumstances, but I still felt guilty. I never was able to put into words why I left my wonderful wife, and then you said it for me. Your explanation of why you left your husband helped me realize that I wasn't a bad person, just someone in a bad situation." As for my ex, Jay kept giving away copies of my book to his friends and business associates, telling them that they were in for a treat!

Thinking about the results of my book, I guess one of my biggest kicks came from getting a good person off the hook. I'm talking about Judy Crowell. Judy received tons of apologetic letters, which is nice, but that doesn't altogether take away from the fact that people had been harsh and quick to judge. The lesson really is not to jump to conclusions about others or to discriminate without knowing the facts. The letters to Judy were great, and our public appearances together were even better. What a joy to watch members of the audience who had been primed to be unkind really warm up to her, and all because they heard her story from a "realiable source."

"No one would have believed me, Kathy," she confided, "but coming from you, they accepted the truth. I can never thank you enough." Hey, I think you've got to go through fire and brimstone to come out on the other side, and Judy's done just that. She's got a healthy relationship going now, she's not looking over her shoulder anymore, and she's never second-guessing. Honestly, I find *her* story inspirational and, once again, I'm proud of the role I played in it.

After *It's Better to Laugh* ... had its QVC run, I was sent on a "book tour." What's a book tour? The truth is, before I went on one, I didn't have a clue. I learned fast. Writing a book, it seems, is only the initial step. A published book has to be sold ... and sold ... and sold. The Pocket Books publicity department

arranged an itinerary that sent me to stores throughout the country. Not an easy task when you're dealing
with a character who has to be in West Chester, PA,
most of the time. My hopping kept Pocket Books hopping. I'd finish a QVC stint, and in the blink of an
eye be on my way to Michigan, Montana, Massachusetts, Idaho, California, Wisconsin ... you name it!
'Course it was a lot easier when I could coordinate
my personal jaunts with the QVC Local, the bus that
travels all over the country looking for new products.
Sure, I was an author. First and foremost, however, I
was a working host on QVC, and my job came before
anything else. I must have been the Pocket Books
publicity department's worst nightmare, because I
couldn't give them large chunks of time, just little bits
and pieces. During those bits and pieces I squeezed
in visits to almost two dozen states, including Hawaii,
and accumulated some 77,000 miles on my frequent-
flyer program. Boy was I pooped!

The whole shebang started off in New Jersey on
September 14, my birthday. My friend Andrea and I
went to the signing, and the viewers had planned a
birthday celebration. My roommate from college
came, and people brought cards and cakes and sang.
And let me tell you, that was a party.

My next stop was in Saugus, Massachusetts, about
twenty miles outside of Boston, where I was doing a
show with the QVC Local. After I finished work, I
was picked up by an escort and drive out to the mall.
(And no, not that kind of escort; rather, these are
people who take celebrities, authors, etc., to book
tours or interviews and help them navigate strange
cities.) "Nervous" doesn't begin to cover my feelings.
All I kept thinking was, Who's going to come? Who's
going to schlep to Saugus for me? My escort told me
that she would drop me off and I would be met by
someone from the bookstore. We drove up to the mall
where the store was, and sure enough there was a

Afterword

woman standing outside holding a sign with the name of the bookstore written in bold letters. I got out, said hello to the sign bearer, and as casually as I could asked, "Is anybody here?" Well, this woman just smiled and kind of shrugged her shoulders, and motioned for me to follow her. My interpretation of the response was an immediate, Uh oh, no one's here—nada, bupkis. There was nothing to do but put my head down and make my way into the mall. The bookstore was on the second level, and I was on my way to the escalator when I heard someone cry out, "There she is!" I looked up quickly to see who "she" was and, lo and behold, she was me!

On the second level a line of people was wrapped around the full length of the mall, and someone in the group had spotted me. I heard my name called again, and as I reached the escalator, the crowd burst into applause! And you know what I did? I cried. I couldn't believe it. I told you I felt like Sally Fields, and I meant it. I was overwhelmed. I went up the escalator, and all I could think was, I've got to thank all these people. I walked the length of the line smiling, nodding, and saying thank you, thank you, thank you. Honest to God, I felt like Miss America. When my triumphant walk was over, I sat down in the bookstore and signed autographs till the cows came home. It was great. I loved it. Later that night, I returned to my hotel and, utterly exhausted, got into bed. Ha. No way could I sleep. My brain was whirling, I was on fire. Now, I thought, I knew what it was like to be an author. What a beginning. What a time. What a night. And that's the way it was on the entire tour.

For the next three months I was in malls everywhere, and frankly, I think plaques honoring me should be placed in every one I visited. Forget plaques, they should put up statues! Oh, I'm not talking about my book, I'm talking about the amount of money I spent. Anywhere I went, I shopped! Nordstram's should declare me their favorite customer. For sure, the Somerset Collection in the Troy, Michigan, mall should put up a notice reading, "While waiting to autograph her book, Miss Kathy Levine went on a buying binge and single-handedly supported the state of Michigan." I bought shoes in at least six states, which is kind of nice because every time I put on a particular pair I think, Oh yeah, these are the Illinois shoes, or the New Jersey shoes, etc. (I also have my California dress, my Massachusetts handbag, and my Idaho pants. Some days I'm just a "cross-section of America" dresser.)

Hectic was my operative word from October through December of 1995. Each time I went to a signing, I was terrified no one would come, and then when I saw the lines, I was terrified that I'd never get finished signing. I was lucky that my plane flights were booked late enough so that I *could* get to everyone. I wasn't the only one on a book tour, either, and I heard many stories about other authors. He doesn't know it, but I actually was on Colin Powell's trail. There's no comparison between us. His signings would attract 10,000 people at a pop. He'd have five books lined up before him and would literally run his pen across them, enabling him to sign a large number of books in a relatively modest amount of time. Not this cookie. I couldn't just sign, I shmoozed! Everyone wanted to talk! It's funny, the person in the back of the line who's shuffling around because she's bored waiting and keeps wishing that people would hurry up and keep moving has a complete turnaround when she actually reaches the signer. She's got to have her three minutes! Don't worry, as I said, I loved every minute of it.

Yep, everyone wanted to talk, and just about everyone experienced the book in the same way. Again and again I was told, "I felt like you were sitting there with me and we were having coffee across the kitchen

Afterword

table." People identified with so much of my story—
the bad hair days, the weight, the dating. And a great
number were moved by the story of my father and
found parallels in my relationship with my dad to their
relationships with their parents. Maybe my father
wasn't Ward Cleaver and not as wonderful as we all
think our fathers should be, but he did at least try.
Other readers were touched by the relationship between my mother and me; either they had the same
kind of connection, or they wished they had. People
were dying to look at my jewelry, and I always wore
the "big" pieces: my Kathy ring, the 8-carat total-
weight diamonique earrings, my bracelets. And I let
everybody try them on. It was like kids playing QVC
shopping mall.

I remember one signing in Pittsburgh where over a
thousand people appeared in a bookstore and some
newspaper guy happened to come in and see the
throngs.

"Who's here?" he asked. "Charlton Heston?"

"Kathy Levine" was the answer.

"Who?" So this guy goes to his office and writes a
gently satirical article along the lines of "Who the hell
is Kathy Levine and why are people standing in line
to meet her?" Not everybody knows me, and just like
that journalist, someone usually would walk by, see
the line, and stop to ask, "Who's that woman?" "You
don't know her?" cried the autograph-seekers. "Why,
she's Kathy Levine from QVC." One lady actually
asked *me* who I was. I told her that I was Kathy
Levine and that I had written a book.

"Yes," she answered, "but who are you?"

"I work on television," I replied, "and this is my
story."

"So, with all due respect, why should I want to read
your book?"

I thought a second before replying. "Got anything
bad happen in your life?" I queried.

294

Afterword

"Yeh, my husband just dumped out on me and left me stuck with my daughter's wedding."

"Buy this book," I shot back. "It'll make you feel better." She bought it. I hope it made her feel better.

Throughout all my travels and in all my signings, it pleases me to report that people were incredibly nice. Some actually broke down in tears telling me what *It's Better to Laugh* ... had done for them—how it got them through the death of a parent, a job layoff, a major illness, a divorce, all of life's slings and arrows. Over and over they kept repeating that my book gave them the courage to know that changes may be scary but they're not always bad, and that you can come out okay. Ladies particularly loved my last bit of advice that because you are alone doesn't mean that you are lonely and because you don't have a man doesn't mean that your life can't be full and enjoyable. And you have to put yourself at the top of the list every once in a while. It was very interesting to me that with all the motivational books out there saying, in essence, the same thing I was saying, for some reason *my* story pointed things out more clearly—maybe because I was my own example!

I have to laugh—my book never seemed to be in the same section in any two bookstores. You'd think it would be under Biography, but oh no, some stores had in Media, others in Self-Help, others in Psychology, others in Entertainment. People were running all over the place trying to locate the thing. By the way, in the Galleria in Sherman Oaks, California, *It's Better to Laugh* ... was sitting in a section entitled Overcoming Life's Adversities. Actually, the way I travel, my book could have been on the Geography shelves or in Fiction right next to *Around the World in Eighty Days.*

I really loved the look of my book. I insisted it be purple, and I got what I wanted. A lot of people were curious as to how the cover was done. The concept was created by Paolo Pepe and the photographer was

Afterword

Kimberly Butler. I went to her studio, and first Kim took a picture of a blank white book. Then she took my photograph, shrank it, and Paolo superimposed it on the blank book. The process was repeated a second and a third time, and that "magic" produced the final product. I thought it was the best cover of the year, and I'll bet if prizes were given for such things it would have gotten the blue, or the purple, ribbon.

What was the hardest chapter for me to write? This was one of those frequently posed questions. Chapter Five (about my divorce) wasn't a piece of cake by any means, but the one I really agonized over was the chapter about my family. My biggest fear was that my mother would never talk to me again because I was airing her laundry even though I used only what was relevant to my life. I was petrified that she would be devastated. At one point Jane Scovell, my wonderful co-author, who knew how anxious I was about my mother's reaction, wrote to my mom to reassure her that I was bending over backwards not to say anything to embarrass her. I sent my mother the first copy, and she got it about two days before the book went on the air. "Mom," I said, "even if you hate this, it's very important for me at this moment for you to tell me that you love it. I just need your support." She called me immediately after reading it and said, "It's wonderful." This wasn't just music to my ears, it was Beethoven's Ninth. She read it quickly the first time, looking for her name. I soon learned that's what all my friends and relatives did. (My girlfriend Dale was upset that she wasn't mentioned, and she should have been since she was much thinner and prettier than I, and got all the dates.) It wasn't just old friends who were looking, either. My co-hosts gave it a close read. It's funny. First you look through to make sure you're *not* in the book, and then when you discover you're not mentioned, you get mad and want to know why you were left out. After her cursory reading, my mother went over *It's Better to Laugh* ... with a fine-tooth comb. "It really is wonderful, Kathy," she told me. "It's a feel-good, happy book and every chapter has a point. There's nothing in it that I'm ashamed or embarrassed about, and I am very proud of you." I think I'd rather have received my mother's approbation than a Pulitzer Prize.

After my brothers read it, Ron, the older one, who shares my assessment of the family picture, told me it was "right on." Bruce, the younger one, had another opinion. "We must've had different fathers," he told me. "I thought Dad was the greatest thing since sliced bread. I never realized you had those feelings. I must've been around for the good part, you got the wrong deal." It just shows you, you can grow up in the same household and, give or take a few years, you can experience something completely different.

Within a week of the book's appearance in the stores, my mother called.

"Kathy, I went to buy lipstick in the West Palm Beach Mall, and there you were in the window of the bookstore! My little girl in a life-size cutout! What a rush I got!" Truthfully? I believe my mom thought my book was going to be some little paperback ditty and it didn't really hit her that this was an honest-to-God book until she saw it on display. Like me, she was overwhelmed, and she hit the telephones as soon as she got home, telling everyone she knew to please go out and buy the book. She bought two copies herself even though she knew I'd send her as many as she wanted. Monica, my best friend, bought two copies, too. I was touched. (*It's Better to Laugh* ... was like a fruitcake. Zillions of people read it, but they all read the same copy! Families passed it around and people had sign-ups in their offices and ran little lending libraries. Please, guys, I want you to read my book, but next time *buy* it also!)

Book signings are a lot like walking the plank.

Afterword

Every time I did one I got the same feeling in the pit of my stomach. There's about ten seconds before you take a deep breath and say, "Here we go," and then you walk out to be dissected. You are literally on display. Your hair, your nails, your weight, your clothes—everything is under a microscope. "You're taller than I thought." "You're younger than you look on TV" (I must look 86 on TV). Television distorts reality and people like to see you up close and personal. People are there to assess and evaluate you and ultimately to decide whether they like you. I'll never forget my visit to my hometown, Allentown. I came in from the back of the mall thinking, I haven't been here in twenty years, nobody really knows me, nobody's going to be here. Once again, Kathy was surprised! There were hundreds of people, relatives, high school friends, my parents' friends, people I hadn't seen in years. Some of my father's patients came and told me that they didn't know I was Dr. Kauffman's daughter; they saw his picture in the book and put two and two together, and they wanted to tell me that he was a wonderful man. Others knew my mother and told me they modeled for her or took her charm school course. "Your other gave me my first break," one attractive, well-dressed woman told me. (She bought three books!) I had a warm and wonderful time in Allentown, and from my experience I'd say you *can* go home again.

For the duration of my book tour I was Miss America, Queen of the May, Cinderella, Snow (off) White, you name it. I was on top of the world. I absolutely forgot that except for weight, what goes up eventually must come down. Way back at the beginning Bob Bowersox had said to me, "Levine, you're going to go on a twelve-week whirlwind. You're going to be a star, you're going to be treated like a lady, you're going to be flying high. It's going to be much different from

298

what you do every day. And when it ends, you're going to fall."

"Oh, no," I argued, "I've got my job to come back to. I'll be fine."

On January 1, 1996, the tour effectively ended. I returned home and immediately went into a terrible blue funk. I had no idea why. I'd forgotten Bob's prophetic words and didn't have a clue that I was experiencing the "withdrawal from the glamour" syndrome. I had won the NIMA award the second year in a row, I had been on television talk shows (three of which were cancelled!—am I the kiss of death or what?) I had been contacted by the major networks, I was on absolute overdrive, full of piss and vinegar, and then—boom, it was over. I was back in West Chester, PA. I had surfaced too fast and was suffering the end-of-the-book-tour "bends." I felt I was at a crossroad and didn't want to do what I was doing anymore. It wasn't depression; I mean, I didn't want drugs or psychiatric help. It was just this terrible funk and I wasn't "me." I was off, way off, and ... fat! I had eaten my way across the country. Every mall has real nice bakeries, and every airport has really bad food and really good cookies. And—thank you very much, Mrs. Fields—I was eighteen pounds bigger. I looked at a map of the U.S. to determine which state my rear-end most closely resembled. Congratulations, Lone-Star State. I had a Tex-ass. After my diet advice was heeded by readers, I'm fat again! I began reading my own book to try and find out what I did to lose weight. I was in poop up to my kansass, and I still didn't know why.

In February, Nick Chavez, the guy who did my hair for the book cover, came to QVC to do some styling for us. I sat in the chair. Nick looked at me in the mirror and said, "How are you, Diva?" I mumbled something.

"The glamour's all gone, isn't it?" he said.

"What do you mean?" I replied.

Afterword

"Hey, babe, you traveled all over the country. You really were the Diva. You were taken by limos to the best places. You had the big brass ring and now it's all gone, isn't it?"

"Yeh," I said, "and I'm fat, and I'm back to doing what isn't bad but sure isn't as exciting."

"Here's a piece of advice," said Nick as he began to comb my bad hair. "You get your ass back into shape and you write another book and you get back out there with the people and do what you love. That's how you stay happy!" Light bulb! I had a terrific haircut and an epiphany at the same time—life doesn't get much better than that.

I love my job but I also love working on books and bringing them before the public, in person. That's what I want to do and that's why I'm watching my weight—AGAIN(!)—and working on my next opus. I really have Nick to thank for the wake-up call that made me understand that part of dealing with why you're down is to know what's bugging you. As soon as I realized that I needed to be out there with all of you as well as working behind the camera, I could take action. I've asked my viewers what they want me to write about, and they've given me ideas. They want to know about life after forty, dating, the weight battle (how to dress as your butt grows larger), those kinds of things. What do you want to know? Any and all suggestions are invited. Just write me care of Pocket Books or QVC, and fasten your seat belts, I'll be out there again! Meanwhile, remember it's better to laugh . . .

JANE SCOVELL (right) has coauthored books with Marilyn Horne, Elizabeth Taylor, Kitty Dukakis, and Maureen Stapleton. She is the author of a forthcoming biography of Oona Chaplin.

9 781451 661910